My
OS X®

EL CAPITAN EDITION

John Ray

Que®

800 East 96th Street,
Indianapolis, Indiana 46240 USA

My OS X® El Capitan Edition

Copyright © 2016 by Pearson Education

ISBN-13: 978-0-7897-56336

ISBN-10: 0-7897-56331

Library of Congress Control Number: 2015913804

Printed in the United States of America

First Printing: October 2015

Trademarks

Warning and Disclaimer

Special Sales

For information about buying this title in bulk quantities, or for special sales opportunities (which may include electronic versions; custom cover designs; and content particular to your business, training goals, marketing focus, or branding interests), please contact our corporate sales department at corpsales@pearsoned.com or (800) 382-3419.

For government sales inquiries, please contact governmentsales@pearsoned.com.

For questions about sales outside the U.S., please contact international@pearsoned.com.

Editor-in-Chief
Greg Wiegand

Senior Acquisitions Editor
Laura Norman

Development Editor
Todd Brakke

Managing Editor
Kristy Hart

Senior Project Editor
Betsy Gratner

Indexer
Erika Millen

Proofreader
Kathy Ruiz

Technical Editor
Paul Sihvonen-Binder

Editorial Assistant
Kristen Watterson

Cover Designer
Mark Shirar

Compositor
Mary Sudul

Table of Contents

2   Making the Most of Your Screen Space   61

3   Connecting Your Mac to a Network   85

4   Setting Up iCloud and Internet Accounts   113

5   Accessing Email and the Web   135

6   Sharing Files, Devices, and Services   187

7   Being Social with Messages, FaceTime, Twitter, and Facebook   221

8   Managing Who, Where, When, and What   **257**

14   Securing and Protecting Your Mac   485

Find the online Chapters 15 and 16 and other helpful information on this book's website at quepublishing.com/title/9780789756336.

About the Author

John Ray is a life-long fan of Apple products; he has been an avid Mac user since its inception in 1984. He relies on OS X both at work and at home because it is a robust, flexible platform for programming, networking, and design. Over the past 16 years, John has written books on OS X, iOS development, Linux, web development, networking, and computer security. He currently serves as the Director of the Office of Research Information Systems at The Ohio State University. When he isn't writing, he is either re-creating a marine disaster in his living room or planning a highly elaborate electronics project that will quadruple his carbon footprint.

Dedication

This book is dedicated to taking a long nap, without any potty breaks.

Acknowledgments

Thanks to the team at Que Publishing—especially Laura Norman and Todd Brakke—for taking random keystrokes typed at 3AM and turning them into words that seem to go in order. Thanks also go to Paul Sihvonen-Binder for sifting through hundreds of screenshots and callouts. It is truly a team effort to make this happen. Thank you all.

We Want to Hear from You!

As the reader of this book, *you* are our most important critic and commentator. We value your opinion and want to know what we're doing right, what we could do better, what areas you'd like to see us publish in, and any other words of wisdom you're willing to pass our way.

We welcome your comments. You can email or write to let us know what you did or didn't like about this book—as well as what we can do to make our books better.

Please note that we cannot help you with technical problems related to the topic of this book.

When you write, please be sure to include this book's title and author as well as your name and email address. We will carefully review your comments and share them with the author and editors who worked on the book.

Email: feedback@quepublishing.com

Mail: Que Publishing
ATTN: Reader Feedback
800 East 96th Street
Indianapolis, IN 46240 USA

Reader Services

Visit our website and register this book at quepublishing.com/register for convenient access to any updates, downloads, or errata that might be available for this book.

Prologue: Getting Started with the Mac

This book explains how your Mac and the latest edition of the OS X operating system, El Capitan, are used to create your ideal working environment. If you've never worked with a Mac before, OS X is the name applied to Apple's desktop operating system—like "Windows" on a PC. iPhones and iPads run iOS, and Macintosh computers run OS X.

Before you can begin climbing El Capitan, let's start by reviewing the hardware capabilities of your system and the prerequisites necessary to use this book.

Getting to Know the Mac Hardware

Each model of Mac includes a wide array of ports and plugs for connecting to other computers, handheld devices, and peripherals such as printers and external displays. For new systems, like the retina USB-C MacBook, you'll need to use an expansion adaptor (sold by Apple as well as third parties) to access additional ports.

I refer to your hardware options by name throughout the book, so it's a good idea to familiarize yourself with the possibilities now.

- **Ethernet**—Ethernet provides high-speed wired network connections with greater speeds and reliability than wireless service. Your Mac can support a very fast version of Ethernet, Gigabit Ethernet, that makes it a first-class citizen on any home or corporate network.

- **FireWire 800**—FireWire 800 is a fast peripheral connection standard available on some systems (or via adaptor) that is frequently used to connect external storage and video devices.

- **Mini DisplayPort**—The DisplayPort enables you to connect external monitors to your Mac. Although few monitors support the DisplayPort standard, you can get adapters from Apple for connecting to both VGA and DVI interface standards.

- **Thunderbolt**—The highest-speed interconnect available on a personal computer, Thunderbolt allows monitors, storage units, and other devices to be daisy-chained together. This means that each device connects to the next device, rather than all having to plug into a separate port on your Mac. Thunderbolt uses the same connector and is compatible with Mini DisplayPort.

- **USB 2.0/3.0**—Universal Serial Bus is a popular peripheral connection standard for everything from mice, to scanners, to hard drives. Mac models released after mid-2012 support USB 3.0, the next, much faster, evolution of USB.

- **SD Card Slot**—SD (Secure Digital) RAM cards are a popular Flash RAM format used in many digital cameras. Using the built-in SD RAM slot, you can create a bootable system "disk" that you can use to start your computer in an emergency.

- **Audio In**—A connection for an external microphone.

- **Audio Out**—An output for headphones, speakers, or a home theater/amplifier system.

- **802.11ac**—The fastest standard currently available for consumer wireless network connections. Your Mac's wireless hardware can connect to any standards-based wireless access point for fast, long-range Internet access.

- **Bluetooth**—Bluetooth connects peripheral devices wirelessly to your Mac. Unlike 802.11ac, Bluetooth has a more limited range (about 30 feet, in most cases) but it is easier to configure and doesn't require a specialized base station.

- **SuperDrive**—An optical drive that can be used to write CDs and DVDs. This is currently only sold as an external add-on item with new Macs.

- **Retina Displays**—The Retina display is an extremely high-resolution display on Apple's new (2014+) MacBook and iMac lines. The display offers near-laser printer quality resolution at the expense of larger application sizes.

- **Force Touch**—Found on all 2015+ MacBooks and MacBook Pros, the Force Touch-enabled trackpad gives uses the ability to trigger actions by applying different levels of pressure to their trackpad.

So what does your computer have? Apple's hardware lineup changes throughout the year, so your features depend on the model and the date it was made. Be sure to consult your owner's manual for a definitive description of what is included in your system.

Built-In Batteries

If you have a portable Mac, its usefulness depends on the built-in battery. Apple has eliminated user-serviceable batteries from all its portable devices. This means that you now get a higher-capacity battery with a longer runtime, but in the event of a failure, you can't repair it yourself.

To replace the battery, you need to visit your local Apple store or registered service center. The battery can be replaced in the store, while you wait, for approximately $130.

Special Keyboard Keys

Take a look across the top of your keyboard. Notice that even though there are "F" (function) designations on the keys, there are also little icons. The keys marked with icons provide system-wide control over important El Capitan features.

- **F1, F2**—Dim and brighten the display, respectively

- **F3**—Start Mission Control and display all application windows

- **F4**—Open the Launchpad

- **F5, F6**—Dim and brighten the backlit keyboard, if available

- **F7, F8, F9**—Act as Rewind, Play, and Fast Forward controls during media playback

- **F10, F11, F12**—Mute, decrease, and increase volume

The Eject key is located in the farthest-right corner of the keyboard and is used to eject any media in your Mac's SuperDrive—if it has one!

Accessing the Function Keys

If you are using an application that requires you to press a function key, hold down the Fn button in the lower-left corner of the keyboard and then push the required function key.

What You Need to Know

If you're holding this book in your hand, you can see that it contains a few hundred pages packed with information about using your Mac with El Capitan. You might also notice books dedicated to the same topic and sitting on the same shelf at the bookstore that include a thousand pages or more! So what's the difference?

My OS X doesn't cover the basics of using a computer; you already know how to drag windows around the screen and move files by dragging them from folder to folder. Instead, this book focuses on using and configuring the core features of OS X—file sharing, Internet access, social networking, calendaring, and entertainment.

If you're switching from Windows, you might encounter a few unique features of OS X. Review these features in the next few sections.

The Menu Bar

The menu bar is universally accessible across all running applications and contains a combination of the Apple menu, which is used to access common system functions; the active application's menus; and menu items, which are global utilities for controlling and monitoring system functions.

Apple menu   Application menus   Menu items

The Dock

The Dock is the starting point for many of your actions when using the Mac. Part application launcher, part file manager, and part window manager, the Dock gives you quick access to your most frequently used applications and documents without requiring that you navigate the Finder to find things on your hard drive.

The Dock

The Finder

In Windows, Explorer provides many of your file management needs. In OS X, you work with files within an ever-present application called Finder. The Finder starts as soon as you log into your computer and continues to run until you log out.

To switch to the Finder at any time, click the blue smiling icon at the left end of the Dock.

Finder —

Tags

Don't like trying to fit all your files in a folder structure that doesn't make sense? In El Capitan, you don't have to. Create tags that represent different attributes of your files (Projects, Important, Personal, and so on) and then apply as many or as few as you'd like. Once applied, you can view your files by tags rather than having to dig through folders.

Tags —

The Launchpad

Applications are installed in folders, nested in folders, or even just lumped together with no organization at all. For simple setups, this is fine; after you've accumulated a few years of downloads, however, finding what you're looking for becomes difficult. The Launchpad offers a consolidated view of all your applications and even lets you group them logically, without having to worry about what folders they're in.

Mission Control

Mission Control is a power-user feature that is easy for anyone to use. With Mission Control, you can manage all your running applications and their windows in a single consolidated display. You can even create new workspaces to hold single or split-screen apps, or navigate between existing workspaces.

Application windows   **Workspaces**   **Current workspace**

Spotlight

Spotlight is a systemwide tool for locating and launching *anything* on your Mac. Use it to quickly locate, preview, and load documents; start applications; find movie showtimes and trailers; even look up information from Wikipedia. Although Spotlight has existed for quite some time on OS X, El Capitan brings new capabilities and a new look to this tool.

Spotlight

The App Store (and Security)

If you've used a modern smartphone or tablet, you've almost certainly used an "app store" of some sort. The Mac App Store is fully integrated with the operating system and provides fast access to screened and safe applications that are installed, updated, and even removed through a simple point-and-click process. El Capitan also implements security controls to prevent undesirable software installation.

The Notification Center and Today View

Does your Mac need to tell you something? If so, it lets you know in the Notification Center. The Notification Center/Today view, activated by clicking the far right side of the menu bar, shows alerts from your applications that help you stay on top of important events. New mail, software updates, meeting invitations, and more are consolidated in this area and presented in a unified fashion.

A special "Today" view contained within the Notification Center gives you instant access to upcoming events in your day and even lets you access widgets for simple tasks—like performing calculations.

Notification
Center

System Preferences

Many configuration options for features in this book require you to access the El Capitan System Preferences. The System Preferences application (accessible from the Dock or the Apple menu) is the central hub for system configuration. You can do everything from setting your password to choosing a screen saver in the System Preferences application.

Window Controls

El Capitan provides three controls at the top of each window. At the top left are the Close, Minimize, and Fullscreen controls. The Close control shuts the window; Minimize slides the window off the screen and into the Dock; and the Fullscreen control switches many applications into a unique fullscreen or split-screen view (click and hold)—sometimes with a very different interface.

Traditionally, the "third" button on Mac windows has been "resize," which sizes windows to fit the content. You can still access this by holding Option when clicking the Fullscreen button.

Minimize ⌐ **Fullscreen**

Close

iOS 9 Preview

The new iPod touch.
And fresh colors for everyone.

Contextual Menus

If you're new to OS X, you might find it hard to believe that the Mac has a "right-click" (also known as the "secondary click") menu in its operating system—and it's been there for a long time! You can invoke contextual menus by right-clicking using a mouse, Ctrl-clicking with your trackpad, or clicking with two fingers simultaneously.

Contextual menus are rarely required in any application, but they can give you quick access to features that might otherwise take more clicks. On new Force Touch trackpads, you can use a hard press on your trackpad to access some features previously exposed via secondary clicks. Find out more about this feature in Chapter 11, "Making the Most of Your Mac Hardware," and by reading the manuals (or help files) that come with your applications.

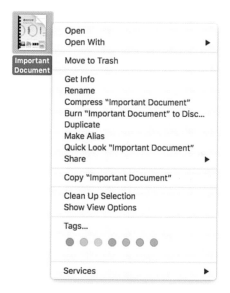

Gestures

Gestures are motions that you can make on your trackpad to control your computer. In El Capitan, gestures are used heavily to navigate between applications and access special features. Gestures can help you navigate web pages, resize images, and do much more with just your fingertips. In fact, without gestures, you'll likely miss out on all OS X has to offer.

Dictation

Don't like typing? With El Capitan, you don't have to. OS X supports dictation into any application where you would normally type—performed either "in the cloud" or locally on your Mac (with an optional install). You learn more about activating dictation in Chapter 11.

>>>Go Further

DON'T LIKE A GESTURE? CHANGE IT!

If you don't like a touch, a click, a force click, or a swipe that you find in El Capitan (including how contextual menus are activated), it's likely that there is an alternative. The Trackpad System Preferences panel provides complete control over your "touching" OS X experience—something you can read about in Chapter 11's "Changing Trackpad and Mouse Options" section.

Understanding iCloud and Apple ID

Apple's iCloud and its corresponding Apple ID deserve special attention during your foray into El Capitan. iCloud provides services such as calendars, notes, and reminders that you can use to synchronize information across multiple Macs and multiple iOS devices. It also offers free email, a means of locating your Mac (if you lose it), a tool for controlling your system from remote locations, and even an online office application suite! You don't need to use iCloud, but you'll see references to it, like the one shown here, as you navigate the operating system.

To use iCloud, you must establish an Apple ID to authenticate with the service. If you've installed El Capitan, chances are you've created an Apple ID in the process and already have everything you need to start using iCloud. If you aren't sure whether you have an Apple ID or you want to generate a new one, I recommend visiting https://appleid.apple.com/ and using the web tools to verify, or start, your setup.

You learn more about configuring iCloud in Chapter 4, "Setting Up iCloud and Internet Accounts."

iCloud Everywhere

Because iCloud makes many of your El Capitan features more useful, it is referenced throughout this book. The information doesn't fit into a single category, so I discuss it in the places where I hope you'll find it most useful.

Windows Compatibility

If you have a Mac, you have a powerful Intel-based computer in your hands—a computer that is capable of natively running the Windows operating system. The goal of this book is to make you comfortable using your Mac with El Capitan, but I'd be remiss in my authoring duties if I didn't mention the options available for running Windows on your hardware.

Boot Camp

Boot Camp is included with El Capitan and gives you the capability to install and boot Windows directly on your Mac. Put simply, when you do this, your Mac becomes a Windows computer. Switching between El Capitan and Windows requires a reboot, so this option is best if you need to work in Windows for extended periods of time.

Apple's Boot Camp Assistant (found in the Utilities folder within the Applications folder) guides you through the process of partitioning your Mac for Windows, creating a disk of drivers for Windows, and configuring your system to boot into Windows or OS X.

You can install Boot Camp at any time, as long as you have enough room (about 28GB) for a Windows installation.

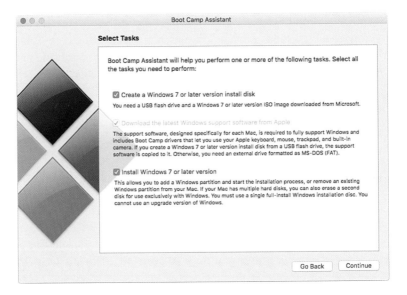

Virtualization

Another solution to the Windows compatibility conundrum is the use of virtualization software. Through virtualization, you can run Windows at near-native speeds at the same time you run El Capitan. Some virtualization solutions even go so far as to mix Mac and Windows applications on the same screen, blurring the lines between the operating systems.

Unlike Boot Camp, virtualization runs operating systems simultaneously. Virtualization requires more resources and has lower performance than a Boot Camp solution, but it is more convenient for running an occasional application or game.

Consider three options for virtualizing Windows on your Mac:

- **VMWare Fusion (www.vmware.com)**—A stable solution from a leader in virtualization software. VMWare Fusion is rock solid and fully compatible with a wide range of virtual "appliances" available for VMWare on Windows.

- **Parallels Desktop (www.parallels.com)**—The widest range of features available of any virtualization solution for OS X, including near-seamless integration with Mac applications.

- **VirtualBox (www.virtualbox.org)**—Free virtualization software that offers many of the same features of VMWare and Parallels. VirtualBox is not as polished as the commercial solutions, but it's well supported and has excellent performance.

Other Operating Systems

Virtualization isn't limited to running Windows. You can also run other operating systems, such as Linux, Chrome, and Solaris, using any of these solutions. In fact, if you have enough memory, you can run two, three, or more operating systems simultaneously.

Use the sidebar to quickly access locations, files, and set tags.

Navigate and customize your workspace in the Finder.

Receive important information in the Notification Center.

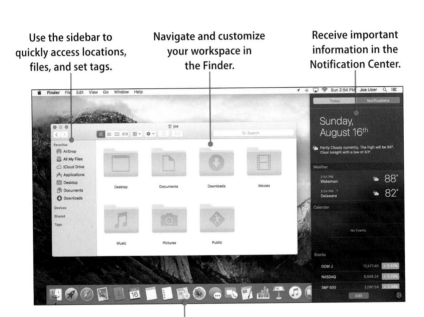

The Dock serves as a launching point for common applications and documents.

In this chapter, you learn how to make efficient use of your screen space.

→ Organizing files using the Dock
→ Navigating folders within the Dock's Grid view mode
→ Customizing the Finder sidebar and toolbar
→ Creating Finder tabs
→ Organizing with File Tags
→ Viewing the contents of files with Quick Look
→ Searching for files and information with Spotlight
→ Keeping track of application events with Notifications

Managing Your Desktop

Your Mac is a powerful machine, capable of working with hundreds of different types of files and managing gigabytes upon gigabytes of data. Back when I got my first 128K Mac (w/floppy), you barely needed folders because only a few files fit on a disk. Today, if you try to count the number of files on your system at any given point in time, the numbers will come back in the hundreds of thousands. The world is more complex, and so are our computers.

To keep things tidy, you can take advantage of a variety of tools built into El Capitan that make working with files and applications fun and efficient, and keep you up-to-date on how your system and applications are performing. You'll see that regardless of how you use your Mac, El Capitan can make both your work and play easier and more intuitive.

Organizing in the Dock

The El Capitan Dock serves as application launcher, filer, and process manager. It enables you to launch applications and documents with a single click, place documents in folders, and even navigate the contents of folders without using the Finder. It also displays running applications so you can easily switch between them. Configuring your Dock to suit your working style and habits can be a big time saver because you don't have to dig through folders within folders just to find a single file.

The Dock is divided into two parts—applications, and files and folders. Applications are on the left of the faint broken line; files and folders are on the right (or top/bottom, if the Dock is oriented vertically). Indicator dots are shown under each active application. If you happen to forget what an icon represents, hover your cursor over the icon to see its name.

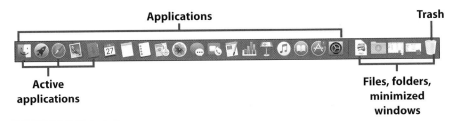

Applications   **Trash**

Active applications   **Files, folders, minimized windows**

Adding and Removing Items from the Dock

Adding files and folders to the Dock is a simple process of dragging and dropping.

1. Use the Finder to locate the icon you want to add to the Dock.

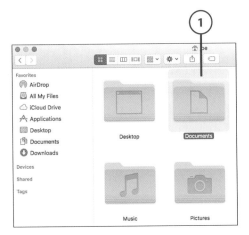

Favorites
- AirDrop
- All My Files
- iCloud Drive
- Applications
- Desktop
- Documents
- Downloads

Devices

Shared

Tags

Desktop   Documents

Music   Pictures

2. Drag the item from the Finder window to the appropriate side of the Dock (apps on the left, docs and folders on the right). As you drag the icon into the Dock, the existing icons move to make room for the addition. Release your mouse when you're happy with the new location.

3. You can rearrange Dock items at any time by dragging them to another position in the Dock.

4. To remove an icon from the Dock, click and drag the icon out of the Dock—holding it until the word "Remove" appears—then release.

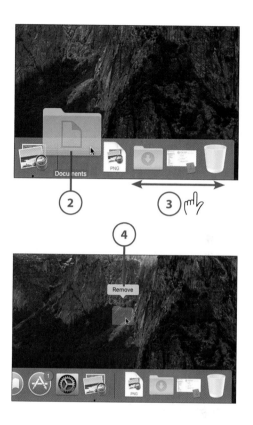

Keep Your Apps Handy

If you start an application and decide you want to keep it in the Dock, click and hold the icon of the running application, and then choose Options, Keep in Dock from the menu that appears.

Using Folders and Stacks in the Dock

Folders that are added to the Dock behave differently from files or applications. When you click a folder residing on the Dock, the contents of the folder are displayed above it in one of three different styles—a Fan, Grid, or List. Additionally, the folder icons themselves can be shown as a simple folder or a stack of files, with your most recent file at the top.

Configuring Folders and Stacks

You can dramatically change the behavior of folders and stacks in the Dock by using the configuration options.

1. After adding a folder to the Dock, right-click or Control-click the folder to open the menu to configure its behavior.

2. Choose to Display as a Folder or Stack to customize the appearance of the icon on the Dock.

3. Choose Fan, Grid, List, or Automatic to set how the content will be displayed when you click the icon in the Dock. The Automatic setting will choose the best option based on the number of items in the folder.

4. Finally, to customize the sorting of the displayed items, choose an option from the Sort by menu.

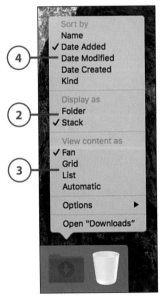

Navigating Files and Folders in Grid Mode

In El Capitan, the Folder Grid mode offers the most functionality for navigating your files. You can navigate through a scrolling list of files, and you can open additional folders.

1. Click a Folder in the Dock that has been configured to Grid mode. A grid popover appears above the folder icon.

2. Scroll through the available files, if needed.

3. To navigate into a folder, click the folder's icon.

4. The Grid refreshes to show the contents of the folder.

5. Click the back arrow in the upper-left corner to return to the previous "parent" folder.

6. Click Open in Finder if you wish to open the current folder as a window in the Finder.

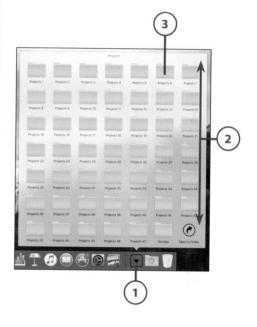

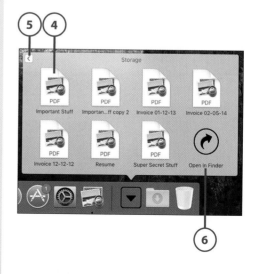

Customizing the Dock's Appearance

The Dock helps keep your desktop nice and tidy by giving you a place to put your commonly used files and folders, but it also takes up a bit of screen space. You can easily customize the Dock's appearance to make it as unobtrusive as possible.

1. Open the System Preferences panel, and click the Dock icon.

2. Use the Size slider to change the size of the Dock.

3. Click the Magnification checkbox. Use the corresponding slider to set the magnification of the icons as you mouse over them in the Dock.

4. Use the Position radio buttons to control the location of the Dock on the screen.

5. To control the way windows animate to and from the Dock, click the Minimize Windows Using drop-down menu to choose between the Genie and Scale effects.

6. Choose Double-Click a Window's Title Bar menu to choose whether a double-click zooms the window to fit the content or minimizes into the Dock.

7. Check the Minimize Windows into Application Icon checkbox to help conserve space in the Dock by putting minimized windows into their applications' Dock icons.

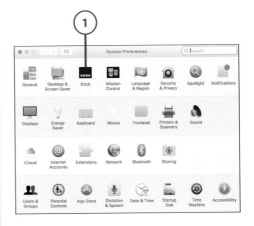

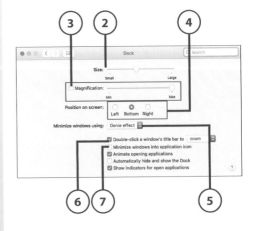

8. By default, application icons "bounce" in the Dock while they're opening. Uncheck the Animate Opening Applications checkbox to disable this behavior.

9. Click Automatically Hide and Show the Dock if you'd like the Dock to disappear altogether when you're not using it.

Hiding the Dock

To quickly hide the Dock, press Command+Option+D. To access Dock settings outside of the System Preferences, right-click the divider line between applications and folders/trash.

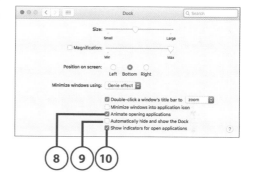

10. Check Show Indicators for Open Applications if you'd like a dot to appear under applications that are running.

Dark-Themed Dock

You can switch your Dock and menu bar from the frosted glass look to a dark theme using the General Preferences panel. Open the panel and check the Use Dark Menu Bar and Dock option.

>>>Go Further

HIDING EVEN MORE!

If you like the extra screen space provided by hiding the Dock, you can also have the El Capitan menu bar hide automatically using the Automatically Hide and Show Menu Bar checkbox in the General preferences.

Customizing Finder Windows

Like the Dock, Finder windows provide an opportunity to configure shortcuts to information that are accessible via a single click. The Finder sidebar and toolbar can be customized with your own files as well as default system shortcuts.

Configuring the Sidebar's System Shortcuts

To change the sidebar's default shortcuts, you need to use the Finder preferences.

1. Open the Finder using its icon in the Dock and choose Finder, Preferences.

2. Click the Sidebar icon at the top of the Finder Preferences window.

3. Use the checkboxes beside Favorites, Shared, Devices, and Tags to configure which folders, network computers, connected hardware, and file tags should be displayed.

4. Close the Finder Preferences window.

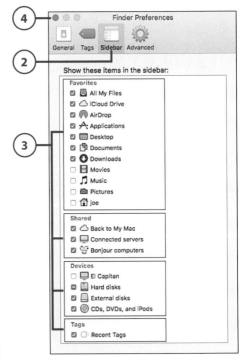

Manually Modifying the Sidebar

In addition to the predefined short-cuts, you can easily add your own icons to the sidebar.

1. To add an icon to the sidebar, first make sure the item's icon is visible in a Finder window.

2. Drag the icon to the Favorites area in the sidebar. If you are *not* dragging a folder, hold down the Command key while dragging.

3. A blue line appears to show where the item will be placed. Release your mouse button to add the item to the list.

4. The icon appears in the sidebar.

5. Rearrange the icons in the sidebar by clicking and dragging them up and down.

6. Remove existing sidebar entries by right-clicking (or Control-clicking) their icons and choosing Remove from Sidebar. Alternatively, just click and drag them from the sidebar—an X appears when the icon is ready to be removed.

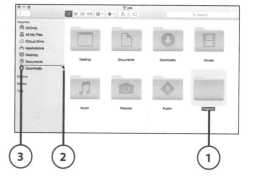

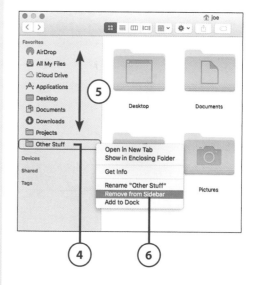

Modifying the Finder Toolbar

Like the sidebar, the Finder window's toolbar can hold shortcuts to files, folders, and applications.

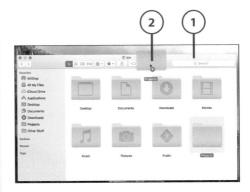

1. Open the Finder window containing the file or folder you want to work with.

2. Drag the icon you wish to add into the toolbar while holding down the Command key. The other interface elements shift to make room for the new addition.

3. To move an icon to a new location on the toolbar, hold the Command key down, and then click and drag. Drag the icon off the toolbar—until a puff of smoke appears—to remove it altogether.

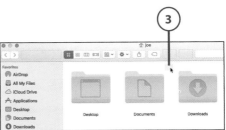

>>>Go Further

DRAGGING ALLOWED!

Toolbar and sidebar items can serve as drag destinations as well as clickable shortcuts. For example, to file a document in a folder, you can drag it to a folder in the sidebar. To save a document to a file server, you can drag it onto a shared drive, and so on.

Using Finder Window Tabs

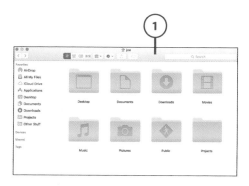

For years your web browser has had tabs to help you browse without having dozens of windows open at a time. In El Capitan, the Finder offers the same feature. You can open a new tab in a Finder window by following these steps.

1. Make sure that a Finder window is open. It doesn't matter what view it is showing.

2. Choose File, New Tab (Command+T) from the menu bar.

3. A new tab appears in the Finder window.

4. After the first tab appears, you can add new tabs by clicking the + icon at the right of the tab bar.

5. You can use each tab as a unique window, browsing different parts of the file system in each.

6. Close a tab by positioning your cursor near its left side and clicking the X box that appears.

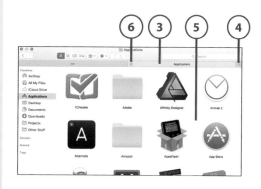

Ever-Present Tabs

If you like seeing the tab bar all the time (even if you don't have multiple tabs open), you can choose Show Tab Bar from the Finder's View menu. This makes the + icon always visible, so adding new tabs becomes easier.

Opening Tabs with a Click

In the Safari web browser (read about it in Chapter 5, "Accessing Email and the Web"), you can open new tabs just by holding Command and clicking. You can do the same with the right preferences set in the Finder. To do this, just complete the following:

1. Choose Finder, Preferences from the menu bar.

2. Make sure the General tab is selected.

3. Check Open Folders in Tabs Instead of New Windows.

4. Close the Finder Preferences window.

5. From this point forward, when you hold Command while double-clicking a folder, the folder opens in a new tab rather than a window.

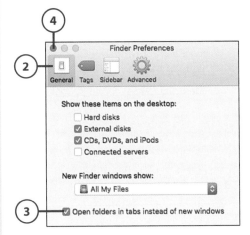

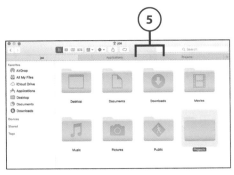

>>>Go Further

TABS ARE A DRAG

Although it may not seem intuitive, you can drag files from one tab to another. Just drag the file into the tab where you want to drop it, keep holding, and after a few seconds the other tab opens, enabling you to continue your drag. Additionally, when you grab a tab itself and drag it out of the window, a new Finder window is created.

Arranging and Grouping Files

You might have noticed that this book doesn't take a bunch of time to tell you about how to sort files, open folders, and all the typical things you do on a computer. Why? Because they work exactly the way you'd expect on a modern operating system. That said, El Capitan has some interesting ways of looking at files that you might not be aware of.

Using All My Files

If you've ever wanted to view all the files you have, the All My Files group will help you. This feature displays, quite literally, *all* your files in your personal account, including files stored in iCloud (see Chapter 4, "Setting Up iCloud and Internet Accounts," for more details). To view your files, follow these steps:

1. Make sure the Favorites section of the Finder sidebar is expanded.

2. Click the All My Files icon, or choose Go, All My Files from the menu bar.

3. All the files that belong to you are shown in the Finder window.

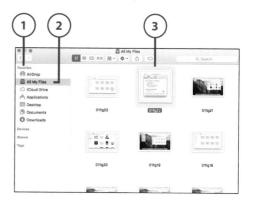

4. Use the view icons to change between icon, list, column, and cover flow views, respectively.

Granted, this isn't the most exciting feature in the world, but when coupled with the Arrange By feature (covered in the next task), it becomes far more interesting.

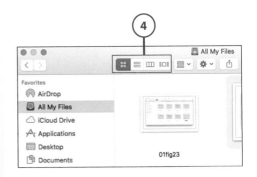

01fig23

Arranging a Finder View

You're probably used to clicking a column heading and sorting files by name, date, modified, or other attributes. This is expanded in OS X with the Arrange By feature. Using Arrange By, you can view your files arranged by more "human" categories, such as the files you've opened today, in the last week, and so on.

1. Open the finder view you want to arrange.

2. Use the Arrange By menu to select a category for grouping your files.

3. Different groups are separated by horizontal lines.

4. When in icon view mode, swipe left or right on a multitouch trackpad or Magic Mouse to scroll through a cover flow-like view of the icons within a grouping.

5. Click the Show All link to turn off the cover flow scrolling and show all the items within the window.

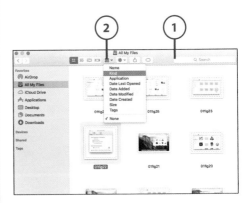

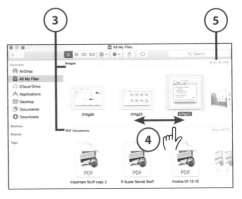

Making Arrangements

To set a default arrangement (among other things) for a folder, choose View, Show View Options from the menu bar when viewing the folder.

Assigning Tags

When choosing an arrangement for a view, you may notice a Tags category. This feature offers the ability to assign tags to your files and folders. These can be anything you want—"Important," "Projects," and so on. They are arbitrary text descriptions that you establish and can use to label any of your files or folders, no matter where they exist on your system.

1. Select a file or folder in a Finder window.

2. Click the Tags button in the Finder toolbar.

3. Either type in a new tag, or choose an existing tag from the menu.

4. Click outside the menu to assign the tag.

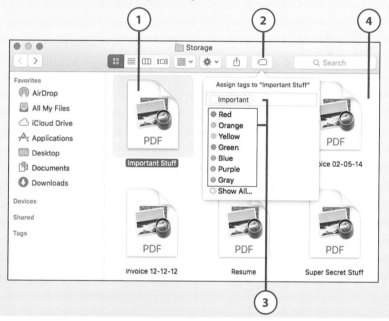

>>>Go Further

EL CAPITAN LOVES TAGS

Truth be told, there are a million and one ways to assign tags in El Capitan. You can do it using the method just described; you can add tags by clicking the file name on a window in many El Capitan applications; you can assign tags by choosing Finder, Get Info when a file or folder is selected. I could write a whole chapter on adding tags, but I suggest you find a method you prefer and stick with it.

Removing Tags

After you start adding tags in El Capitan, you'll quickly discover that you can add as many tags to an individual file or folder as you want. As a result, you might want to remove a tag you added in error.

1. Select a file or folder in a Finder window.

2. Click the Tags button in the Finder toolbar.

3. All of the assigned tags appear in the field at the top of the drop-down menu.

4. Click to highlight a tag, and either press delete or drag it to the trash.

5. Click outside of the menu to save the new tag list.

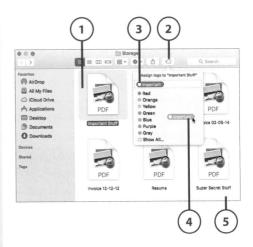

Viewing Tags

After you've assigned tags, you can view them using the Tags section in the Finder sidebar.

1. Make sure the Tags section is visible.

2. Click the tag you want to view or All Tags if your tag list is long and the one you want isn't visible.

3. Files and folders matching the tag are displayed.

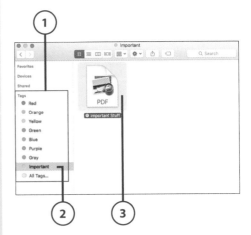

Spotting Tags

If the tag has an assigned color, it appears as a color-coded dot beside the file in many of the standard Finder views.

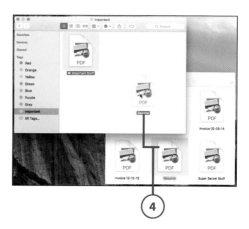

4. You can drag new files and folders into the window to assign them to the tag. (I told you there are a million ways to assign tags!)

>>>*Go Further*

TAGS—SERIOUSLY, THEY'RE EVERYWHERE

When you open files, notice that Tags now appear in the sidebar within the File Open dialog box. You can use these to quickly view all the files matching a tag and open a file without having to find its folder.

The "Finding Information with Spotlight" section later in this chapter explains how Spotlight can be used to search for files matching certain tags and other criteria (for example, "All images with the tag 'Vacation' created between the dates of June 2015 and August 2016").

Managing Tags

To see, edit, and assign colors to your tags, use the Finder preferences.

1. Choose Finder, Preferences from the menu bar.

2. Click the Tags tab at the top of the Preferences window.

3. Use the checkboxes to control which tags are visible in the Finder sidebar.

4. Click the circle beside a tag to choose a color for it.

5. Click a tag's name to edit it.

6. Drag Tags to the rectangular list of Tags at the bottom to have quick access to them through Finder contextual menus or the Finder's File menu (yet *another* way to add tags to files and folders!).

Missing Tags?

If the Tags section is missing from your Finder sidebar, you might have disabled it accidentally. You can add the Tags section back using the Sidebar Finder preferences (Finder, Preferences).

Previewing Document Contents

Launching applications takes time and resources. Frequently, when you want to open a file, all you really want is to see the contents of the file. Using the equivalent of X-Ray vision, called Quick Look, you can view many of your documents without the need to open an application.

Viewing a File with Quick Look

Using Quick Look doesn't require anything more than your mouse and a press of the spacebar.

1. Select a file from the Finder or desktop by clicking once, but don't open it!

2. Press the spacebar to open Quick Look.

3. Click the circle with double arrows to expand Quick Look to fullscreen.

4. Use the Share menu to send the file via email, add images to iPhoto, etc.

5. Some files might show additional controls above the preview or below when in fullscreen mode. When multiple images are selected, for example, fullscreen mode includes a button to play a slideshow.

6. Press the spacebar again to exit Quick Look (not shown). Note that if you are in fullscreen mode, you need to press Escape (Esc) on your keyboard or press the onscreen >< (two arrows facing each other) button to exit fullscreen mode before exiting Quick Look.

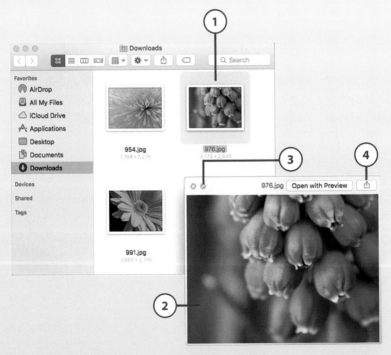

⑤

>>>Go Further

INSTANT SLIDESHOWS!

If you start Quick Look on multiple files, you can run a slideshow. The fullscreen Quick Look window includes play, forward, and backward arrows to start and control the slideshow. You can also use an index sheet icon (four squares) to show previews of all the files in a single Quick Look window (also available in windowed mode).

Quick Look even works on music and video files, enabling you to play back media without opening a dedicated application.

Adding a Finder Preview Panel

New to El Capitan is the ability to keep a Quick Look preview panel open in any finder window.

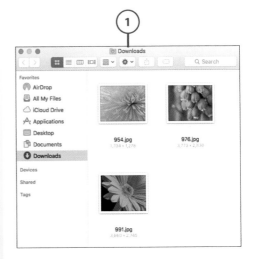

1. To add a file preview to your Finder, first make sure you have a Finder window open.

2. Choose View, Show Preview.

3. A preview of the currently selected file is shown on the right side of the Finder window. Notice this also provides yet *another* way to add tags to file!

4. Click and drag the divider at the left edge of the preview area to change the size of the preview.

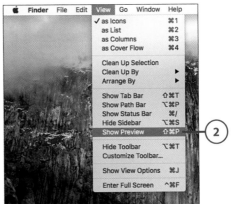

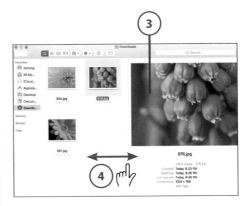

Previewing Files Using Finder Icons

The Finder includes Quick Look-like capability for some files just by mousing over them.

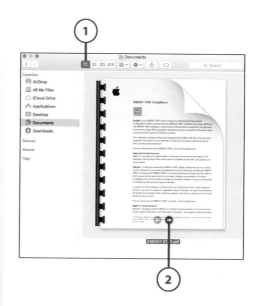

1. To preview a file using icons in El Capitan, make sure you're in icon view mode.

2. Mouse over the file, and use the controls that appear to navigate the contents of the file. As with Quick Look, even media files can be played in this manner.

Adjust Icon Size

For quick access to a slider for changing your icon sizes, choose View, Show Status Bar from the menu bar. Alternatively, you can adjust a window's icon size by choosing View, Show View Options from the menu bar.

Finding Information with Spotlight (New!)

When the Finder's file organization features can't help you find what you want, the amazing Spotlight search system in El Capitan makes it simple. Spotlight can search across files, email messages, the built-in dictionary, and even Internet resources to find information.

Searching for Files and Information

Spotlight searches can be started at any time, without needing to launch any additional applications.

1. To start a search, press Command+Space, or click the magnifying glass icon in the upper-right corner of your screen. A search field appears in the center of the screen.

2. Begin typing in the search field.

3. As you type, files, images, folders, and even Internet sources that match your terms are displayed in a list. You can even type the names of movies, or queries such as "weather in Cleveland" to find information using Internet sources.

4. Click a result to see a preview on the right.

5. Double-click a matched item in the list to open the item.

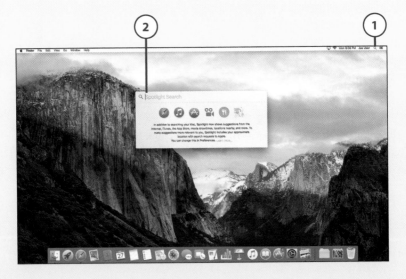

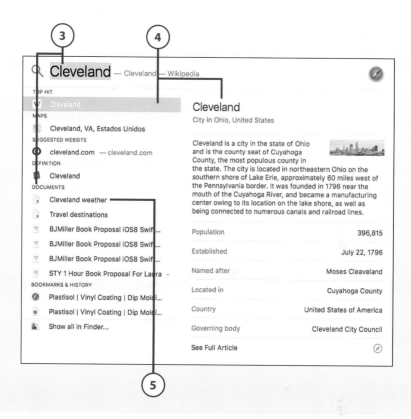

Quick Launching via Spotlight

You can use Spotlight searches to quickly launch applications. Begin typing the name of the application in the search, wait until a match appears, and then press Return. Your application launches!

Customizing Spotlight Searching

Spotlight searches can turn up tons of information. More, perhaps, than you'd like. To choose exactly what you want to display, you need to configure the Spotlight System Preferences panel.

1. Open the Spotlight System Preferences panel.

2. Within the Search Results panel, check items you want to be returned as part of the search results. Uncheck the items you want to exclude.

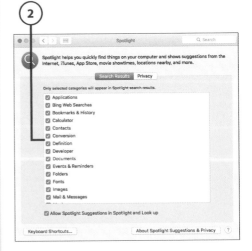

3. To restrict what volumes are searched, click the Privacy button. You can choose to have Spotlight ignore specific folders or disks.

4. Click the + button to choose a folder or disk that you don't want to be searchable. Alternatively, drag folders directly from the Finder into the Privacy list.

5. Click Keyboard Shortcuts to change how Spotlight is started or disable keyboard shortcuts altogether.

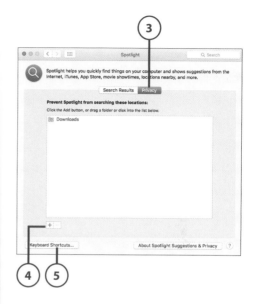

Saving Searches as Smart Folders in the Finder

Spotlight file searches can be saved and reused in the form of Smart Folders. If you'd like to create a search that shows all your image files—regardless of where they are stored, for example—you can create and save a Show All Images search.

1. Use a Finder window's search field to type the name or content of a file you want to find.

2. Choose what the search should include (such as a filename). The default is to include file content, kinds, and other metadata.

3. Adjust whether you want to search your entire Mac (indicated by the words "This Mac") or just the folder you're currently in.

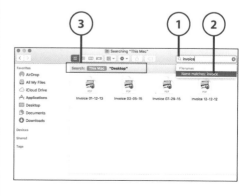

4. Use the + and – buttons below the search field to add or subtract additional search criteria lines.

5. Use the pop-up menu at the start of each search line to configure search attributes such as file, kinds, or size.

6. To add even more search criteria, choose Other. A window listing the available search attributes displays. Choose an attribute and click OK.

7. When you're satisfied with your search, click the Save button.

8. You are prompted for a name for the search and where it should be saved.

9. Click Add to Sidebar.

10. Click Save.

11. If you choose to add the search to your sidebar, it is accessible immediately from your Finder window. Otherwise you need to navigate to the saved location and double-click the search's Smart Folder icon to run it again.

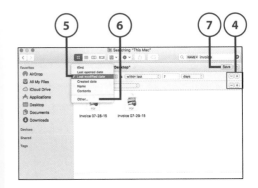

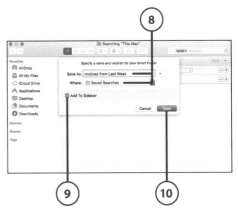

Less Is More

After you've configured a few search criteria beyond the text for the file name or file content, you can erase the search text and El Capitan includes all of the files that match your other criteria.

Managing Your "Today" and Notifications (New!)

At any given time, both you and your computer have quite a bit going on—mail being checked, potential FaceTime invites, software updates, bills to calculate, calendars to watch, and so on.

El Capitan's Notification Center contains a view of system notifications (alert messages, warnings, and so on) along with a Today view that you can customize with information and tools you use everyday. The Notification Center keeps you in touch with your virtual and real lives—without needing to leave the El Capitan Finder.

Receiving Notifications

To receive a notification, you technically don't need to do anything, but you should know what to expect:

1. Notifications, as they occur, appear along the right side of the display.

2. Most notifications go away after a few seconds and require no interaction. Some might include options to immediately react to the notification. Clicking the buttons performs the action described.

Viewing Notifications in Notification Center

If a notification "goes away" before you have a chance to read it, you can catch up with the latest notifications in the Notification Center.

1. Click the bulleted list icon in the upper-right corner of the menu bar. You can also open the Notification Center with a trackpad gesture by sliding two fingers to the left, starting off the right side of the trackpad.

2. The desktop slides over to reveal the Notification Center.

3. Switch to the notifications view by clicking the Notifications button at the top.

4. Clicking a notification reacts appropriately—clicking a missed FaceTime call, for example, opens FaceTime and returns the call.

5. To dismiss an application's notifications, click the X icon in the upper-right corner of its list of notifications.

6. To close the Notification Center, click on the desktop or the menu bar icon, or slide two fingers to the right on the trackpad.

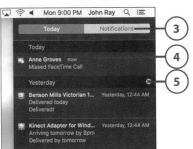

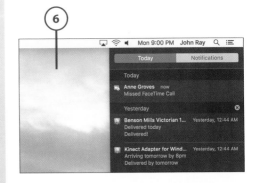

Customizing the Notification Display

How each application presents notifications (or if they present notifications at all) can be customized in OS X.

1. Open the Notifications System Preferences panel.

2. Choose an Application to customize from the list on the left.

3. Use the alert style buttons to choose from None (no visual at all), Banners (automatically close), and Alerts (stay on the screen until manually dismissed).

4. Check Show Notifications on Lock Screen if you want to see the notifications when your Mac's screen is locked.

5. Uncheck Show in Notification Center if you prefer to not receive any notifications (visual or audio) from the application.

6. Use the Recent Items pop-up menu to choose how many notifications are shown at a time.

7. Check the Badge App Icon checkbox to show the count of notifications (such as new messages) on the application's icon.

8. Check Play Sound for Notifications to enable the application to provide an audio alert.

9. Select whether to Sort Notification Center manually or according to the time a notification was received. If sorting manually, you can drag the icons up and down in the application list to choose how they appear in the Notification Center.

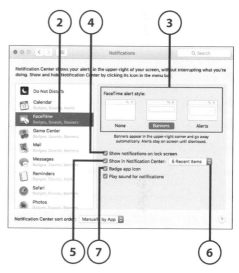

Quick Settings Access Within Notification Center

In the lower-right corner of the Notification Center itself is a small gear icon. Clicking this button opens the Notification Center preferences.

Activating Do Not Disturb Mode

If you're like me, you probably have (potentially) several dozen apps wanting to tell you something via notification. For the times you'd prefer not to hear all the sounds and see the notification windows, you can activate a Do Not Disturb mode that lasts until the next morning. Begin by opening the Notification Center, and then follow these steps:

1. Scroll the Notification Center content down. (It doesn't matter which Notification Center section you're in.)

2. An On/Off button is revealed. Click Off to quiet your notifications or On to let them be seen and heard.

3. The Notification Center icon becomes dimmed when in Do Not Disturb mode.

Do Not Disturb Me NOW!

Want to activate Do Not Disturb mode in a flash? Just hold the option key and click the Notification Center icon in the menu bar. The icon will gray to show it is disabled. Repeat the process to turn it back on.

Customizing Do Not Disturb Mode

It's simple to activate Do Not Disturb when you need it, but you can customize the feature to automatically activate in situations where you typically don't want notifications to appear.

1. Open the Notifications System Preferences Panel.

2. Select the Do Not Disturb option.

3. Provide a time range (and check the checkbox) to automatically apply Do Not Disturb during a common time period (for example, night time).

4. Click When the Display Is Sleeping to activate Do Not Disturb when your Mac's screen is asleep.

5. Check When Mirroring to TVs and Projectors to keep notifications from showing up when you're displaying content on a TV or a projector.

6. Use the Allow Calls from Everyone to allow any contact to call you via FaceTime during Do Not Disturb hours.

7. Click the Allow Repeated Calls checkbox to disable Do Not Disturb for individuals who have called repeatedly (in case of potential emergencies).

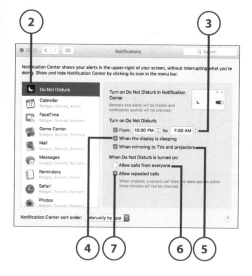

Using Notification Center's Today View

Also available in the Notification Center is the Today view. The Today view doesn't show you system notifications, but it does keep you up-to-date on your real world events, and it gives you access to commonly used utilities for communicating with social networks, checking your calendar, and much more.

Working in the Today View

You can access the Today view any-time the menu bar is visible. Just fol-low these steps:

1. Open the Notification Center.

2. Click the Today button at the top of the Notification Center column.

3. Widgets are included to show you a summary of your day, the weather, stocks, calendar events—even the location of your friends if they have iOS devices. If widgets are off your screen, you can scroll up and down to view them.

4. Position your cursor over a widget's name (here, Stocks) to reveal an "i" icon that, when clicked, configures features of that widget.

5. Close the Today view by clicking the desktop or the Notification Center icon in the upper-right of the screen.

>>>Go Further
YOUR SOCIAL CENTER

The Notification Center's Today view can serve as your interface to social media. If you add social networking accounts (see Chapters 4 and 7), you'll automatically get a widget added to the Today view for interacting with those accounts.

Managing Today View Widgets

The Today view isn't static. You can customize it by rearranging widgets and adding new widgets from the Mac App Store. To manage the Today view, follow these steps:

1. Open the Notification Center and click Today to switch to the Today view.

2. Click the Edit button at the bottom of the view; an additional column appears.

3. Click the – buttons to remove widgets.

4. The right column displays available widgets to add. Click + beside a widget name to add it to your Today view.

5. To the right of each widget within the Today view is an icon consisting of three lines. Click and drag on these icons to move widgets up and down in the view.

6. To find and download new widgets, click the App Store button in the bottom center of the Notification Center.

7. Click Done to save your edits.

Using Utilities in the Dashboard

The Today view in the Notification Center is the future of OS X widgets. The past, however, is a feature called Dashboard. Although I have my doubts about the longevity of the Dashboard, it remains a useful tool. So, what is this thing…?

The Dashboard is an overlay of widgets you can call up and dismiss with a single keystroke. Widgets you add to the Dashboard persist between reboots, so when you've configured your Dashboard the way you like it, it's there to stay!

Turning on the Dashboard

To turn on the Dashboard feature, follow these steps:

1. Open the Mission Control System Preferences panel.

2. Use the Dashboard menu to choose whether the Dashboard is displayed over the top of your windows, or as a separate "space." You'll learn about spaces in the next chapter. For consistency with the rest of El Capitan, choose "space."

3. Close the System Preferences.

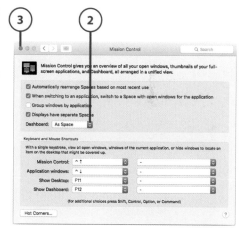

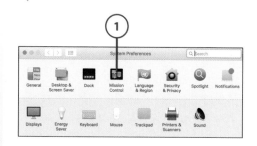

Showing the Dashboard

The El Capitan Dashboard appears and disappears with a keystroke or a click.

1. To show the Dashboard, click the Dashboard icon in the Applications folder, or, even easier, swipe with four fingers to the right across your Magic Trackpad (not shown).

2. The desktop slides out of the way and a default set of Dashboard widgets displays.

3. You can now interact with any of the widgets, including dragging them around to rearrange them, just as you would with normal applications.

4. Exit Dashboard by clicking the arrow in the lower right of the Dashboard or swiping with four fingers to the left.

Tweaking Your Shortcuts

To configure additional shortcuts to the Dashboard, you can visit the Mission Control System Preferences panel. Read more in Chapter 2, "Making the Most of Your Screen Space."

Adding and Removing Dashboard Widgets

One of the best things about widgets is that you can keep adding them to your screen, and they'll always be there until you choose to remove them.

1. To add (or remove) a widget in the Dashboard, start the Dashboard and click the + icon in the lower-left corner. A screen of widgets displays.

2. Click More Widgets to open a web browser with a page listing additional downloadable widgets.

3. If you have many widgets, use the search field, if needed, to find what you are looking for.

4. To add a widget to your desktop, click its icon. The list of widgets disappears and you return to the Dashboard with the new widget visible.

5. To remove widgets, click the – icon in the lower-left corner, and all the widgets display the X icon in their corner. Tap the X for each widget you want to remove.

Configuring Dashboard Widgets

Widgets are unique applications that each behave differently, but, in general, you configure them one of two ways. Some widgets, when you add them to your screen, automatically prompt you with the information they are expecting. Other widgets must be configured to show the proper results, as follows:

1. Mouse over a widget you want to configure. A small "i" appears in the corner of the widget. Click the "i" icon.

2. The widget flips over, revealing the configuration details.

Installing Widgets

When you download a widget (see "Adding and Removing Dashboard Widgets"), it downloads a file in your Downloads folder. To install the download, just double-click the icon; OS X takes care of the rest.

>>>Go Further

LAUNCHPAD IN DISGUISE

The view for adding widgets to the Dashboard is really just a feature called Launchpad but customized to only show Dashboard widgets. You can use the same techniques you'll learn about Launchpad in Chapter 2 to organize and manage your widget library.

Navigate Desktop spaces and applications.

Create new spaces to make room for your work.

View active applications and windows in Mission Control.

In this chapter, you learn how to take control
of your applications and windows, including:

→ Finding your way around Mission Control

→ Managing applications and windows

→ Creating new spaces

→ Launching applications with Launchpad

→ Creating application groups in Launchpad

→ Uninstalling applications through Launchpad

→ Managing auto open and save features

Making the Most of Your Screen Space

As applications become more complex, so does the task of managing them. Software is installed everywhere, windows are spread
out over your desktop, and just trying to find your way through
the maze of information overload can be nightmarish. El Capitan
attempts to bring the madness under control by way of Mission
Control.

Mission Control, combined with features such as Spaces,
Launchpad, fullscreen apps, auto application, and window restoration, makes it easy to navigate the most cluttered computer. The
biggest problem? Many of these features are hidden until you
invoke them. In this chapter, you learn how to do just that!

Swimming the Sea of Application Windows with Mission Control (New!)

One of the big benefits of modern operating systems is that they enable you to run multiple applications at once. Unfortunately, no matter how much screen space we have, we always need more! To help manage the ever-expanding collection of windows that you need to work within, Apple provides Mission Control as part of OS X El Capitan. Mission Control helps you view your running apps, see the windows they have open, and even expand the amount of desktop real estate you have available.

As you're about to see, in Mission Control terms, a "space" is a single screenful of information. It can be your Dashboard screen, your typical desktop, a full-screen app, or even additional desktop views that you create.

Opening and Closing Mission Control

To manage Mission Control and access its features, follow these instructions:

1. Slide three fingers up your trackpad, double-tap two fingers on the Magic Mouse, or press the Mission Control key (F3) on your keyboard. Mission Control opens. Spaces appear on the top; the current space is in the center of the screen.

2. Slide three fingers down on the trackpad, double-tap two fingers on the mouse, or press the Mission Control key again. Mission Control closes.

Docking Mission Control

If you prefer to start Mission Control by clicking, you can use the Mission Control icon. It's in the Dock on machines without a multitouch trackpad—but you can add it from the Applications folder on any Mac.

Navigating Applications and Windows

When you start Mission Control, your current space (probably your desktop, if you're starting Mission Control for the first time) is front and center, along with representations of each app running in the space and its windows.

To switch between applications and their windows, do the following:

1. Start Mission Control.

2. Click a window to exit Mission Control and bring the chosen window to the front.

3. To preview the contents of a window, position your pointer over the window and then press the spacebar. Press the spacebar again to hide the preview.

>>>*Go Further*

I MISS MY APPLICATION ICONS AND WINDOW GROUPINGS!

In previous versions of OS X, Mission Control grouped application windows by application. This is turned off, by default, in El Capitan. If you want to re-enable this feature, skip ahead to the section "Configuring Mission Control Features and Shortcuts" later in this chapter.

Creating and Populating a New Space

Modern applications look like the cockpit controls of advanced aircraft; it can be overwhelming finding your way around a single application—let alone 10. With Mission Control you can create new desktop spaces dedicated to whatever applications you'd like. To do so, start Mission Control and follow these steps:

1. Move your mouse to the upper-right corner. The top of the screen expands to show thumbnails of your spaces, and a + button appears as your mouse approaches the corner; click it.

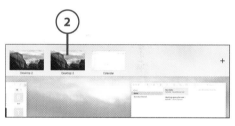

2. A new space is created and a depiction of its contents is added to the top of Mission Control.

3. Drag application windows from the current space to the thumbnail of the new space.

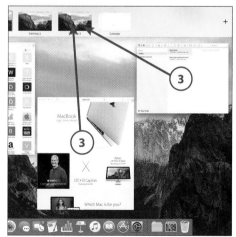

Switching Between Spaces

After you've created a new space, you can switch to it via Mission Control or using a trackpad gesture:

1. Start Mission Control.

2. Click the space thumbnail you want to display, or swipe left or right with three fingers to move between spaces.

3. Click on the background to exit Mission Control.

Even Faster Space Switching

The fastest way to switch between Mission Control spaces is without even starting Mission Control. Swipe left or right with three fingers on your trackpad (or two fingers on the Magic Mouse) at any time to move between spaces.

Closing a Space

It's so easy to create spaces, you might find yourself with some extra ones you need to get rid of. To close out a space, follow these steps:

1. Start Mission Control.

2. Position your cursor over a space at the top of the screen.

3. An X appears in the upper-left corner of the space thumbnail. Click the X to close the space. Any windows within it move back to the primary desktop space.

Creating Fullscreen Application Spaces

Spaces are great for providing more, um, space for your windowed applications, but they also serve as a "container" for your fullscreen apps. Rather than a fullscreen application eating up one of your desktop spaces, it automatically creates a new dedicated space when it starts and removes it when it stops.

1. Click the green double-arrow button in the upper-left corner of an application window to enter fullscreen mode.

2. A new space is created and is visible in Mission Control.

3. Switch to and from the space exactly as you would any other. When you're done using the fullscreen app, either quit the application or exit fullscreen mode by pressing the Escape key or moving your cursor to the top left of the screen and clicking the green button again. The space is automatically removed from Mission Control.

Creating Split-Screen Application Spaces

New to El Capitan is the ability to create split fullscreen spaces—that is, a space shared by two fullscreen applications. To do this, follow these steps:

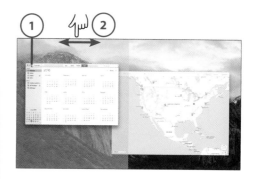

1. Click and *hold* the green double-arrow button in the upper-left corner of an application window to enter fullscreen mode.

2. While continuing to hold the mouse/trackpad button, drag the window to the left or right of the screen. The screen side will highlight to show it is selected.

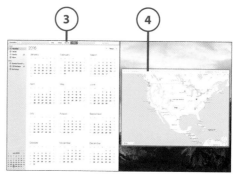

3. Release the mouse button to enter split-screen mode with the application.

4. El Capitan displays the options for your second application window (other open apps) beside the app you've chosen. Click a window to expand it to fill the second half of the screen.

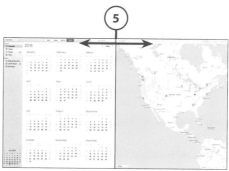

5. Drag the divider line to change the amount of screen space allocated to each app.

6. Switch to and from the split-screen space exactly as you would any other. When you're done using the either app, either quit the application or exit fullscreen mode by pressing the Escape key or moving your cursor to the top left of the screen and clicking the green button again. The space is automatically removed from Mission Control once both apps have exited.

>>>Go Further

QUICKLY ADD WINDOWS TO A SPACE OR CREATE NEW APPLICATION SPACES

If you're working with an app and you want to quickly add its window to another space (or turn it into its own fullscreen space), drag the window up "past" the top of the menu bar. Mission control automatically launches and allows you to drag the window into an existing space, on top of an existing fullscreen space, to create a split-screen space, or to the right of any existing spaces to create a new space.

Choosing Between Application Windows

When you just need to navigate your windows, the Mission Control Application windows option comes in handy. Using this, you can show all your application windows, or just the windows for a specific program, with a single click.

1. To display all the windows open within an application, click and hold an active application's icon in the dock and choose Show All Windows. Alternatively, press Control+down arrow.

2. The screen refreshes to show miniature versions of your windows. Minimized windows appear in the bottom portion of the display; active windows appear at the top.

3. Press the Tab key to switch between active applications, limiting the miniaturized windows to the highlighted application.

4. Click a window to select it and move it to the front.

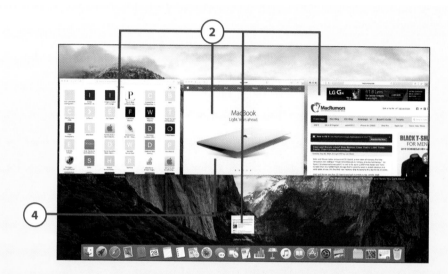

Showing the Desktop

Sometimes you need quick access to the files on your desktop, and rearranging windows (or using the Finder's Hide menu) isn't very efficient. Mission Control's Show Desktop feature comes in handy here:

1. To clear all the windows off the screen so that you can temporarily work with the desktop, press F11 (you need to hold down the function key).

2. You can now work within the desktop with no obstructions. Press F11 again to return the windows to their original positions.

If Only Real Life Were So Easy…

To quickly drop a file from the Finder into another application (such as an attachment into an email message), start dragging a file while the desktop is cleared, press F11 to return the windows to the screen, and then finish dragging and dropping the file into an application.

Configuring Mission Control Features and Shortcuts

If you have a specific way of working and want to customize how Mission Control or any of its features is activated, just follow these steps:

1. Open the System Preferences application, and click the Mission Control panel icon.

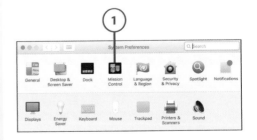

2. Uncheck Automatically Rearrange Spaces Based on Most Recent Use if you prefer that El Capitan keeps your spaces in the same order you add them, regardless of your usage patterns.

3. In most cases, leave When Switching to an Application, Switch to a Space with Open Windows for the Application checkbox checked. This indicates that when you switch to an application (using the Dock or Command+Tab), you automatically switch to the space that contains its open windows.

4. If you prefer application windows to be grouped under their application icon in the Mission Control display, check Group Windows by Application.

5. If you're lucky enough to have multiple monitors connected to your Mac, check Displays Have Separate Spaces to have each display act as a separate work area with its own collection of fullscreen apps and workspaces. To use the monitors as a single unified space, uncheck this option.

6. Use the Dashboard pop-up menu to choose whether Dashboard should be its own space, displayed as a transparent overlay, or turned off entirely.

7. At the bottom of the panel, use the pop-up menus to configure keyboard and mouse button combinations to invoke the Mission Control features and Dashboard.

8. To trigger these features by moving the mouse to the screen corners, click the Hot Corners button.

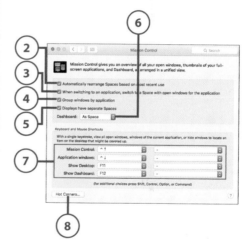

9. Use the pop-up menus beside each screen corner to choose among the different options. After you've made a selection, just move the mouse into that corner to invoke the feature.

10. Click OK when finished.

11. Close the System Preferences.

Remember Your Gestures!

As you know, you control Mission Control through gestures, and these aren't set in stone! Use the trackpad or Mouse System Preferences panels to configure the gestures used by Mission Control.

Managing and Launching Applications with Launchpad

Whereas Mission Control helps you find your way through your windows, the Launchpad eliminates the need to open them. Launchpad brings iOS-like application management to your Mac. Instead of digging through folders to launch an application, you simply start Launchpad and all your installed apps are visible in one place. No digging required.

Starting Launchpad

Like Mission Control, Apple wants to keep Launchpad at the ready. Unlike other applications, it takes no time to start and can be invoked through a gesture:

1. Open Launchpad by performing a pinching gesture with your thumb and three fingers on your trackpad. Alternatively, press the Launchpad key (F4), or click the Launchpad icon in the Dock or in the Applications folder.

2. The Launchpad appears, blurring out your background.

3. Reverse the pinching gesture, or click on the background to exit Launchpad.

Navigating Launchpad

If you've used an iPad or an iPhone, you immediately know how to navigate Launchpad. If you haven't, don't worry—it takes about a minute to learn everything you'll need to know.

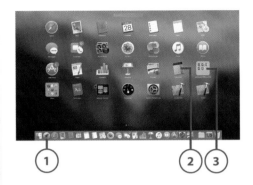

1. Open Launchpad to access your applications.

2. Click an application icon to launch it.

3. Click a folder icon to open it.

4. Click outside the folder to close it.

5. There can be multiple pages of icons, represented by the dots at the center bottom of the screen.

6. Move between pages by swiping left or right with your fingers, clicking the dots, or clicking and dragging left or right.

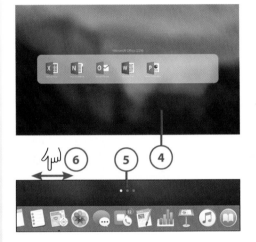

Searching Launchpad

If you can't find an application you're looking for, you can easily search for it directly in Launchpad.

1. Open Launchpad.

2. Click to type in the search field.

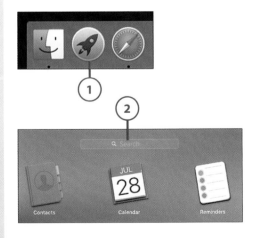

3. Enter a few characters of the name of the application you're looking for.

4. Launchpad refreshes to show the search results. The best match is highlighted.

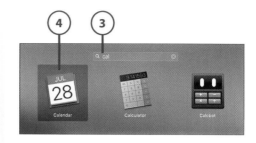

Rearranging Icons

The Launchpad display is completely customizable. To rearrange the icons on your screen, follow these instructions:

1. Open Launchpad.

2. Click and drag the icon to a new location—even a new page. Release the mouse to place the icon.

It's Not All Good

A Mac Disguised as an iPad

Launchpad suffers from a bit of an identity crisis. It follows the same "click and hold to enter icon wiggle mode," just like iOS. This behavior, however, isn't necessary for rearranging or even deleting icons as it is in iOS. Whether you use it is up to you and completely superficial. You can even make the icons wiggle manually by pressing and holding the Option key on your keyboard.

Creating New Folders

Unlike folders in the Finder, Launchpad folders are created on the fly and automatically disappear when all their contents are removed. To create a folder in Launchpad, follow these steps:

1. Open Launchpad.

2. Drag an icon on top of another icon that you want to group it with.

3. A new folder is created and opened, and the icons are added.

4. Click the title of the folder to rename it.

5. Click on the background outside the folder to close it.

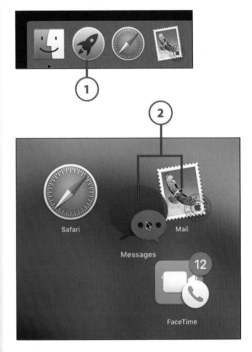

The Folder That Wasn't There

Folders you create or delete in Launchpad do not alter your file system. They are purely logical groupings and do not affect the location of your actual files.

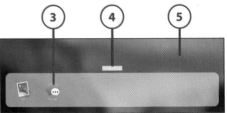

Deleting Folders

To remove a folder from Launchpad, follow these instructions:

1. Open Launchpad.

2. Click the folder that you want to remove.

3. The folder opens.

4. Drag each item out of the folder.

5. When you reach the last item, the folder vanishes automatically.

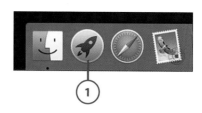

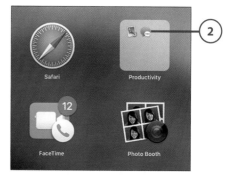

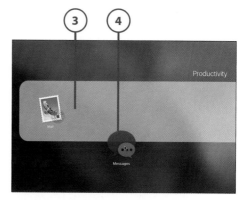

Deleting Applications

In addition to providing a quick way to access your applications, Launchpad offers an easy way to uninstall applications that you've installed from the Mac App Store. (See Chapter 10, "Installing and Managing Applications and Extensions on Your Mac," for details.)

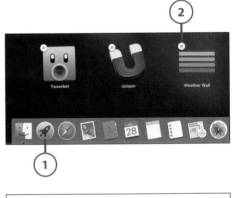

1. Open Launchpad.

2. Click and hold on the icon until an X appears in the upper left, and click the X. (Alternatively, drag the item to the Trash icon on the Dock.)

3. You are prompted to confirm the deletion.

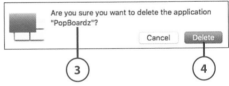

4. Click Delete. The application is uninstalled from your system. You can reinstall it through the App Store if needed.

It's Not All Good

The Not-So-Universal Uninstaller

You can only use Launchpad for uninstalling applications you've added through the Mac App Store. To remove other apps, you need to revert to the old-school method of using an uninstaller (if one came with the application) or manually dragging the application files to the trash.

Managing Auto Open and Save Features

El Capitan offers some unique features that save you time when you boot your system after some downtime, start an application you use frequently, or even just save files. Although these can be useful, they can also be disconcerting to users who expect more conventional behavior—such as explicitly choosing when to open applications and save files.

Toggling Application Auto Open

By default, applications and windows open at login exactly as you had them when you shut down your computer. This is a nifty feature, but it also means you might have software starting at boot that you didn't intend. You can toggle this feature on and off by following these steps:

1. Choose Log Out from the Apple menu.

2. Uncheck Reopen Windows When Logging Back In to disable automatic application startup, or check the box to re-enable it.

3. Click Log Out or Cancel. Your preference will be maintained regardless of your choice.

Setting Window Restoration

In addition to restoring applications, El Capitan can restore the open files and windows that you were using when you quit an application. By default, this feature is turned off, but you can easily toggle it on.

1. Open the System Preferences application and click the General icon.

2. Uncheck Close Windows When Quitting an App. This causes your applications to save their current state when they quit. Check the box to disable the behavior.

3. Close the System Preferences.

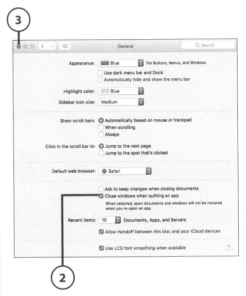

>>>Go Further

TEMPORARILY ENABLE OR DISABLE WINDOW SAVING

If you're not sure you want to use the window restoration feature, or you don't want to use it with specific applications, you can temporarily toggle it on and off. To do this, just hold down the Option key when quitting your application. The Quit menu selection changes to Quit and Keep Windows or Quit and Close All Windows, depending on your setting in the General preference panel.

Enabling Manual File Saving

When you start working in El Capitan, you'll notice something "missing" when you work with files: Frequently, you aren't asked to save them when you close them. El Capitan automatically saves your files, even if you prefer that it didn't. To change this, complete these steps:

1. Open the System Preferences application and click the General icon.

2. Check Ask to Keep Changes When Closing Documents.

3. Close the System Preferences.

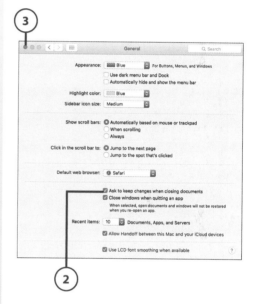

**Use the Wi-Fi status
menu to find and join
wireless networks.**

**Configure and control your network
interfaces in the Network System
Preferences panel.**

In this chapter, you learn how to get your Mac online, including tasks like:

→ Connecting to wired networks
→ Connecting to secure wireless networks
→ Configuring network address, DNS, and routing information
→ Verifying network connections
→ Creating VPN connections
→ Managing multiple connections with Locations

Connecting Your Mac to a Network

Being connected to a network gives you access to information, files, and services such as email or the Web. Your Mac comes with the latest networking technology—802.11ac Wi-Fi and gigabit Ethernet, making it a snap to connect to existing wired or wireless networks.

In this chapter, we explore the connection options available to you on your Mac.

Connecting to a Wired Network

The most common type of network connection in the business world is a wired Ethernet connection. The cables used to connect to the network look like oversized phone connectors and, as luck has it, plug directly into your Mac's Ethernet port. (New Air and Retina Mac owners will need to buy Apple's USB or Thunderbolt Ethernet adapter.) Almost all Macs support Gigabit Ethernet, making them capable of exchanging information at extremely high speeds.

It's Not All Good

There aren't many things that upset a network administrator more than a person who attempts to guess at the proper configuration of his computer when attaching it to a network. An improperly configured computer can potentially disrupt an entire network, so please make sure you have all the information you need from your administrator or ISP before attempting the things in this chapter!

Making an Ethernet (Wired) Connection

On a network that is set up to automatically configure your computer using DHCP, the most complicated thing you need to do is plug in the network cable!

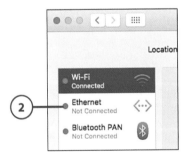

1. Open the System Preferences panel and click the Network icon.

2. The network preferences panel displays. All of the active network interfaces are listed here. Red dots indicate that no connection is present on the interface.

3. Plug the network cable into the back of your Mac. After a few seconds, the interface should update, showing a green dot for an active connection. The pane to the right of the interfaces displays the information that your computer is using to communicate online.

It's Not All Good

Things Not Working?

If your network connection is showing a yellow dot, you might have to configure your settings manually, or if you're using a DSL connection, you might have to use PPPoE to make your connection. If this is the case, skip ahead to "Manually Configuring Network Settings."

If, however, you see a red dot, you need to check your cable or the device you're plugging into because your Macintosh can't detect *any* type of network.

Connecting to a Wireless Network

When wireless network cards first started appearing, they were limited to portable computers. Over the past decade, however, Wi-Fi has taken off as a networking standard for both laptops and desktop computers. Current wireless network speeds are approaching wired connections, so, slowly but surely, wireless is taking over.

Apple makes your wireless life easy. Your Mac comes ready (and able) to connect to wireless networks with a minimal amount of fuss. Using the built-in AirPort wireless card in your Mac, you can connect to almost any type of wireless network.

>>>Go Further
WIRELESS NETWORKS TYPES

The latest Macs can make use of 802.11ac, 802.11n, 802.11a, 802.11b, and 802.11g networks! This represents the full range of consumer and business wireless networking standards. Your Mac is also capable of talking to a wide range of 802.1x authentication protocols and encryption methods. Setup is usually automatic, so you won't need to know the specifics unless your administrator tells you otherwise.

To learn more about wireless security, read http://en.wikipedia.org/wiki/Wireless_security.

Finding and Connecting to a Network

If you haven't already made a wired connection, your Mac's Wi-Fi (wireless) card will be active and searching for networks that it can connect to.

1. If your Mac finds an available network, it prompts you to make a connection.

2. Choose the network name to connect to. Note that the network signal strength and security are denoted by icons to the right of the name. If a lock is present, the network requires authentication. This is covered in "Authenticating on a Wireless Network" later in this chapter.

3. Click Join to connect to the selected network.

4. If you've been given the specific name of a network (called an SSID) by a network administrator and it doesn't appear in the available networks list, click the Join Other button to enter the name and attempt to find the network.

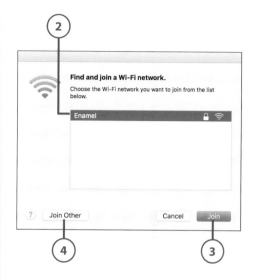

It's Not All Good

Things Not Working?

If you've successfully connected to a wireless network, but it doesn't seem to work, you might need to configure the network settings manually. Keep in mind that you need to get those settings from your wireless network administrator.

If this is the case, skip ahead to the "Manually Configuring Network Settings" task.

Manually Choosing a Wireless Connection

If you want to manually choose a wireless network connection, you can use the Wi-Fi menu in your menu bar.

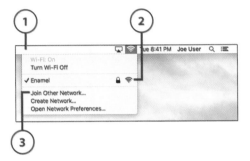

1. The Wi-Fi menu displays a list of all of the available wireless access points, their signal strengths, and their security requirements.

2. Choose the network name to which you want to connect from the list. If you're connecting to a network that shows a lock icon, it requires authentication. This topic is covered in "Authenticating on a Wireless Network" later in this chapter.

3. If you want to connect to a network using only its name, choose Join Other Network to enter the name and attempt the connection.

>>>Go Further
ALTERNATIVE WI-FI CONFIGURATION

If you'd prefer to manage all your network connection information in one place, you can access these same options by opening the Network System Preferences panel and selecting the Wi-Fi interface.

You can also use the Show Wi-Fi Status in Menu Bar checkbox to remove or add (if it's missing) the Wi-Fi status menu item.

Authenticating on a Wireless Network

When your Mac connects to an open (unsecured) network, it works immediately. If you're connecting to a network that is secure, however, you need to authenticate, which means you need to provide a password or other identifying information.

1. If you attempt to connect to a network that has a security requirement, you are prompted for a password.

Look for the Lock

Secure networks are usually denoted by a lock icon next to the network's signal strength icon. (Refer to the previous task.)

2. Enter the password (or other information, depending on the security settings).

3. Click Show Password if you'd like to see the password instead of dots while you type.

4. To make sure that the network can be used again in the future without requiring that you retype the password, check the Remember This Network button.

5. Click Join to finish and authenticate to the network.

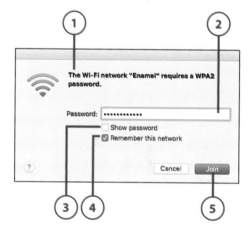

Disabling (and Enabling) Wireless Networking

Not everyone *wants* to have wireless networking always enabled. It can potentially expose you to network attacks on poorly secured wireless networks. Disabling the Wi-Fi network interface, and re-enabling it, is just a menu option away.

1. To disable the Wi-Fi card, choose Turn Wi-Fi Off from the Wi-Fi status menu.

2. The Wi-Fi menu updates to an outline of the usual multiline symbol. The Wi-Fi hardware is now powered down.

3. To re-enable the Wi-Fi card, choose Turn Wi-Fi On from the Wi-Fi status menu.

Need More Wi-Fi Detail? No Problem.

To see all the stats about your Wi-Fi connection, hold Option while clicking the Wi-Fi menu. You'll see signal strength, speed, and more!

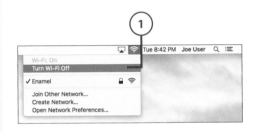

Manually Configuring Network Settings

Network connections, when automatically configured, seem to work almost like magic. Your computer finds a signal (wired or wireless), makes a connection, and everything just "works." Behind the scenes, however, there are a handful of network settings that make this happen. If a network doesn't support auto-configuration, using a protocol known as DHCP, you need to make these settings manually.

Your network administrator needs to provide the following settings in order to manually set up your network:

- **IP Address**—A numerical address that uniquely identifies your computer.

- **Subnet Mask**—A value that helps your computer determine what network it is on.

- **Router**—The address of a device that moves network traffic between other local computers and remote networks (such as the Internet).

- **DNS**—The address of a device providing domain name lookups to your network. This service translates human-readable names (such as www.apple.com) into IP addresses and vice-versa.

- **Proxy Settings**—A device that sends and receives network traffic on your behalf, acting as a middleman for services.

Configuring TCP/IP and Proxy Settings

To manually change your TCP/IP and Proxy settings, follow these simple steps:

1. Open System Preferences and click the Network panel icon.

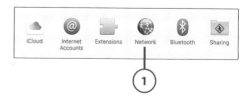

2. The network panel opens, showing all the available interfaces. Click the interface you want to configure (usually Ethernet or Wi-Fi).

3. Click the Advanced button to view the full manual interface for network settings.

4. The Advanced configuration screen appears. Click TCP/IP in the button bar to access the common TCP/IP network settings.

5. Use the Configure IPv4 drop-down menu to change your settings to be configured Manually.

6. Enter the IP address, Subnet Mask, and Router, as provided by your network administrator.

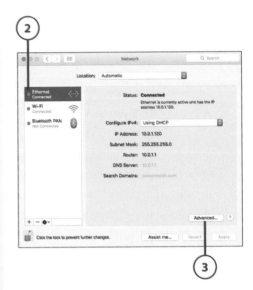

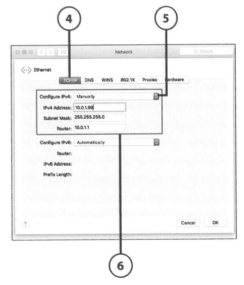

7. Click DNS in the button bar to change your domain name server settings.

8. Click the + button below the DNS Servers list to add a new server to the list. Your ISP or network administrator usually provides at least two addresses to use; be sure to type it exactly as provided. (Use the – button to remove unused DNS Servers. Search Domains are not required unless specified by your administrator.)

9. If your network requires the use of a proxy, click the Proxies button in the button bar. If not, skip ahead to step 13.

10. Click the checkboxes beside the protocols that you want to configure.

11. Click the protocol names to configure each proxy. Setup fields appear to the right of the protocol list.

12. Enter the proxy information as provided by your network administrator.

13. Click OK to exit Advanced setup.

14. Click Apply to activate and begin using your new network settings.

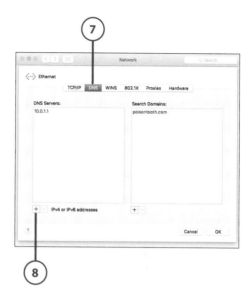

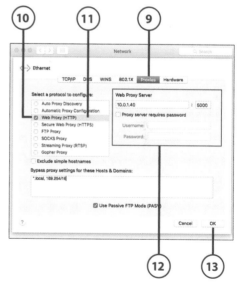

Switching to Automatic Configuration

To revert back to the default "automatic" configuration of a network interface, you need to select Using DHCP from the Configure IPv4 drop-down menu.

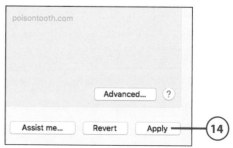

Activating PPPoE for DSL Connections

In some cases, most typically when using a DSL modem, you need to activate PPPoE (Point-to-Point Protocol over Ethernet) in order to make a connection.

1. Open System Preferences and click the Network panel icon.

2. Select your active Ethernet Interface.

3. Choose Create PPPoE Service from the Configure IPv4 drop-down menu.

4. Choose a name for the connection. (The default, PPPoE, is fine.)

5. Click Done.

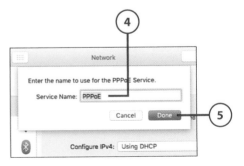

6. Enter the PPPoE information as provided by your ISP. Choose to remember the password if desired.

7. Click the Show PPPoE Status in Menu Bar checkbox to add a convenient menu option for connecting and disconnecting to the service.

8. Click the Advanced button.

9. Click PPP to open a variety of options for configuring your connection.

10. To help maintain a stable connection, check Connect Automatically When Needed and uncheck the Disconnect checkboxes if desired.

11. If required by your ISP, configure the TCP/IP settings manually as described in the "Configuring TCP/IP and Proxy Settings" task.

12. Click OK to close the Advanced settings.

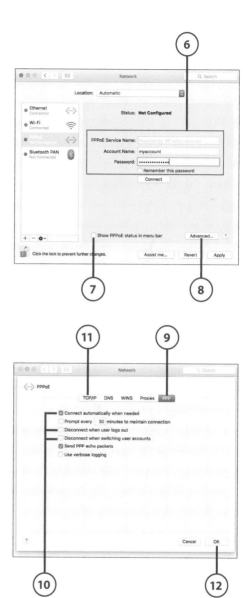

13. Click Connect to begin using the PPPoE interface you've configured.

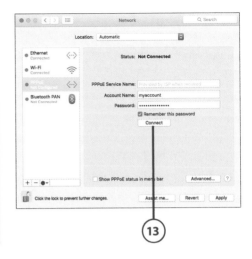

Making Connections with Cellular Data Modems and iOS Devices

When you're on the go, you have a variety of options available to stay connected with your Mac. Cellular modems are fast, small, and convenient. On the other hand, you probably already have an iPhone or iPad, don't you? El Capitan can work with both of these devices to get your Mac online with a minimal amount of hassle.

There are a wide variety of WWAN (Wireless Wide Area Network) modems that work out of the box on El Capitan—you'll need to check with the vendor for support, but most popular USB options support OS X.

Configuring a WWAN Modem for Use with Your Mac

Using a supported WWAN module is easy, as long as the card has been properly provisioned by your service provider!

1. Plug the WWAN modem into your computer (not pictured).

2. Open the System Preferences panel and select the Network icon.

3. The Network panel opens, showing the new device. Make sure it is selected in the interface list.

4. Configure the settings using the information provided by your ISP. In most cases, you won't need to do *anything*.

5. Click the Show WWAN Status in Menu Bar button to display a menu item for the card.

6. Choose to connect automatically, if desired.

7. If you have been given specific network settings instructions by your ISP, click the Advanced button and enter the options as described in "Manually Configuring Network Settings."

8. Click Apply to begin using your WWAN card.

Managing Your WWAN Connection

If you chose to add the WWAN status to your menu bar as described in the previous section, you can use it to monitor and manage your connection.

1. The WWAN menu bar displays the signal strength of your device.

2. Use the Connect and Disconnect options under the menu to connect or disconnect from the Internet.

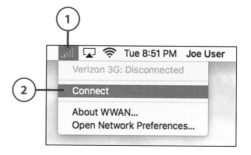

Using Your iOS Instant Hotspot

El Capitan provides the ability to quickly access your iOS device's cellular Internet connection—assuming your plan already includes support for personal hotspots.

To use this feature, you don't need to do anything except make sure that your devices are signed into the same iCloud account (see Chapter 4, "Setting Up iCloud and Internet Accounts") and that your iOS device is on and has a cellular connection. From there, just open the Wi-Fi menu and select the personal hotspot item that appears.

That's it. No more configuration, no passwords—you're immediately online! Use the Wi-Fi menu to monitor the signal strength and battery life of your iOS device.

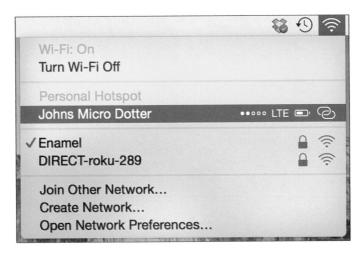

It's Not All Good

Change Is Bad

If you've made changes to your Bluetooth settings on your iOS device or Mac, this feature might not work for you. Read through Chapter 12, "Using El Capitan with Your iDevices," and make sure that El Capitan's Handoff feature is properly configured and then try again.

Creating Virtual Private Network Connections

You have many different ways to connect to networks wherever you are. Many companies, however, only give you access to certain resources when you're connected directly to their networks. This puts a small crimp on the idea of "working at home" or "on the go."

To get around the access problem, many organizations provide Virtual Private Network (VPN) servers. Using a VPN server, your Mac can use its current network connection (wireless, wired, or using a WWAN card) to securely connect to your company's network. You are able to access all the same resources that you see when you're sitting in your office chair.

Creating a VPN Connection

El Capitan supports four types of VPN connections—L2TP, PPTP, Cisco IPSec, and IKEv2. You need to find out from your network administrator which option is right for you, along with the settings you need to make the connection.

1. Create a new VPN connection by opening the System Preferences and clicking the Network icon.

2. Click the + button at the bottom of the interfaces pane.

3. Choose VPN as the interface.

4. Set the VPN type to the type specified by your network administrator.

5. Enter a meaningful name for the VPN service, such as "Work VPN."

6. Click Create.

7. A new VPN interface is created and added to the list of network interfaces. Make sure the VPN interface is highlighted.

8. Configuration options appear on the right side of the network preferences panel. Enter the server address and account information provided by your network administrator.

9. Click the Show VPN Status in Menu Bar checkbox. This adds a menu item to the menu bar so you can quickly connect and disconnect from a VPN.

10. Click the Authentication Settings button.

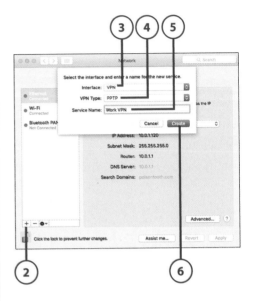

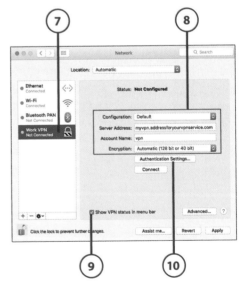

11. You are prompted for a method of authentication. Enter a password or choose one of the other available options as directed by your network administrator

12. Click OK.

13. If you have been given specific network settings by your network administrator, click the Advanced button and enter the options as described in "Manually Configuring Network Settings."

14. Click the Connect button to connect to the VPN.

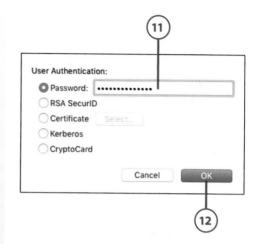

Managing Your VPN Connection

If you've chosen to show the VPN status in your menu bar, you can use the menu item to quickly connect and disconnect at any time. In addition, you can show the amount of time you've been connected, in case connection charges apply.

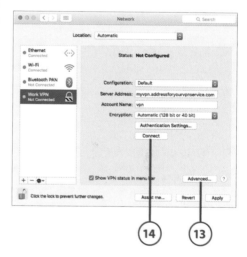

Managing Multiple Connections with Locations and Configurations

If you have a Mac, chances are you're not one to sit still. One day you might be connecting from a beach in Maui, and the next, from a coffee shop in Columbus, Ohio.

To help keep things straight, El Capitan includes Configurations and Locations—two important tools for keeping multiple sets of network information.

For interfaces such as VPNs or other devices that might have multiple "versions" of their settings, you can create configurations. A configuration holds information such as the server you're connecting to and your specific network settings.

A location, on the other hand, has a much broader scope. Locations enable you to create new configurations across all your interfaces and swap them out instantly. Creating a new location is like establishing an entirely new network setup—making instant reconfiguration a snap.

Creating Configurations

To create a configuration, do the following:

1. To create a configuration (if supported by your network interface), first open the System Preferences and click the Network icon.

2. Click the interface for which you want to create a new configuration.

3. Using the Configuration pop-up menu, choose Add Configuration.

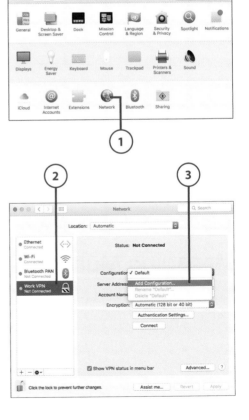

4. Enter a name for the configuration.

5. Click Create. You may now configure the network interface as described in the chapter.

6. Your new settings are stored and accessible under the configuration name you provided so that you can easily switch from one to another. (You can also remove or rename configurations under this menu.)

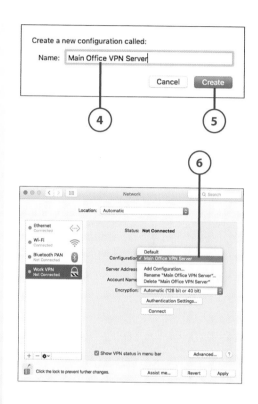

Adding and Using Locations

Locations are like configurations on steroids. Lots of steroids. Using locations, you can create entirely new sets of network interfaces and options and switch between them easily.

1. Open the System Preferences and click the Network icon.

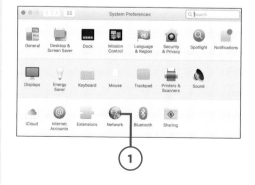

2. The default location of Automatic is set at the top of the network panel.

3. Choose Edit Locations from the Location drop-down menu.

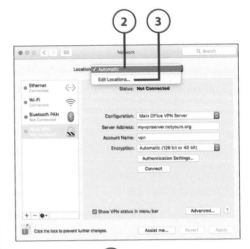

4. A dialog box that lists any configured locations displays.

5. Click the + button to add an entry for a new location. (Use – to remove locations you no longer want.)

6. Type a name to describe the location, such as "Office Intranet."

7. Click Done.

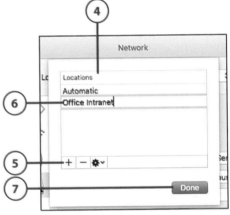

8. All your network settings are now set to their defaults for the new location. All VPN connections and other interfaces are gone. You are, in effect, starting fresh with configuring your Mac network setup.

9. Configure your network settings as described in this chapter.

10. After you've completed your setup, you can switch between locations using the Location drop-down menu within the System Preferences Network panel. Remember that you can return to your original network settings by choosing the location named "Automatic."

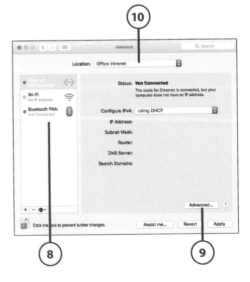

Seeking Automated Network Assistance

The El Capitan operating system provides a few automated tools to help you configure and diagnose your Mac's network settings. Be aware that the automated tools might not be able to fully set up your connection; and if you have complicated network configurations, you might want to manage the settings manually anyway. Let's review what you need to do to use these tools.

Launching Diagnostics

To launch the diagnostics system, follow these steps:

1. Open the System Preferences panel and click the Network icon.

2. Click the Assist Me button at the bottom of the window.

3. Click Diagnostics in the dialog box that displays.

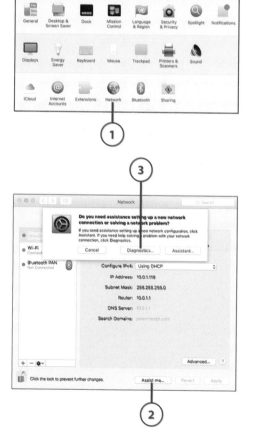

4. Choose the Network interface to run diagnostics on. If you've configured locations, you are first prompted to choose your location.

5. Click Continue.

6. Review the results and follow the onscreen instructions.

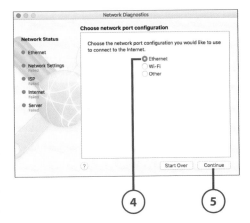

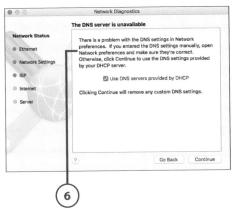

Launching the Setup Assistant

To launch the setup assistant, follow these steps:

1. Open the System Preferences panel and click the Network icon.

2. Click the Assist Me button at the bottom of the window.

3. Click Assistant in the dialog box that appears.

4. Provide a location where you will be using the network connection. This process creates a new location, as described in the previous "Adding and Using Locations" section.

5. Click Continue.

6. Choose the type of connection you are making.

7. Click Continue.

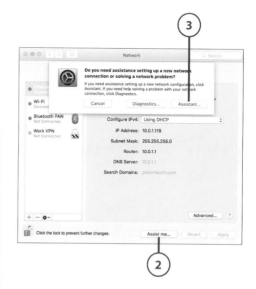

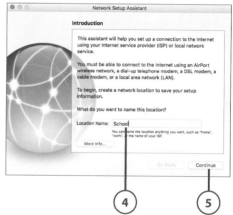

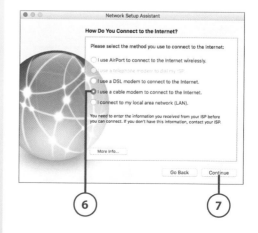

8. Follow the onscreen instructions to let El Capitan attempt to configure your network settings for you.

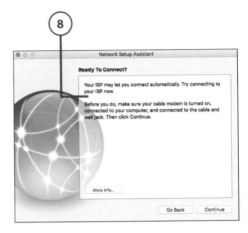

It's Not All Good

Don't Discount Your Admin!

It is impossible for me to stress this enough: Your network administrator or ISP is your best resource for correcting network problems. Using the assistant tools in El Capitan is not a silver bullet; if you don't have the information required to make a network connection (IP address, and so on), it won't "just work"!

Explore iCloud features and options.

Establish accounts to popular Internet services.

In this chapter, you learn about iCloud services and unified account management in El Capitan, including:

→ Activating iCloud services
→ What iCloud is and does
→ Interesting iCloud services
→ How to navigate iCloud Drive
→ How to use iCloud Photo Sharing
→ How to manage your myriad of Internet accounts

Setting Up iCloud and Internet Accounts

One of the coolest features of El Capitan isn't really located on your Mac—it's "in the cloud." iCloud enables you to keep all of your information in sync in your digital life. Your iPhones, iPads, and Mac—coupled with iCloud—make up the perfect digital workplace and playground.

In this chapter, you find out how to establish and configure iCloud accounts and get to know some of the basics of using iCloud services—including the all-new iCloud Drive. You also learn how El Capitan manages all of the accounts that you may use on popular social network sites, email, and online sharing services.

Setting Up iCloud

One of the most convenient features of using multiple Apple devices is the difficult-to-describe iCloud service. iCloud provides data synchronization between your computers and iOS devices (such as synchronizing your files, web browser bookmarks, passwords, and even credit card information). It also gives you free email, contact storage, beautiful online office applications, and it even provides the ability to connect to your home Macintosh from your work computer. Best of all, all you need to do to use iCloud is establish an account and click a few checkboxes.

Integrated iCloud

I mention iCloud where relevant throughout this book, but keep in mind that Apple is continuously upgrading iCloud services and adding new features. The goal is for your computing life to be more intuitive and seamless without having to worry about what is going on in the background.

The first step in using iCloud is configuring your Mac to log into your account. If you have an Apple ID, chances are you already have an iCloud account. If not, the setup process guides you along the way.

Configuring iCloud for the First Time

To access your iCloud account for the first time, follow these steps:

1. Open the iCloud System Preferences panel. A sign-in window displays.

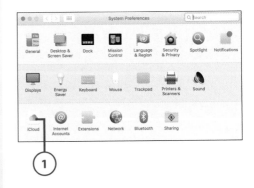

One-Time Deal

Note that you only need to follow these steps once—after that, you remain logged in even if you reboot your Mac.

2. Enter your Apple ID and Password, or click Create Apple ID to generate a new safe ID.

3. Click Sign In to log in to the iCloud service.

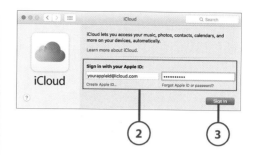

4. iCloud prompts to automatically install basic services—contacts, calendar, reminders, notes, and bookmark syncing as well as Find My Mac. You can either enable these now, or you can do it later by following the instructions in the "Activating iCloud Services" task.

5. Click Next.

6. You might be prompted for information as some services start. If you're using Find My Mac, for example, you're prompted to allow Location Services. Click Allow to move on.

7. You are shown the list of active iCloud services. Close the System Preferences, or proceed to the next section to learn more about the available services.

Browsing iCloud Services

Your iCloud account comes with many free services that work across your OS X systems and iOS (iPhone/iPad) devices. The following list summarizes the available services at the time of this writing:

- **iCloud Drive**—This makes it possible to save files to iCloud rather than your local hard drive. Using this feature, you can start editing a document on one machine and finish it up on another (discussed later in this chapter in the "Using iCloud Drive" task).

- **Photos**—Photos automatically makes the photos you take on your iPhone or iPad available on your Mac (and vice versa) and enables you to share albums with anyone. (This is discussed later in this chapter in the "Using Photo Sharing" task.)

- **Mail**—When activated, Mail sets up an El Capitan email account associated with your iCloud account. This will be an @icloud.com address that you established when registering for an Apple ID (discussed in Chapter 5, "Accessing Email and the Web").

- **Contacts**—Moves your contacts to iCloud storage, making them accessible and editable on any device that has iCloud configured. (See Chapter 8, "Managing Who, Where, When, and What," for more details.)

- **Calendars**—Sets up shared calendars between all iCloud devices. (See Chapter 8 for more details.)

- **Reminders**—Creates shared lists—everything from shopping lists to to-do lists that are shared between all iCloud devices. (See Chapter 8 for more details.)

- **Safari**—Enables syncing of your Safari bookmarks and your reading list across devices as well as providing a list of open Safari tabs on other devices. This makes it possible to start browsing in one location and finish in another. (Read more in Chapter 5.)

- **Notes**—Connects your Mac Notes application to iCloud storage, making all your notes available across all your Macs and iPhone/iPad (see Chapter 8 for more details).

- **Keychain**—Enables syncing of secure passwords and credit card information between your devices. This will be used for auto-fill data in Safari. Note that when enabling this feature, you'll need to bounce back and forth between your Mac and iOS devices to ensure that they are all properly authorized to share the data. (Read more in Chapter 5.)

- **Back to My Mac**—When activated, this unique iCloud feature makes your computer visible to any other computer where you have activated Back to My Mac. Using this, you can access your home computer from any other network-connected Mac—no network configuration required. (See Chapter 6, "Sharing Files, Devices, and Services," for details.)

- **Find My Mac**—If your Mac is lost or stolen, Find My Mac attempts to locate it. Using the icloud.com website, you can track your Mac on a map and even lock or erase it. (This is discussed later in this chapter in the "Using Find My Mac" task.)

Activating iCloud Services

To activate an iCloud service, first make sure you have completed the task "Configuring iCloud for the First Time" and then follow these simple steps:

1. Open the iCloud System Preferences panel.

2. Click the checkboxes in front of the services you want to use. If prompted to provide access to additional system services (Find My Mac requires you to grant access to your location, for instance), click the appropriate response.

3. Close System Preferences when satisfied with your selections.

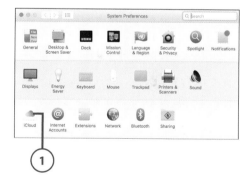

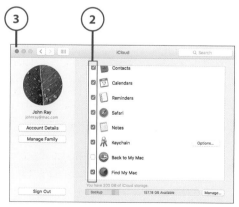

More Storage Is a Click Away

At the bottom of the service list is a bar showing how much storage you have left. By default, iCloud includes several gigabytes of free storage—but storing documents and data, backups of your iOS devices, and other information can eat the space up quickly. Click the Manage button to buy more storage, based on a variety of monthly subscription plans.

Exploring Unique iCloud Services (New!)

It's pretty easy to describe the use of features like Contacts and Safari bookmark syncing, and they fall neatly into place in many of this book's chapters. There are a few "unique" iCloud services that are important to cover, but don't quite fit as cleanly elsewhere. One such service, for example, enables you to find your Mac on a map, should it be lost or stolen. Another provides direct access to your contacts, events, and mail from a web interface no matter where you are. Rather than leave these topics out, they are covered in the following tasks.

Accessing iCloud Applications Online

After you activate iCloud services like Mail, Calendar, and Reminders, you can log into Apple's online iCloud service and use web applications that resemble their Mac counterparts. To access iCloud applications, do the following:

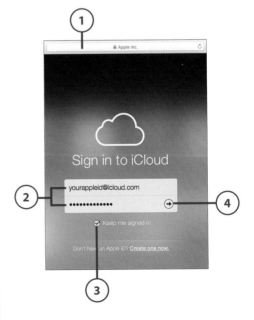

1. Open a current version of a web browser (Safari, Internet Explorer 8+, Firefox, or Chrome) and browse to www.icloud.com.

2. Enter your Apple ID and Password.

3. Click the Keep Me Signed In checkbox if you'd like to be able to access iCloud from your computer without logging in again.

4. Click the arrow to log in.

5. Click the icon of the application you want to launch.

Automatic Saves

Use the web application as you would the desktop version. If your app makes changes to data, those changes will be pushed out to all your iCloud-connected devices.

6. Click the iCloud menu (upper-left corner) to jump to other applications.

7. Close your browser when finished.

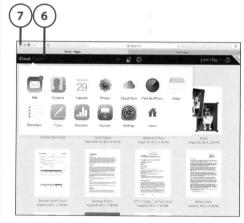

Using Find My Mac

To turn on Find My Mac and make your Mac location available via the iCloud website, follow these steps:

1. If you haven't already, activate Find My Mac using the technique described in "Activating iCloud Services," earlier in this chapter.

2. If prompted, click Allow on the Allow Find My Mac to Use the Location dialog.

3. If you need to find your Mac, go to iCloud.com in a browser on any Internet-connected device and log in. Click Find My iPhone.

4. Click All Devices to show the list of tracked devices.

5. Click the name of your Mac in the list.

6. The Mac's location is highlighted on the map.

7. The web app displays options for sending a message/playing a sound on the computer, locking it, or wiping the contents of the hard drive.

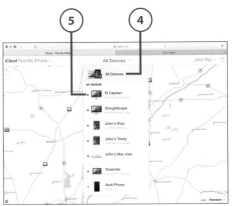

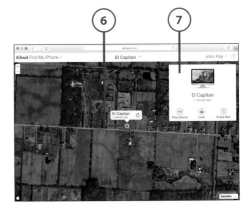

Using iCloud Drive

The iCloud Drive feature of iCloud makes it easy to work on a document in one location, and then open it again in another. If you've used other "cloud drives" like Box, Dropbox, or OneDrive, this works in much the same way.

Before starting, be sure to activate iCloud Drive using the steps described at the end of the "Activating iCloud Services" section, earlier in this chapter.

Navigating the iCloud Drive

The iCloud Drive is fully integrated into the El Capitan Finder. Access it by following these steps:

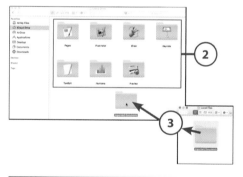

1. Click iCloud Drive in the Finder sidebar or via the Go menu.

2. Within the iCloud Drive, you'll see folders for each application you use. By default, files created by these applications are saved within their own folders.

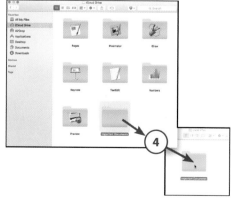

Arrange as Needed

Organize your iCloud Drive as you see fit. You don't *have* to save files within folders named for your applications (or within any folder at all, for that matter). This is simply how Apple keeps things arranged by default.

3. Drag folders and files from outside the iCloud Drive into the iCloud Drive, and they will appear on your other iCloud-connected devices.

4. Drag folders and files out of the iCloud Drive to move them to your local computer.

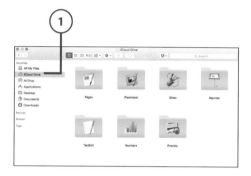

5. When prompted, click Move to confirm that you really want to move the files out of iCloud Drive.

Pick and Choose

If you find yourself running low on space and don't want to buy more, you can pick and choose which applications can interact with iCloud Drive by clicking the Options button beside it in the iCloud preferences panel.

Opening iCloud Files Within an Application

iCloud Drive files can always be opened by double-clicking in the Finder, the same as any other file—but when you go to open them in an application, things look a bit different. To open a file that you've saved in iCloud (from any iCloud-connected device), first complete the actions you normally would to open a file within an application of your choosing and then follow these steps:

1. Use the sidebar to select iCloud Drive.

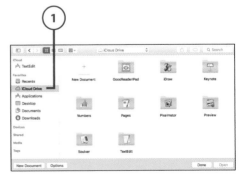

2. Double-click the folder for the application that created the file (if following Apple's default organization), use the drop-down menu at the top of the dialog box to choose the application name, or click the application name under the "iCloud" heading in the sidebar.

3. Select the file you want to open.

4. Click Open. The file opens and you can begin working with it wherever you left off, no matter which device you were using.

When It's in iCloud, It's in iCloud

When you open and edit a file in iCloud, it stays in iCloud. You don't need to worry about moving it from your local computer to iCloud after editing it, or anything of the sort. Just think of iCloud storage like any other disk, except that you have access to it no matter where you are or what iCloud-enabled device you are using.

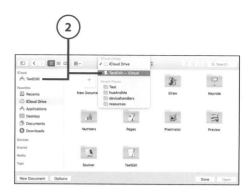

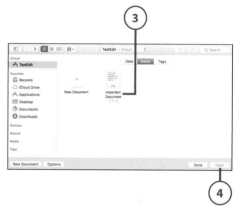

Saving iCloud Files from an Application

To save a file to iCloud from within an application, just edit the file as you normally would and then follow these steps when it's time to save.

1. Choose File, Save (or Save As/Move if editing a file you've already saved).

2. Use the sidebar to pick iCloud. (Expand the dialog box, if needed.)

3. Double-click the folder for the application that created the file (if following Apple's default organization), use the drop-down menu at the top of the dialog box to choose the application name, or click the application name under the "iCloud" heading in the sidebar. This will store the file in a directory specifically for that application.

4. Provide a name for the file.

5. Click Save.

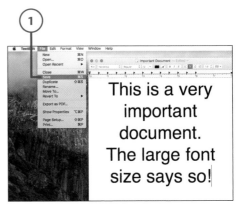

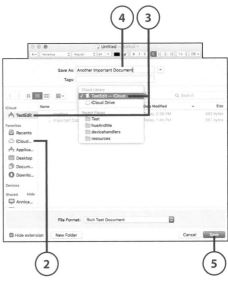

It's Not All Good

Upload Delays

If you aren't connected to the Internet (or have a slow connection), El Capitan will delay uploading changes in your iCloud Drive files until the connection improves. You'll still be able to make changes; you just won't see them reflected on other devices immediately.

You can tell when a file hasn't been uploaded by the "Waiting" label displayed underneath the file in the Finder—as well as a progress indicator beside the iCloud Drive entry in the Finder sidebar.

Opening iCloud Files on the Web

If you save a file to iCloud using Pages, Keynote, or Numbers on your Mac or iOS device, you can open and edit the file with nothing more than your web browser. To do this, make sure you've added the files you want to access to iCloud Drive and then follow the steps in the earlier task "Accessing iCloud Applications Online."

1. Use the iCloud webpage to choose the application whose files you want to open.

2. The application opens, displaying all the files you saved to iCloud from your Mac.

3. Double-click a file you want to work with.

4. The file opens and you can begin working with it directly in your browser.

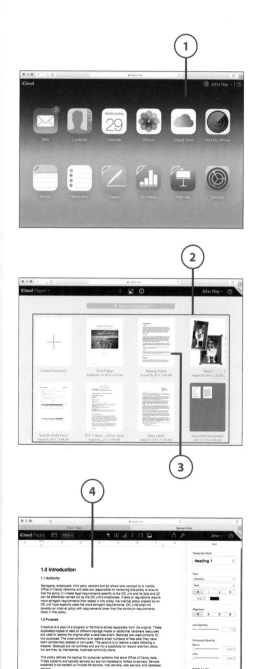

>>>*Go Further*
WHERE DID I PUT THAT?

iCloud Drive integrates so cleanly with El Capitan that you don't have to worry about whether something is "in the cloud" when you go looking for it. Spotlight and Finder searches (including the "All My Files" feature of the Finder) automatically include the files that are stored on your iCloud Drive.

Using Photo Sharing

Another extremely useful (and fun) feature of iCloud is Photo Sharing. Photo Sharing automatically keeps copies of your most recent 1,000 photos taken using iOS devices and makes sure that your Mac has copies of them all. It also enables you to share collections of photos with anyone you'd like.

Enabling iCloud Photo Sharing

To get started, enable and configure Photo Sharing in iCloud. To enable the service, follow these steps:

1. Open the iCloud System Preferences panel.

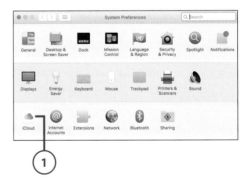

2. Enable the Photos item.

3. Click the Options button beside the Photos line.

4. Check the iCloud Photo Library checkbox to keep your entire photo library in iCloud.

5. Click the My Photo Stream check-box to keep all of your latest photos synced between devices.

6. Enable the iCloud Photo Sharing option to share photos with individuals that you select.

7. Click Done.

8. Close the Preferences window.

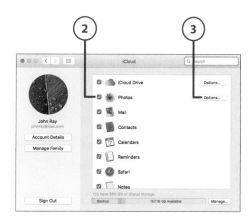

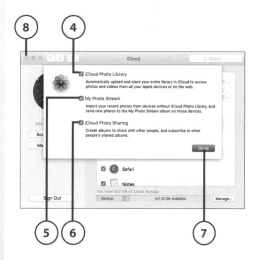

Viewing Shared Photos

To view your shared photos and photo stream, you need to use Photos, which comes with El Capitan.

1. Open Photos from the Applications folder or Launchpad.

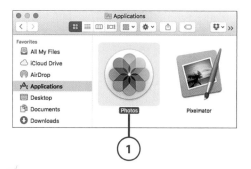

2. Click the Photos button to show all your photos in chronological order.

3. Click Albums to show photos arranged by album.

4. Use the back arrow to "zoom out" of a particular collection of photos and show the album or year/location where they are located.

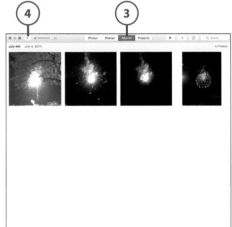

Sharing Photos

To share your photos with others, you also use the Photos application.

1. Open Photos from the Applications folder or Launchpad.

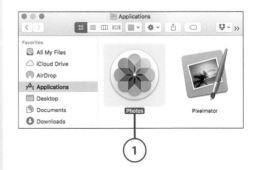

2. Navigate to a photo collection (Events, Albums, Faces, Places, and so on) or select a group of photos from the Photos section or from within an album.

3. Click the Share button and choose iCloud Photo Sharing.

4. Enter a comment to describe the shared photos.

5. Choose an existing shared album, or click New Shared Album to create a new shared album.

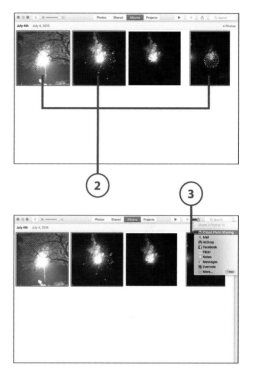

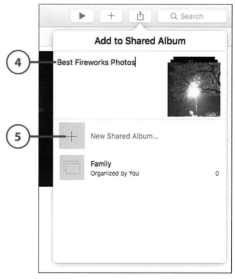

6. Enter the name of the album, the addresses for people who should be able to access the shared album, and any comments.

7. Click Create to begin sharing!

8. Use the Shared button to access all your shared Photo libraries.

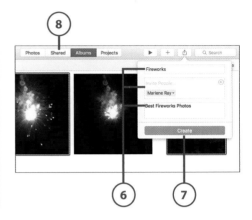

Getting Started with Accounts

For all the fun and information the Internet has brought us, it has also created a mess in terms of managing all the accounts we use to communicate online. If you're like many people, you have multiple email accounts—possibly one through iCloud, one from work, and even others you use for personal email or online services. You have accounts for chatting with instant messenger. You have accounts for sharing contacts and calendars. In other words, you've got multiple usernames and passwords that need to be configured in different applications, just so you can be connected.

In OS X, Apple has recognized the problem of account overload and worked to consolidate all your online account management in a single centralized preference panel—Internet Accounts. Here you can set up email, instant messenger, Exchange, Calendar, and other account types—without needing to figure out where they're managed in your individual applications.

I show the use of this panel as needed in the relevant chapters, but let's take a very brief look at how you interact with this tool on your Mac.

More iCloud Settings?

When you use the Internet Accounts panel to manage your accounts, you'll notice that it also includes iCloud. The iCloud settings in this panel are identical to what you configured in the iCloud panel shown earlier in this chapter—this is just a different way to access them.

Adding an Account

To add an account for an online service (email, contacts, calendars, Exchange, etc.), follow these steps.

1. Open the Internet Accounts System Preferences panel.

2. Choose an online service provider that you want to configure by clicking its name. Select Add Other Account from the bottom of the list to pick from additional service types.

3. Provide the credentials you use to log into the account and click Sign In.

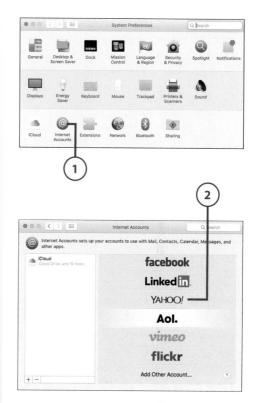

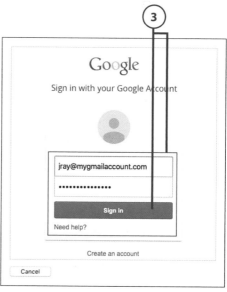

4. Choose which applications you want the account to be able to interact with on your Mac. Click Done when you're finished.

5. The completed account is listed in the preferences panel with its settings available on the right.

6. Close System Preferences when finished.

Exploration Is Rewarded!

Although the Internet Accounts panel is a great place for establishing new accounts and performing high-level configuration, you might still find yourself needing to dig for various esoteric settings (such as specific server addresses, proxies, and other technical tweaks) within your individual Internet applications.

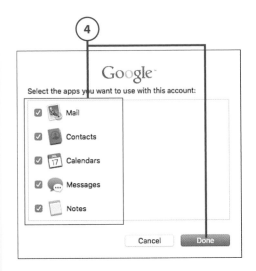

Browse the web and keep track of your favorite articles in Safari.

Create beautiful email in the Mail application.

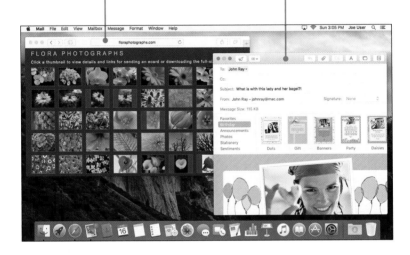

In this chapter, you learn how to use your Mac for common Internet uses, including:

→ Connecting to email servers
→ Using VIP and Smart Mailboxes
→ Browsing the Web
→ Muting noisy tabs
→ Creating web clippings
→ Using Safari extensions

5

Accessing Email and the Web

The Internet (for better or worse) is everywhere we turn. To be effective in our professional (and frequently social) lives, we need best-of-breed Internet tools on our Mac. The good news is that we've got 'em.

In this chapter, you find out how to use some of the unique features of the Mail and Web applications in El Capitan. Even if you're working in a Microsoft-centric environment, you'll find that your Mac's tools are up to the job.

Getting Started with Mail (New!)

The first thing that many of us do when we have an Internet connection is check our email. Email is now a way to exchange rich media—such as photos, files, and movies—in addition to a way to exchange written messages. The email application, Mail (found in the Dock or Applications folder), is provided with your Mac. With Mail, you can connect to a variety of different mail servers, including Microsoft Exchange, with only a few clicks of your mouse.

Things You Need Before Setting Up an Email Connection

As with the networking information in the last chapter, configuring your email account isn't a matter of guessing. Apple's Mail application can automatically set up several popular email services (such as Google and Yahoo!), but if you're connecting to a corporate email server, you should collect as much information as possible from your email system administrator or ISP before proceeding. This includes your email address, password, email server, email server type (POP, IMAP, or Exchange), and SMTP server:

- **Incoming Mail Server**—The server that you connect to when retrieving your email.

- **Incoming Mail Server Type**—The type of server that you're connecting to. Apple's Mail application supports Exchange, IMAP, and POP servers.

- **Outgoing (SMTP) Server**—The server that sends your messages.

- **Authentication**—Typically, a user name and password required to retrieve or send messages.

Note that if you've already activated iCloud email, your account is already set up! You don't need to do anything else.

Adding an Email Account

If you have an email account that El Capitan recognizes, configuration couldn't be easier—you just need your email address, name, and password to make a connection. El Capitan attempts to identify and configure your account. If for some reason it fails, you can continue with an advanced manual configuration (see the next task).

1. Open the Internet Accounts System Preferences Panel.

2. Choose an email service that you want to configure by clicking its name on the right.

3. The Add Account window displays. Type your email address and password for the account.

4. Click Sign In.

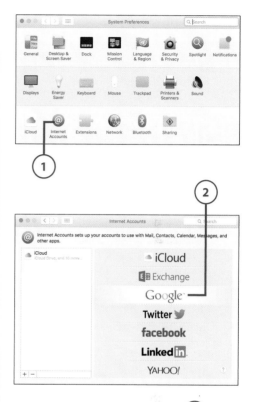

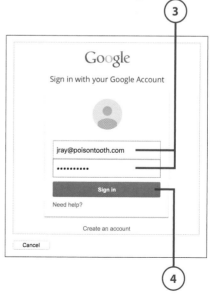

5. El Capitan attempts to automatically configure your account. If additional features are determined to be available from the email provider, they are listed in the window. Choose which services you want to use by checking/unchecking the checkboxes.

6. Click Done to finish adding the account.

7. If it's successful, the newly configured email account appears in the account list. If the setup fails, cancel setup and skip ahead to the next section, "Configuring Advanced Account Settings."

8. Clicking the account name in the list displays the account details on the right.

9. You can click Details to edit the basic account settings if, for example, you want to change your display name or the name of your account.

10. Close System Preferences and begin using your account in Mail.

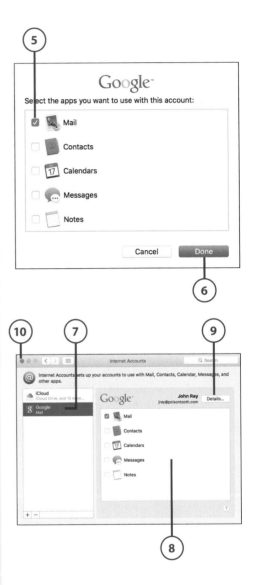

Configuring Advanced Account Settings

Email accounts that aren't immediately recognized by El Capitan require more information to be entered before they can be used. First, set up an account as best you can using the process described in the previous task, then follow these steps:

1. Open the Mail application from the Dock or Applications folder.

2. Choose Preferences from the Mail menu.

3. Click the Accounts button within the Mail preferences window.

4. Click the account that you want to configure with advanced settings.

5. Use the Incoming Mail Server fields to set a specific server that will handle your incoming messages.

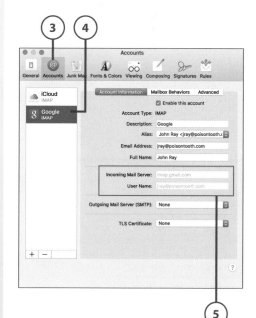

6. To set an SMTP server, Choose Edit SMTP Server List from the Outgoing Mail Server (SMTP) drop-down menu.

7. Use the +/− buttons to add and remove servers.

8. Configure the server by setting the description and address (Server Name) in the fields below the list.

9. Choose a security certificate, if any, using the TLS Certificate drop-down menu.

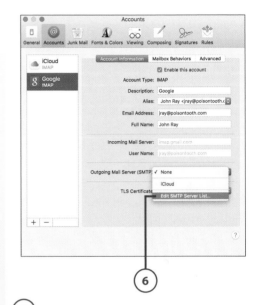

Troubleshooting Your Connection

To troubleshoot your account settings, from within Mail choose Window, Connection Doctor. Your Mac tests all your email account settings and shows you exactly where any errors are occurring.

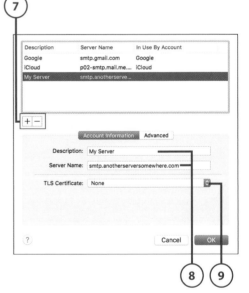

10. Click Advanced to access port and authentication settings.

11. Click OK when finished. The server you configured will be accessible from the Outgoing Mail Server (SMTP) menu.

12. Set a TLS certificate for your incoming mail server (if any) using the TLS Certificate.

13. Finally, make sure that the Enable This Account checkbox is selected so you can begin using your account settings.

14. Close the Mail Preferences.

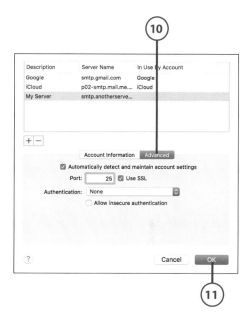

Multiple Email Addresses, One Account

It isn't uncommon for one email account to have multiple addresses associated with it. I might have a single account with addresses, such as *myMac@placeforstuff.com* or *johnray@me.com*, which I want to appear when I send a message. To configure multiple addresses for a single account, open Mail's preferences, click Accounts, and then click the account you want to add an alias to. Enter the alias email addresses, separated by commas, in the Email Address field in the account details. The email addresses are then available in a pop-up menu when you compose a new message.

Finding Your Way Around Mail

After your email account is configured, Mail connects and retrieves your messages. The Mail application workspace is split into three columns, from left to right: mailboxes, a message list, and message content.

On the left, the mailbox list shows different mailboxes (or folders) for categorizing your messages. Apple has decided to conserve as much space as possible by hiding the mailboxes by default. There's also a quick hide/show mailboxes button to show the mailbox column and links to the important mailboxes (Inbox, Sent, and so on) directly below the toolbar.

When you click a mailbox, the message list refreshes to show all of the email within the mailbox, including a several-line preview of the contents. Any message that you click in the Message list is displayed in the message content area on the right.

Now that you know the basics of finding your way around Mail, take a look at the common tasks you should familiarize yourself with.

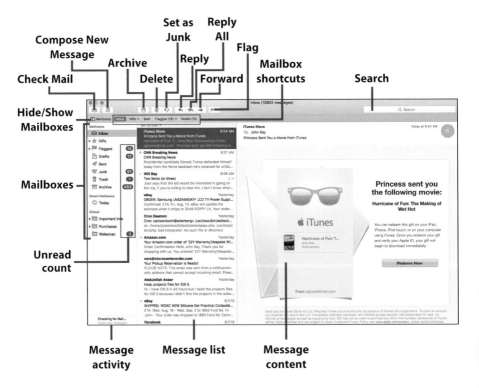

Reading Email

Reading messages is typically a matter of finding a message in the message list, clicking it, and reading. Even so, you can improve the experience by taking advantage of several tools built into Mail.

Additionally, El Capitan now supports iOS-like gestures in Mail's message list. To delete a message, swipe with two fingers to the left while the cursor is over the message in the message list. To mark a message as unread, swipe with two fingers to the right

Sorting Mail

You're certainly used to sorting information by clicking column headings, right? In the Mail application, however, the message list doesn't have columns, so you need to follow this approach:

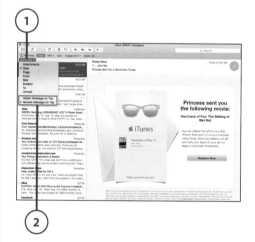

1. Use the Sort By drop-down menu above the message list to choose a message attribute to use as your sorting criteria.

2. Use the same menu to set the order of your sorting preferences.

Viewing Additional Attributes

Much as you can set the mail attributes you want to use for sorting, you can also set the attributes displayed in the message list. Use the View, Message List menu to set which attributes will be visible in the message list items.

Previewing Attachments

In Chapter 1, "Managing Your Desktop," you learned about the Quick Look system for previewing files in the Finder. In Mail, if your message contains an attachment, you can also use the Quick Look system.

1. Choose a message with an attachment—represented by a paperclip in the message list.

2. Position your cursor near the top of an email to show buttons for interacting with the message.

3. Click the Attachment button.

4. Select Quick Look from the menu that appears.

5. A Quick Look window appears, displaying the selected content.

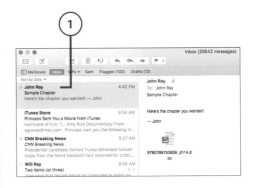

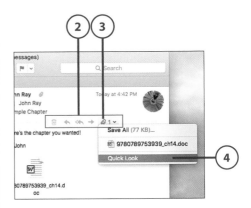

Saving Attachments

You can easily save one or more attachments to your Mac's hard drive, and even add images to iPhoto, directly from Mail.

1. Choose a message with an attachment—represented by a paperclip in the message list.

2. Position your cursor near the top of the message and click the Attachment button.

3. A menu appears, enabling you to Save All, choose an individual file to save, or, if applicable, add the file to iPhoto.

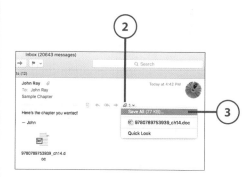

>>>Go Further
WORKING WITH ATTACHMENTS

If you prefer a more Finder-like approach to dealing with attachments, you can also work with attached files as icons. Scroll through your email and you'll see the attached files represented as icons in the message (usually at the bottom). You can drag these icons to your desktop (or anywhere you'd like to store them). You can also click an icon to immediately open it in a compatible El Capitan application.

Viewing Web Pages within an Email

Have you ever gotten a link to a web page in email and wanted to view it without having to launch Safari? In El Capitan, you can. To preview a web link directly in Mail, follow these steps:

1. Position your cursor over the link within the message content, but do not click!

2. A small downward-pointing arrow appears to the right of the link. Click it.

3. A pop-over window appears displaying the web page.

4. Click Open with Safari to open the full page in your web browser, or Add to Reading List to save the page to your Safari reading list.

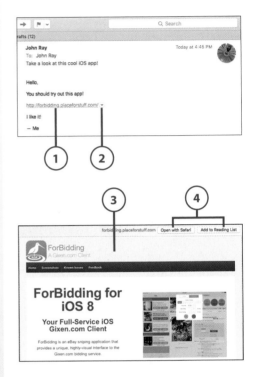

Using Data Detectors

The icon that appears at the end of a web link in mail (and the subsequent preview of the page) is an example of an El Capitan "Data Detector" in action. You may notice other icons beside dates, addresses, phone numbers, and so on. Clicking these icons will do similar helpful actions, such as setting appointments, adding information to a contact, or tracking shipments.

Organizing with Email Conversations

Email conversations can grow quite lengthy with back-and-forth replies. To help keep long conversations under control, Mail, by default, collapses your conversations into a single entry in your message list. You can expand the entry to show the individual messages whenever you need to see one.

1. Conversations are denoted by a number within an entry in the message list.

2. Click the message list entry to show all the messages in the conversation within the content area.

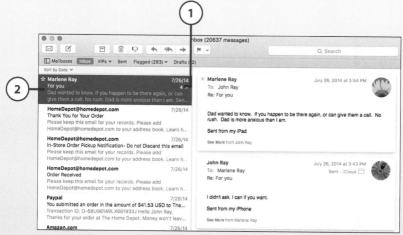

3. To focus on a single message, click the arrow beside the number in the message list to show a list of individual senders and dates.

4. Click the individual name/date to show only that message.

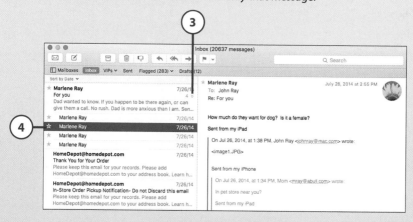

It's Not All Good

Silence the Conversation!

Many people find the conversation view to be disorienting in Mail. If you're one of those people, you can turn it off entirely by choosing Organize by Conversation from Mail's View Menu.

>>>Go Further

SEE MY SMILING FACE!

To see your friends' (and other contacts') photos beside each message summary in the message list, open Mail's preferences (Mail, Preferences from the menu), and within the Viewing section, click the Show Contact Photos in the Message List checkbox.

Managing Spam Filtering

Mail can learn (with some help) which messages in your inbox are spam and then filter similar messages so you don't have to see them. To manage your spam filtering, follow these steps:

1. Choose Mail, Preferences from the menu bar.

2. Click the Junk Mail toolbar icon.

3. Click Enable Junk Mail Filtering to turn on spam filtering. You can disable it by unchecking this box at any time.

4. Choose where Mail should file spam messages. Moving messages to the Junk mailbox is a good choice.

5. To help prevent getting false positives, use the spam exemptions to identify types of messages that you don't consider to be spam.

6. If your ISP offers spam filtering (and you trust it), make sure the Trust Junk Mail Headers in Messages option is set.

7. Close the Mail Preferences.

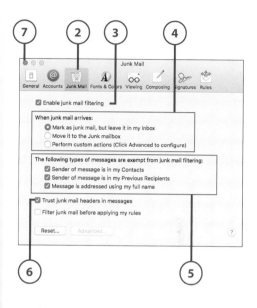

Classifying Spam

If you receive spam mail, select it and click the Junk icon (thumbs down) in the Mail toolbar. This classifies messages as spam. When new messages recognized as spam come in, they are automatically placed in the Junk folder. If *good* mail is accidentally classified as spam, use the thumbs up icon in the toolbar to tell Mail it made a mistake.

Changing How Often Mail Is Retrieved

You can force Mail to retrieve messages using the Get Mail toolbar button, but to change the frequency with which it forces a check, you need to access the preferences.

1. Choose Mail, Preferences from the menu bar.

2. Click the General icon in the preferences toolbar.

3. Use the Check for New Messages pop-up menu to set how frequently Mail looks for new messages.

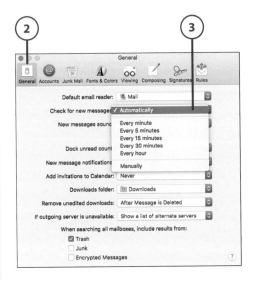

Composing Email

Email today is a bit more than just typing a message—it can include sending photos, files, or even professionally designed invitations and announcements. Mail on your Mac enables you to do all of these things.

Sending Messages with Attachments

Mail can attach virtually any type of file to your messages with ease. Follow these steps to add Windows-compatible attachments to a Mail message.

1. Start a new message by clicking the new message icon (pencil and paper) in the Mail toolbar or reply to an existing message.

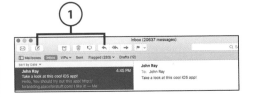

2. If you want to re-attach any attachments from the original message (in the case of a reply), click the Include Attachments icon (paperclip on paper) in the New Message window.

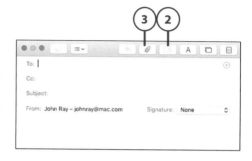

3. To add new attachments, click the Include Attachments icon (paperclip) in the New Message window.

4. Choose the files or folders to send from the file chooser dialog. Select multiples by holding down the ⌘ key and clicking.

5. Click Options to show additional options.

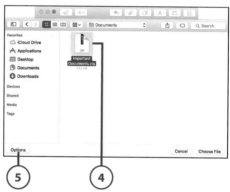

6. Check the Send Windows-Friendly Attachments checkbox to ensure that anyone (regardless of their platform choice) can open the attachments.

7. Click Choose File to add the attachments.

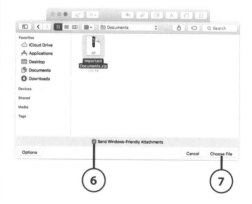

8. Compose the message as normal and then click the send icon (paper airplane).

Attaching Pictures from iPhoto

To quickly attach photos from Photos, click the Photo Browser button to open a small window that shows your Photo galleries. Choose your photos and drag them into the message to attach them!

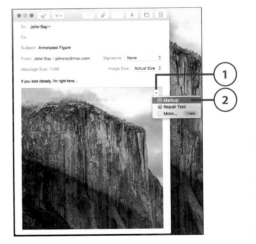

Annotating Attachments with Markup

El Capitan includes a Markup extension for images. When working with an image in an email (added as an attachment or automatically included when replying to a message with an image), you can access tools to quickly annotate the image without leaving Mail.

1. Position your cursor over the image; a down arrow appears in the upper-right corner. Click the arrow.

2. Choose Markup from the menu that appears.

3. The Markup window displays.

4. Use the Freehand tool to add freehand drawings and fancy arrows to the image.

5. Use the Shapes tools to access a variety of geometric shapes along with a magnifying loupe.

6. Click the T icon to insert a line of text over the image.

7. Use the signature tools to add your signature to the image.

8. All these tools' appearances can be modified using the line width, line color, fill color, and font menus located to the right of the tool icons.

9. When finished annotating, click Done.

10. The modified image is inserted into the message and is ready to send!

Extend Yourself

The Markup tool is an example of an El Capitan extension. It adds features to an application without changing the application itself. You can find and download additional extensions from the App Store. Read Chapter 10, "Installing and Managing Applications and Extensions on Your Mac," for more details!

Using Stationery Templates

If you'd like to send an invitation or a fancy greeting, you can make use of prebuilt templates, called "Stationery," that come with the Mail application. Stationery is available whenever you begin composing a new message:

1. Start a new message by clicking the new message icon (pencil and paper) in the Mail toolbar.

2. Click the Show Stationery icon (paper with dots) in the New Message toolbar.

3. Choose a category of templates on the left side of the Stationery bar.

4. Click the thumbnail of the template you want to apply.

5. Click to edit the text within the template.

6. If the template contains images, replace them by dragging photo files from the Finder onto the template image or use the Photo Browser button to locate an image and drag it in.

7. Click the send icon (paper airplane) when you are finished with the message.

Changing Templates

After you change the content of a template, you can choose another template and your changes will be maintained as much as possible.

Creating Signatures

When you send a lot of email, you probably get a bit tired of typing the same thing at the end of each message—your name, email, and other contact information. To add this information automatically to the end of each message you write, create a signature.

1. Choose Mail, Preferences from the menu bar.

2. Click the Signatures icon in the preferences toolbar.

3. Choose an account that the signature should be used with, or choose All Signatures to not associate the signature with a specific account.

4. Click + to add a new signature.

5. Type a name for the signature.

6. Enter the text for the signature in the space to the right.

7. Click Always Match My Default Message Font so that the signature always matches the font you're using.

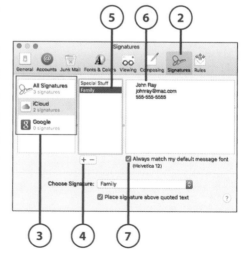

8. If you're adding the signature to an account, use the Choose Signature drop-down menu to choose which signature is automatically added when you write a message. You can also manually choose a signature using the Choose Signature drop-down menu in the message composition window.

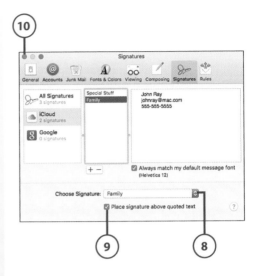

9. Click Place Signature Above Quoted Text to have Mail position your signature above earlier (quoted) text when replying to messages.

10. Close the Mail Preferences window.

Adding a vCard

To attach your personal information to your signature as a virtual business card, you can drag a card out of your Contacts application into the signature.

Managing Your Email with Mailboxes

Email can be overwhelming, especially if you have several different accounts and dozens of incoming messages each day. To help you cope with the incoming mail, you can create mailboxes in which to file or copy messages. You can also set up smart mailboxes that automatically display messages that match certain criteria.

Creating Mailboxes

To create a new mailbox, follow
these steps:

1. Position your cursor over the Mailboxes label in the mailbox list.

2. Click the + button that appears.

3. Using the Location pop-up menu,
   choose where the mailbox should
   be stored. You see all of your
   existing Mailboxes in the menu,
   as well as On My Mac. Choosing an existing location creates
   the new mailbox inside of that
   location.

4. Enter a name for the new
   mailbox.

5. Click OK.

6. The new mailbox is created and
   displayed in the mailbox list.

Make Room for Your Mail

Remember: Because the mailbox display eats up a bunch of room on your
screen, Apple has made it simple to
hide and show the mailbox column
using the Mailboxes button in the
upper-left corner of the Mail window.
In addition, you can quickly change
between your Inbox, Sent, Drafts,
and Flagged folders using the links
directly in the Mail toolbar.

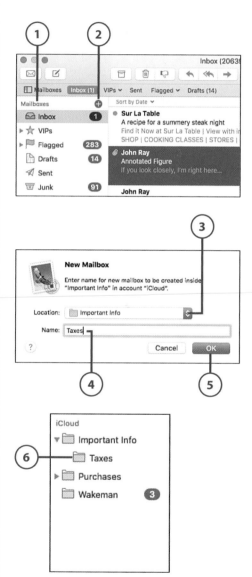

Deleting and Renaming Mailboxes

If you find yourself with extra mailboxes or mailboxes that are no longer serving their original purposes, you can delete or rename them.

1. Right-click the mailbox you want to change in your mailbox list.

2. Choose Delete Mailbox or Rename Mailbox as needed. Any messages stored in a mailbox being deleted are also deleted.

Nesting Folders

Even though you chose where to put your mailbox when it was first created, you can easily move it within your mailbox hierarchy. Mailboxes can be moved inside of other mailboxes by clicking and dragging their folder icons into (or out of) another mailbox.

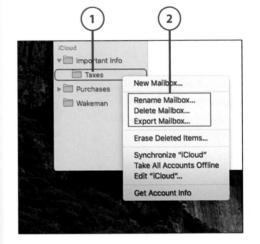

Filing Messages in Mailboxes

Mailboxes are only useful if you file your messages in them. You can copy or move messages one at a time or en masse to a mailbox. You can do this either manually, as described here, or automatically using Smart Mailboxes or Email Rules, discussed in the tasks following this one.

1. Select a message by clicking it in the message list. You can select a contiguous range of messages by holding down Shift and clicking another message, or select several scattered messages by holding down the Command key, ⌘, and clicking multiple messages.

2. Move the messages to a mailbox by dragging them onto the desired mailbox. To copy—rather than move—the messages, hold down the Option key while you're dragging the messages. The messages are moved (or copied) to the other mailbox.

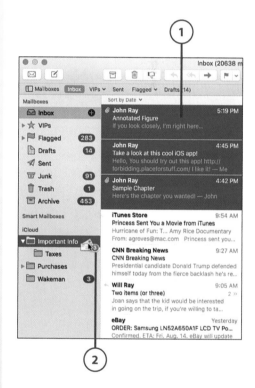

Filing Without Dragging

If you have a large number of mailboxes, or just find the process of dragging to the mailbox list to be cumbersome, you can select the messages and then use Move To or Copy To from the Messages menu to file the email without any dragging required.

Automatic Email Organization with Smart Mailboxes

Much as smart folders in the Finder can help you keep track of files that share certain attributes, Smart Mailboxes can do the same for your email. Using information such as the sender, recipient, and even attachment names, you can group messages together in a Smart Mailbox, regardless of what mailbox, or even what email account, they're associated with. Apple includes one Smart Mailbox by default—"Today"—showing all the messages you've received today.

1. Hover your mouse over the Smart Mailboxes heading in the mailbox list and then click the + icon that appears.

2. Type a name for the mailbox.

3. Choose whether the mailbox should match any or all conditions.

4. Configure your search criteria. Use the first pop-up menu to choose a message attribute (such as Subject), the second to choose a comparison, and the field (where applicable) to provide the value that you are comparing against.

5. Use the + and – buttons to add or remove additional criteria.

6. To include messages from the Trash mailbox or Sent mailbox, click the appropriate Include Messages checkboxes.

7. Click OK when you're finished configuring the Smart Mailbox.

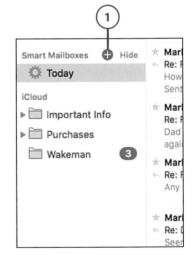

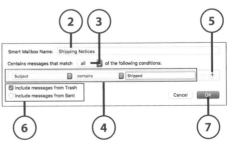

8. The new mailbox is created and displayed in the Smart Mailboxes section within the mailbox list.

Nesting Smart Mailboxes

Smart Mailboxes can't be arranged hierarchically inside one another as normal mailboxes can. To create a hierarchy of Smart Mailboxes, you must create a Smart Mailbox Folder (Mailbox, New Smart Mailbox Folder). This special folder is added to the Smart Mailboxes section and can be used to organize any Smart Mailboxes you create.

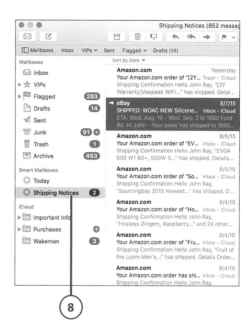

Keeping Track of Your Very Important People with VIP Mailboxes

Mail includes a feature that makes it very simple to track and view all messages from a specific person—the VIP Mailbox. VIP Mailboxes are like smart folders, but with a targeted purpose—showing you all messages from an individual person. To create a VIP mailbox, follow these steps:

1. Choose a message from a sender you want to designate as a VIP.

2. Position your mouse beside the sender's name in the content window and click the star that appears.

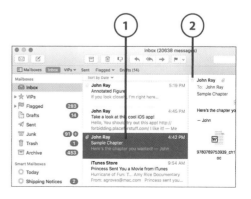

3. The sender is added to a new VIP mailbox.

4. Clicking the VIP mailbox shows all messages from the sender.

5. Click the star in the content view again, or select the new VIP mailbox and choose Remove from VIPs from the Action pop-up menu (gear) to remove VIP status (and the corresponding VIP mailbox).

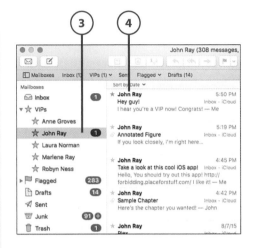

Searching for Messages

Mail makes it easy to quickly search all of your email for particular content, and to turn that search into a Smart Mailbox for future reference.

1. Type the text you are looking for into the search field in the upper-right corner.

2. Using the links below the toolbar, click the mailbox where the search should be performed.

3. Potential search options appear in a drop-down list for matched people, mailboxes, subjects, and message content. Choose what best matches what you want to find.

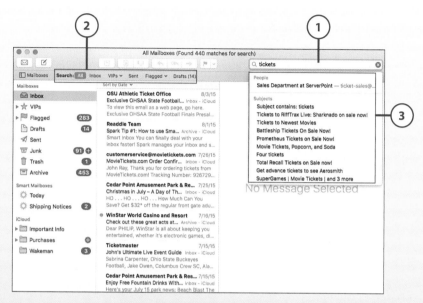

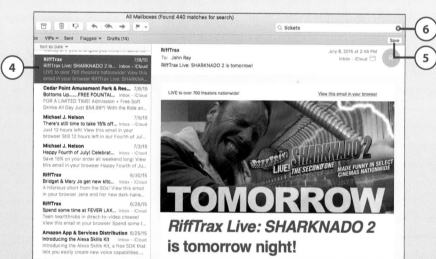

4. The results appear in the message list.

5. Click Save to save the search as a Smart Mailbox. (See steps 2–8 of the "Automatic Email Organization with Smart Mailboxes" task.)

6. Alternatively, click the X button in the search field to clear the search results.

Writing Email Rules

If you'd prefer to have messages filed to actual mailboxes rather than Smart Mailboxes, you can write email rules. Email rules can file messages, highlight messages in the message list, and even forward them to another account. To write a rule, follow these steps:

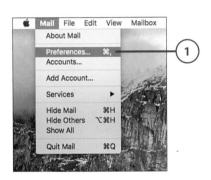

1. Choose Mail, Preferences from the menu bar.

2. Click the Rules icon in the Preferences toolbar.

3. Click Add Rule.

4. Enter a description for the rule so that you can identify it later.

5. Use the Any pop-up menu to choose where any or all rules must evaluate as "true" in order for the rule's actions to be carried out.

6. Configure the conditions under which the rule executes. The first pop-up menu chooses what is evaluated, the second the comparison to be made, and field is the value that should be used in the comparison.

7. Use + or – to add or remove additional conditions.

8. Configure the actions that are performed when the conditions are met.

9. Use + or – to add or remove actions.

10. Click OK to save the rule.

11. Close the Mail Preferences.

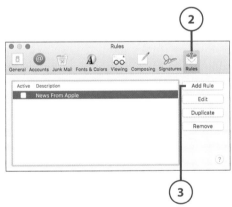

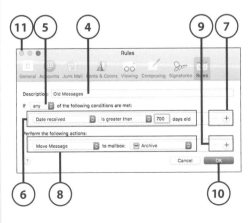

Web Browsing in Safari (New!)

Although similar in many ways to other web browsers, Safari offers a few unique features that set it apart. You can open Safari from its icon on the Dock or Launchpad, or in the Applications folder.

Safari has seen dramatic improvements over the past few years. Safari uses a web browsing engine called Webkit that was, although not an Apple product, engineered by mostly Apple developers. This engine is the same engine on many platforms, including WebOS, some versions of Android, Adobe Air, and others. This means that Safari is treated as a standard, rather than an exception, by most websites.

It's Not All Good

Bring Your Own Flash

If you're browsing with Safari and your web pages seem a bit "bare," it might be because El Capitan doesn't include Adobe Flash by default. To add the Flash plug-in to your browser, visit http://www.adobe.com/products/flashplayer/ in Safari.

Managing Your Bookmarks, Bookmarks Menu, Favorites, Top Sites, and Reading List (Whew!)

In Safari, there are many areas where you can store links to content for easy access. Understanding them can be a bit of a challenge.

First, there is the Bookmarks menu, which appears under the Bookmarks menu item.

Next are Favorites displayed in the main Safari window when opening a new window (and under the URL when you've clicked within it). These are intended to be "quick" access items that you use frequently.

Third, you have the Top Sites list, which shows the sites you (or Safari) have identified as being frequently visited. Access this list by clicking the grid-of-dots icon when viewing Favorites.

Fourth is a sidebar that contains a master view of bookmarks. This includes groups for your favorites, the Bookmarks menu, and anything else you want to add that shouldn't be included in the Favorites or Bookmarks menu view.

Think we're done? Nope. There's still more!

The sidebar, in addition to the master Bookmarks view, also contains the Reading List (denoted by an icon of eyeglasses). It holds pages and links that you want to visit at a later time, but aren't planning to keep as a permanent bookmark.

When Safari first starts, it displays the Favorites view with the sidebar active. If you set up access to a social networking site via El Capitan (see Chapter 7, "Being Social with Messages, FaceTime, Twitter, and Facebook"), your sidebar takes on an additional type of information—shared bookmarks. Bookmarks posted by friends on your social networking accounts will automatically be visible in the sidebar.

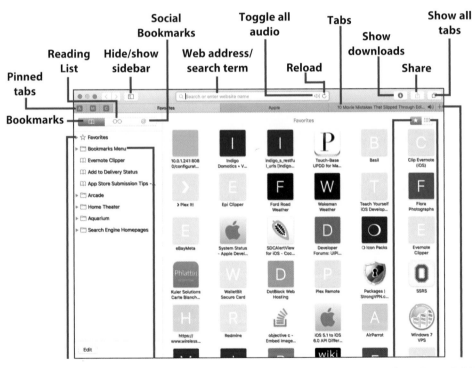

It's Not All Good

Searching for Search?

The first time you start Safari in El Capitan, you may notice something is missing—the search field. Apple has taken the approach of many other browsers and combined the search with the URL field. To go to a particular URL, type in a URL. To perform a search, type in the search. It can be a bit disconcerting at first, but it works just fine.

Adding a Web Page to Bookmarks, Bookmarks Menu, Favorites, Reading List, or Top Sites

To add a web page to the Reading List, Bookmarks, or even Top Sites, you simply need to know what site you want to bookmark, and then follow these steps:

1. Visit the site you want to bookmark by typing its address into the URL field.

2. Click and hold the + button to the left of the URL.

3. Choose where to file the bookmark (Reading List, Top Sites, Favorites, Bookmarks, Bookmarks menu, or a folder within one of these areas).

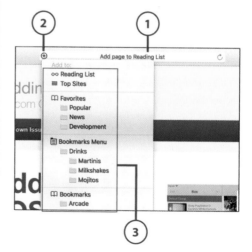

Organizing Bookmarks

After you've added a few bookmarks, you can re-categorize them using these steps:

1. Click the button to show the sidebar.

2. Click the Edit button to display a view for managing bookmarks.

3. Click the New Folder button at the bottom of the window to add a new folder, if desired.

4. Provide a name for the folder by clicking and typing the high-lighted field.

5. Drag bookmarks from anywhere in the list into the order you want. You can drag them into folders, or even place folders inside other folders.

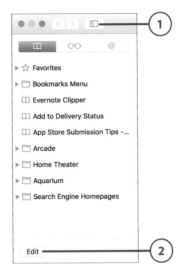

6. To view the contents of a folder, simply click the arrow beside it and the bookmarks contained are displayed.

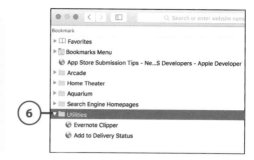

Organizing Top Sites

As you browse, Safari identifies your "top sites." The Top Sites button switches to display previews and marks sites that have updates with a star. Clicking a site opens it in Safari.

To manage the ordering and display of the Top Sites in Safari, follow these steps:

1. Open a new Safari window.
2. Click the Top Sites button (grid of dots).
3. ·Position your cursor near the top left of one of the Top Sites to show the management controls.
4. Click the X button by a site to remove it.
5. Click the pin button to make sure the site always stays on the screen.
6. Rearrange the sites by clicking and dragging their preview images.

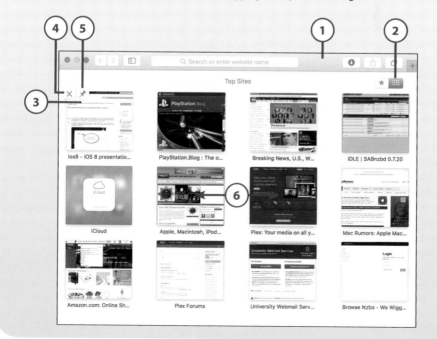

Adding Your Top Sites

You can add to your Top Sites by dragging items from the URL field, sidebar, and so on—pretty much anywhere you see a URL.

A HISTORY LESSON

You can access (and search) your browsing history through the History menu. For a more detailed view (with search), choose History, Show History from the menu bar. For fast access to recently browsed sites, click in the URL and scroll to the bottom of your favorites list. Your recent browsing history is displayed there.

Managing Your Reading List

After you add things to your list, you want to read them, right? To manage your list, just follow these steps:

1. Open the Safari sidebar.

2. Open the Reading List by clicking the Reading List icon.

3. Click a Reading List entry to load the page in Safari.

4. While hovering over an entry, click the X icon in the upper-right corner to remove it from the list.

5. Click the hide/show sidebar icon again to hide the list when you're finished.

Sidebar-Free Reading List Additions

If you get in the habit of using the Reading List, Apple provides some shortcuts to make additions while you're browsing. Shift-click links to add them to the Reading List, or press Shift-⌘-D to add your current page to the list. If you're more of a click-and-drag person, you can drag individual links to the sidebar.

Advanced Browsing Features

It might seem that there isn't much else a web browser could do beyond displaying a web page. Each year, however, Apple adds new features to make browsing faster and easier—and to keep up with (or ahead of) the competition.

Using Tabbed Browsing

In Safari, separate browser windows are combined under a single window with tabs representing each individual website you have open. To use tabbed browsing in Safari, follow these steps:

1. Click the + button near the far right of the Safari toolbar.

2. A new tab is added with your homepage (by default, the Favorites view).

3. Enter a URL (or choose a bookmark) to browse to a new site in that tab.

4. Use the tabs to quickly switch between web pages. Note that while you're browsing, you can hold down Command as you click links. The links create a new tab in the Safari browser window.

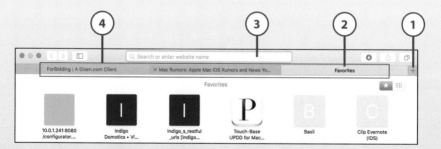

Fine-Tune Your Tabs

To fine-tune your tabbed browsing behavior (or disable it entirely), use the Tabs section of the Safari Preferences. (Choose Safari, Preferences, from the menu bar.)

Viewing All Tabs

If you find yourself lost in tabs, not knowing what they all are, you can view all the tabbed web pages at once in a pretty scrolling view. To do this, follow these steps:

1. Click the Show All Tabs icon at the far right of the Safari toolbar, or perform a pinch gesture on the Magic Trackpad.

2. The tabs appear in a grid view so you can easily identify your content.

3. Click within a page to go to that page.

4. Click the + page to create a new empty tab.

5. Use the links at the bottom to browse to tabs open on your other iCloud-connected devices.

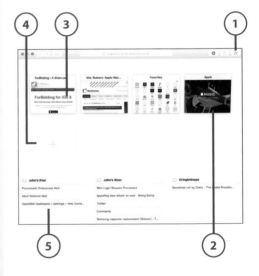

Enable the Safari iCloud Service

Browsing tabs across your devices requires the Safari service to be active on your iCloud account. This is managed in the iCloud preference panel.

Silencing Tabs

Ever find yourself browsing the web, only to hear audio that is coming from *somewhere*? Rather than forcing you to search through your tabs to silence unwanted sounds, Safari makes it easy:

1. When you hear audio, look for the speaker icon at the right side of a tab. Click the speaker to toggle the sound off and on.

2. Alternatively, click the speaker icon in the address field to toggle the sound in *all* tabs off and on.

Pinning Tabs

If you want to create a set of tabs that exist each time you start Safari, you can "pin" them. Follow these steps to pin and unpin your favorite sites:

1. Open the site you want to pin in a new tab.

2. Right-click the tab and choose Pin Tab.

3. A miniature version of the tab appears on the left. Add as many pinned tabs as you want.

4. Right-click a pinned tab and choose Unpin to convert it to a normal tab or close to remove it altogether.

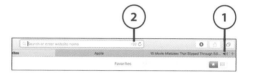

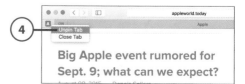

Viewing PDFs Online

In El Capitan, Apple has included
a helpful PDF viewer that makes
reviewing PDF documents a breeze.
When you click a PDF link, the viewer
opens. To control the viewer, follow
these steps:

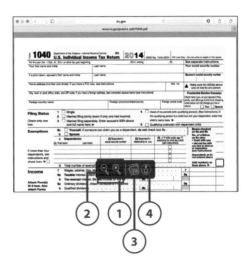

1. Position the cursor near the bottom center of the browser window to show the PDF controls.

2. Click + or – to zoom in and out.

3. Click the Preview icon to open the PDF in the El Capitan Preview (an Image/PDF viewer) application.

4. Click the Download button to save the PDF to your Downloads folder.

Distraction-Free Reading with Reader

Web pages, unfortunately, are rarely
dedicated to getting you just the
information you need. They are filled
with ads and other distracting content, and frequently require you to
click multiple links to get the whole
story. To provide a distraction-free
reading experience, Apple includes a
Reader feature with Safari that strips
out all the unnecessary cruft. To use
Reader, follow these instructions.

1. When viewing a web page with a story you want to read, check to see if the Reader icon (four horizontal lines) is visible on the left of the URL field. Click it.

2. You are now viewing a clean version of the content.

3. Click the AA button in the address field to access font and background color controls.

4. Click the Reader icon again to close Reader.

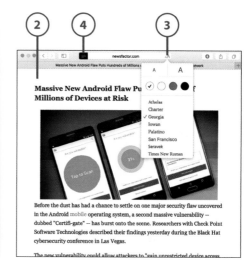

It's Not All Good

Disabled Reader Icon? C'est la Vie!

The Reader feature of Safari does not work with all articles—only those that it can correctly identify and reformat. If the button shows up as disabled, Reader can't work with the content you're viewing and no amount of reloading or fiddling with settings is going to help.

Saving and Sharing Account Information

In El Capitan, if you've enabled the Keychain option in iCloud (see Chapter 4, "Setting Up iCloud and Internet Accounts"), Safari tracks auto-completion information, stores credit cards, and shares all of the data between all your devices.

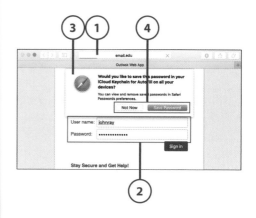

1. Browse to a login form on a website where you'd like to log in.

2. Enter your login information.

3. Safari prompts to save your information.

4. Choose to save the information, or not.

Managing AutoFill Data

In addition to the information stored as you browse, Safari can also fill in forms using your Address Book data, or credit card information that you store. To manage all of this data, you need the Safari Preferences:

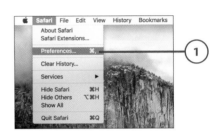

1. Choose Preferences from the Safari menu.

2. Select Autofill from the toolbar.

3. Check the sources of information you want to use for auto-completing web forms.

4. Click the Edit button to edit that category of information. (Editing the Contacts information opens Address Book.)

5. Close the preferences.

Editing AutoFill User Names and Passwords

To edit user names and passwords that you've stored while browsing, complete the steps in "Managing AutoFill Data" and then do the following:

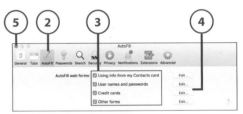

1. Click the Edit button beside User Names and Passwords.

2. Use the search field to locate stored information.

3. Click a stored URL and press delete to remove it.

4. Click Show Passwords for Selected Websites to display passwords in clear text. (You'll be prompted for your password if you haven't authenticated recently.)

5. Close the preferences.

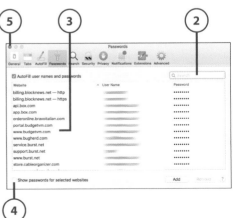

Editing AutoFill Credit Cards

While you're checking out in popular online websites, Safari may prompt you to save credit card details. To edit and manage the saved information, complete the steps in "Managing AutoFill Data" and then follow these additional steps:

1. Click the Edit Button beside Credit Cards.

2. Select a card and click Remove to delete it.

3. Click Add to create a new card entry.

4. Fill in the data for each field.

5. Click Done to save the card.

6. Close the preferences.

And All the Rest...

The final type of AutoFill information you can edit is Other forms. This is just other information that Safari stores as you provide data on various web forms. If you click the Edit button for Other forms, you have the ability to browse for web addresses and remove stored data, not edit or view the data.

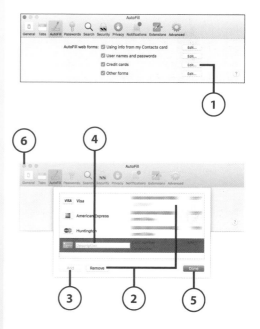

Sharing with Others

To share the page that you are currently reading with someone else via email or Messages, you can use the Safari Share icon.

1. Click the Share icon when browsing a page you like.

2. Choose to share the page via one of the methods displayed.

3. When sharing via email, a new email is created and you can choose whether to share a reader version of the page, the full web page, a PDF of the page, or just the link!

More on Sharing

Sharing, including how to add Twitter to the Share menu, is covered in more detail in Chapters 6, "Sharing Files, Devices, and Services," and 9, "Entertainment on the (Big) Little Screen."

Enabling Private Browsing

When private browsing is enabled, no website content is saved to your Mac—it's as if you were never there:

1. Choose File, New Private Window from the menu bar.

2. Use the new Safari window as you would normally, but your session is private—as indicated by a dark background in the URL field.

3. Close the window when finished browsing.

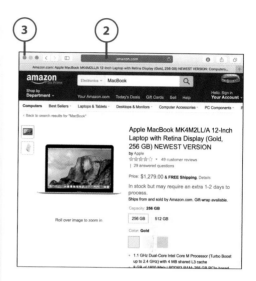

Why Private?

Enabling private browsing is useful if, for example, you share a computer with other people, and there's a chance that they might stumble upon something in your web history that you'd prefer they didn't (holiday gift orders, for example).

Protecting Your Mac and Yourself Online

Safari offers several tools to help protect you from fraudulent activity online. To ensure that you have the most secure browsing experience possible, complete the following configuration:

1. Choose Safari, Preferences from the menu.

2. Click the Security toolbar icon.

3. Check the checkbox beside Warn When Visiting a Fraudulent Website.

4. Check the checkbox beside Block Pop-up Windows.

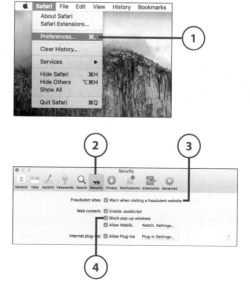

5. Click the Privacy toolbar icon.

6. Be sure that the Cookies and Website Data option is set to Allow from Websites I Visit.

7. Choose whether Safari should deny all access to your location information, or to prompt you if a website requests it. Note that some online services can provide valuable customized information using your location.

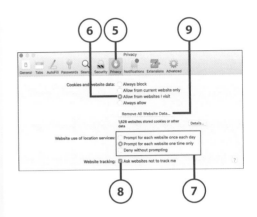

8. Click Ask Websites Not to Track Me to request that your website visits be logged as little as possible. Note that web service providers may not pay attention to this setting.

9. To remove all information stored on your computer by the sites you've visited, click Remove All Website Data. You might want to repeat this from time to time.

10. Use the Notifications Preferences section to manage which websites can post notifications to the El Capitan Notification Center.

11. Close the Safari Preferences.

Go with What You Know

As a general rule, you should never download files online unless you trust the source. By default, Safari opens files that it has identified as safe. If you prefer to prevent Safari from opening *any* file it downloads, you can find this option under the General Safari Preferences.

Adding Web Content to the Dashboard

Many of us visit a web page just to see a tiny piece of content, such as the latest weather report or breaking news. With Safari and the Dashboard, you can create your own widget, called a web clipping, that is accessible directly from your Mac's Dashboard.

1. Visit the web page with the content you want to add to the Dashboard.

2. Choose File, Open in Dashboard.

3. Position the box on the page so that the content you want to capture is highlighted as best as possible, and then click your mouse.

4. Fine-tune the selected area by dragging it within the Safari window and using the handles on the sides to resize it.

5. Click Add when you are satisfied with the results.

6. The Dashboard opens and the new web clipping widget is displayed.

Automatic Updates

Clipped web content even updates automatically as long as you are connected to the Internet.

>>>Go Further
CHANGING THE CLIPPING APPEARANCE

To customize the web clipping even more, click the i icon in the lower-right corner of the widget in Dashboard. You are given the option of several different borders that can be applied to stylize the clipping.

Extending Safari's Capabilities with Extensions

Safari supports developer-created extensions that can add functionality to your browsing experience—such as the ability to quickly access Twitter, eBay, and other services without leaving your current web page. Safari extensions are supported by the individual developers, so after you install one, you need to refer to the documentation for further support.

Installing an Extension

Installing extensions doesn't require anything more than clicking a link on a website.

1. Choose Safari, Safari Extensions from the menu bar.

2. An Apple website opens listing all registered extensions.

3. Use the website to browse to an extension you are interested in, and then click the Install Now button beside the extension.

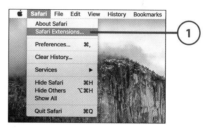

4. After a few seconds, the extension is installed and activated. Depending on how it works, you might see a new button or area added to the Safari toolbar. Follow the developer's instructions to use the extension.

Managing Extensions

To manage the extensions you've installed—including configuring them, if configuration is necessary—use Safari Preferences. Follow these steps to access your extension preferences:

1. Open the Safari Preferences by choosing Safari, Preferences from the menu bar.

2. Click the Extensions button in the top of the Preferences window.

3. Click an individual extension to view its configuration options.

4. Use the Enable checkbox to enable or disable individual extensions.

5. Click Uninstall to remove the extension entirely.

6. Make sure that the Automatically Update checkbox is selected to ensure that your extensions will be updated as needed.

7. Close the Preferences panel when finished.

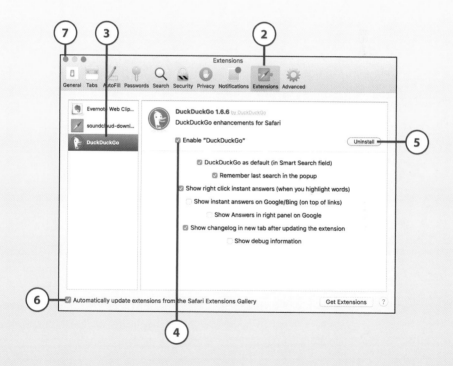

Configure file, printer, screen, and Internet sharing in the Sharing System Preferences panel.

Point and click to browse available servers on your network.

Connect directly to a wide range of servers using their Internet addresses.

- → Sharing files and folders using AirDrop and File Sharing
- → File sharing with Windows computers
- → Setting Share Permissions
- → Using the Share menu to quickly share files online
- → Sharing and accessing network printers
- → Sharing your screen and viewing remote systems
- → Turning your Mac into an Internet Access Point

Sharing Files, Devices, and Services

Your Mac is a self-contained workstation that packs all the power you need into a highly integrated package—and one that is fully capable of integrating with new or existing networks. El Capitan can share and access a variety of resources with other computers on your network. Files and folders can be shared with other Macs and Windows PCs; printers can be shared with other Macs; even your screen can be made available to other computers on your network.

To make the most use of the information in this chapter, the assumption is that you've already established a network connection and have connected any printers or scanners to either your Mac or another El Capitan-based Macintosh on your network. You might want to refer to Chapter 3, "Connecting Your Mac to a Network," and Chapter 12, "Using El Capitan with Your iDevices," for more details on networking and peripherals, respectively.

File Sharing on Your Mac

The most common network activity (beyond email and web surfing) is file sharing. Your Mac comes ready to share files using several popular protocols—AFP (Apple Filing Protocol) and SMB (Simple Message Block) are the most popular. AFP, as the name suggests, is a Mac-to-Mac file sharing protocol, but recently Apple has switched to SMB as the preferred protocol. SMB is traditionally used in Windows environments and offers significant performance improvements over AFP.

In addition to the *protocols* for sharing files, you also have different *methods* for *how* you share them. Traditional file sharing requires that you turn on file sharing, choose what you want to share, tell another person how to connect, and so on. With El Capitan, your Mac includes a zero-configuration version of file sharing called AirDrop. AirDrop enables you to wirelessly share files with other users who are in your vicinity—with no setup required!

Authenticate to Make Changes!

Many of the settings in this chapter require you to authenticate with El Capitan before the settings can be made. If you find yourself in a situation where a setting is grayed out, click the padlock icon in the lower-left corner of the window to authenticate and make the necessary change.

AirDrop is a fast and easy file-sharing system that enables you to send files to another Macintosh without any setup—no usernames, no passwords, nothing except a Wi-Fi adapter that is turned on! Unlike traditional file sharing, AirDrop's simplicity does present a few challenges that might make it less than ideal for your particular file-sharing situation. Specifically, AirDrop requires the following:

- All computers sharing files must be using the Lion (or later) operating system.

- All systems must have recent wireless-AC or N Wi-Fi hardware—2011 or later Macs will work fine.

- Your computer will not be able to browse the contents of other systems, only send files.

AirDrop Everywhere

AirDrop works with iOS clients! To learn more about this feature, be sure to check out Chapter 12.

Configuring AirDrop

Before you get started using Air-
Drop, you might want to make a
few changes to help restrict or open
access to the service. To modify who
can see you (and whom you can
see!), complete the following:

1. Open a new Finder window and
   make sure the Favorites sidebar
   section is expanded.

2. Click the AirDrop icon.

3. Click the Allow Me to Be Dis-
   covered By option to choose
   whether you are visible to everyone, just people in your contacts,
   or no one.

4. Click the Don't See Who You're
   Looking For? link to enable support for some older Macs.

5. After making your changes, you
   should see other AirDrop clients
   begin to appear in the AirDrop
   window.

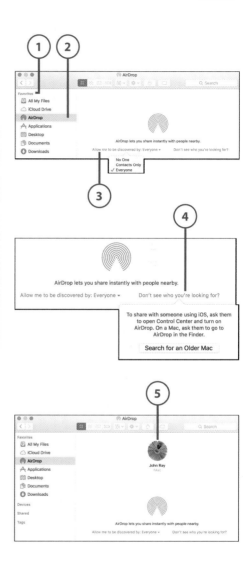

It's Not All Good

Set Your Options. Then Set Them Again!

The settings you make in AirDrop windows do not currently persist. You'll
need to make these settings repeatedly each time you use AirDrop.

Sending Files with AirDrop

To use AirDrop, be sure that your Wi-Fi adapter is turned on (see Chapter 3 for details), identify the files that you want to share with another person, and then follow these steps:

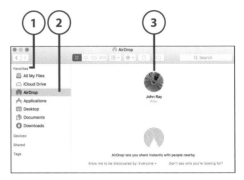

1. Open a new Finder window and make sure the Favorites sidebar section is expanded.

2. Click the AirDrop icon to browse for other OS X computers.

3. Other devices are shown using the owner's avatar picture (set in Address Book) as their icon.

4. Drag the files you want to transfer to the icon of another computer or device.

5. You will see "Waiting" shown below the remote computer's icon while the receiving user confirms the transfer.

6. The files are copied to the remote system. A blue circle around the receiving computer indicates progress.

John Ray
Waiting...

7. Close the AirDrop window to stop being visible on the network. After you've closed the AirDrop window, you can go your merry way. You don't need to disconnect or change your network settings. You're done!

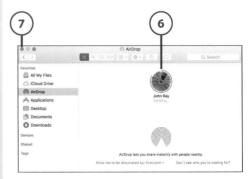

Receiving Files with AirDrop

Receiving files with AirDrop is even easier than sending them. When a nearby El Capitan user wants to send files to your Mac, follow these steps:

1. Open a new Finder window and make sure the Favorites sidebar section is expanded.

2. Click the AirDrop icon to become visible to other AirDrop users.

3. When prompted to receive files, click Accept or Accept and Open to accept the transfer, or Decline to cancel.

4. The files are transferred to your Downloads folder.

5. Click the X on the downloading file or folder to cancel the download, or click Cancel in the notification that appears.

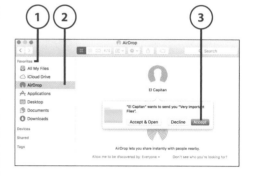

6. Close the AirDrop window to stop being visible on the network. That's it! Your AirDrop session is automatically ended when the window closes.

No AirDrop? Your Mac Might Be Too Old.

AirDrop uses peer-to-peer ad hoc wireless networking, which is only supported in recent Macs (2011 and later). Although this may seem limiting, this hardware is what makes it possible to communicate with zero configuration and without using a common Wi-Fi access point.

Using the Share Menu to Send via AirDrop

The Share menu is a relatively new user interface (UI) element and feature in OS X. It enables applications to share files and folders from almost anywhere—even file open and save dialog boxes, as you'll see here.

1. Select a file (or open a file) within an application.

2. Look for the Share icon. Click it to show the Share menu.

3. Select AirDrop from the list of sharing options.

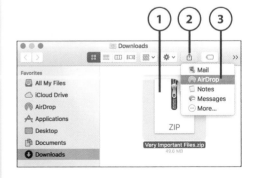

4. A new window appears listing all nearby users with AirDrop open in the Finder.

5. Enable support for older Macs, if necessary, by clicking the Don't See Who You're Looking For? link.

6. Click the person or machine you want to send the file to.

7. The copy begins as soon as the recipient accepts the transfer. Click Done to exit and the copy will continue in the background.

Beyond the 'Drop

The Share menu is much more powerful than just sharing via AirDrop. We look at a few other sharing scenarios that use this feature later in this chapter.

Configuring Traditional File and Folder Sharing

When AirDrop won't do (you need to browse another computer's files or share with Windows/older Macs), you need to turn to the traditional file sharing features built into OS X. El Capitan provides consolidated controls for sharing files, regardless of what type of computer you want to share them with. You set up file sharing by first enabling sharing for your Mac and then choosing the protocols available for accessing the files. Finally, you decide which folders should be shared and who should see them.

Enabling File Sharing

Before your Mac can make any files
or folders available over a network,
you must enable File Sharing.

1. In the System Preferences, click
   the Sharing icon.

2. Click the checkbox in front of the
   service labeled File Sharing.

3. The details about your sharing configuration are displayed
   on the right side of the sharing
   window.

4. Close the Sharing Preferences
   panel, or continue configuring
   other sharing options.

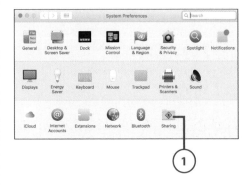

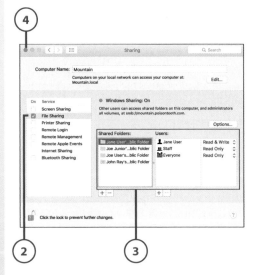

Choosing File Sharing Protocols

Files can be shared over AFP (Legacy OS X) or SMB (current OS X and Windows). If possible, stick to SMB for the best speeds.

To choose which protocols can be used to access the files on your Mac, follow these steps:

1. In System Preferences, click the Sharing icon.

2. Click the File Sharing service label.

3. Click the Options button to display the available sharing protocols.

4. Check or uncheck the protocols that you want to use. If you are only sharing between El Capitan machines, all you need is SMB.

5. If you want to use SMB to share specifically with Windows systems, you must enable each account for access. Within the Windows File Sharing section, check the box in front of each user that should be *allowed* to connect.

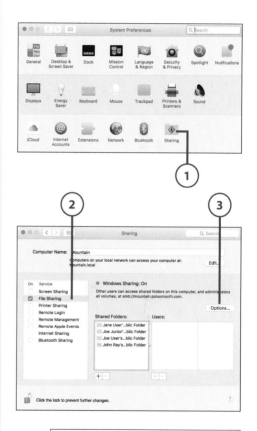

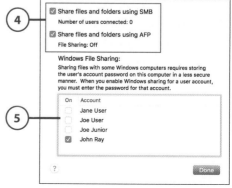

6. Enter the password for each account and click OK.

7. Click Done.

8. Close the Sharing Preferences, or continue configuring sharing options.

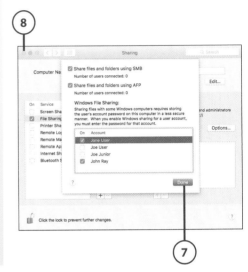

>>>Go Further

WHAT IS WITH THE ACCOUNT CHECKBOXES AND PASSWORDS FOR WINDOWS FILE SHARING?

To share with Windows clients, the El Capitan SMB implementation requires that user accounts and passwords be stored in a different format than how they are used natively by OS X. By enabling or disabling accounts for Windows File, you are creating the user authentication information that Windows users will need to connect.

Selecting Folders and Permissions

After enabling file sharing and choosing the protocols that are used, your next step is to pick the folders that can be shared. By default, each user's Public folder is shared and accessible by anyone with an account on your computer. (See Chapter 14, "Securing and Protecting Your Mac," for configuring user accounts.)

1. In the System Preferences, click the Sharing icon.

2. Click the File Sharing service label.

3. Click the + button under Shared Folders to share a new folder.

4. Find the folder you want to make available and then click the Add button.

5. Close the System Preferences, or continue configuring sharing options.

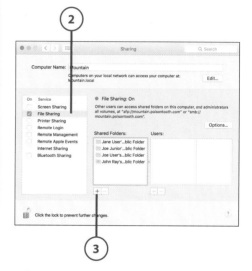

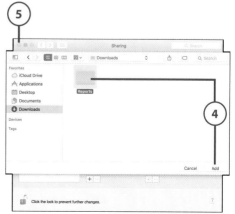

Setting Folder Access Permissions

By default, your user account has full access to anything that you share. The default user group named Staff, and everyone with an account on the computer, has read-only access.

To change who can access a file share, complete the following steps:

1. In the System Preferences window, click the Sharing icon.

2. Click the File Sharing service label.

3. Click the Shared Folder name that you want to modify.

4. Click the + button under the Users list to add a new user (or − to remove access for a selected user).

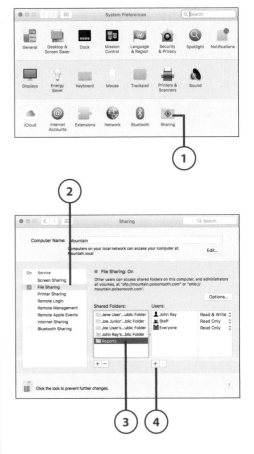

5. A window for selecting a user displays. Within the Users & Groups category, pick the user or group and click Select.

6. Use the pop-up menu to the right of each user in the Users list to choose what the user can do within the shared folder.

7. Close the System Preferences.

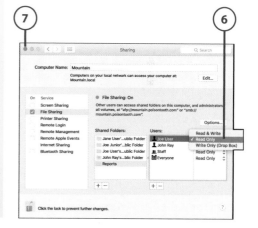

>>>Go Further

WHAT PERMISSIONS CAN BE APPLIED TO A SHARED FOLDER?

Shared folders can have the following permissions set on a per-user or per-group basis:

- **Read & Write**—Grants full access to the folder and files within it. Users can add, edit, and delete items within the folder.

- **Read Only**—Provides access to the files in the folder, but users cannot modify or delete them, nor can they create new files or folders.

- **Write Only (Drop Box)**—Allows users to write to the folder, but not see its contents.

- **No Access**—Available only for the Everyone group; disables access for all user accounts except those explicitly granted access in the permissions.

Browsing and Connecting to Network Shares

Browsing and connecting to a local network share to find shared files you want to access is similar to browsing through the folders located on your Mac. To browse for available network shares, do the following:

1. Open a new Finder window and make sure the Shared sidebar section is expanded.

2. Click the computer that is sharing the folders and files that you want to access.

3. If you have not logged into the computer before and saved your password, a list of the publicly accessible file shares is displayed in the Finder window.

4. Click the Connect As button on the upper right of the Finder window.

5. Enter the username and password that you have established for accessing files on the server.

6. Click Remember This Password in My Keychain to enable browsing directly to the file shares in the future.

7. Click Connect.

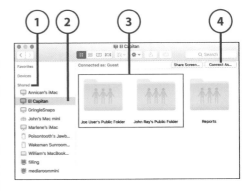

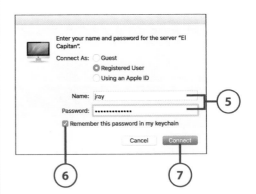

8. The file share list updates to display all the shares that your user account can access. Double-click the share you want to use.

9. The share is mounted as a disk and can be used as if it were local to your Mac.

Browsing Large Networks

If there are many different computers sharing files on your network, you can browse them in a Finder window rather than the Finder sidebar. To open a Finder window that browses your network, choose Go, Network from the menu bar or click the All... icon within the Shared section of the Finder sidebar.

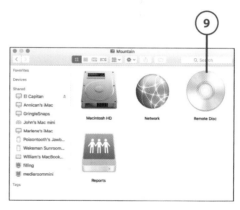

>>>Go Further
ONE PASSWORD TO RULE THEM ALL

You might notice when connecting to other El Capitan, Yosemite, or Mountain Lion servers that you are given the option of connecting with your Apple ID and iCloud Password. This works if your account has had an Apple ID associated with it on the remote server. This association is made when first creating a user account on an OS X system. Existing users can opt-in to using their Apple ID and iCloud password by opening the Users & Groups System Preferences panel and then clicking the Change Password button and selecting the Use iCloud Password button.

Connecting to Remote Shares

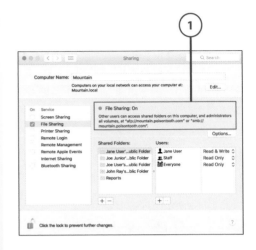

Sometimes file shares aren't directly browseable because they're hiding their available shares, or they are located on a different network from your Mac. To access remote shares by URL, follow these steps:

1. When you create a new file share on your Mac, El Capitan provides you with a list of URLs that can be used to access that file share (see step 3 of "Enabling File Sharing"). You can use these URLs to directly access a file share rather than browsing.

2. Choose Go, Connect to Server from the Finder menu.

3. Enter the URL for the file share in the Server Address field.

4. Click + if you want to add the server to the list of favorite servers.

5. Click Connect to connect to the server and view the available shares.

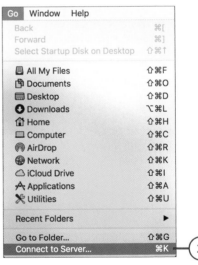

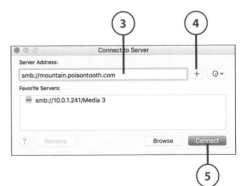

Talking the (Windows) Talk

Your Windows friends might give you network shares to connect to in the format \\servername\sharename. You can translate this into a "Mac-friendly" URL by adding the prefix smb: and reversing the direction of the slashes—that is, smb://servername/sharename.

Sharing Files via the Share Menu

El Capitan includes a way of sharing files from almost anywhere via Share menu. You can use a Share menu (indicated by an icon of an arrow pointing out of a rectangle) to quickly send a file through a variety of different means, including AirDrop (discussed earlier in this chapter), Messages, and other online services.

Sharing Files via Messages

A simple example of the Share menu is using it to share a file via Messages. To do this, either open the file or select it in the Finder, and then follow these instructions:

1. Click the Share icon.

2. Choose Messages from the drop-down menu.

3. A panel appears with the file added as an attachment.

4. Add the user that you want to send the file to.

5. Click Send to send the file and get back to work!

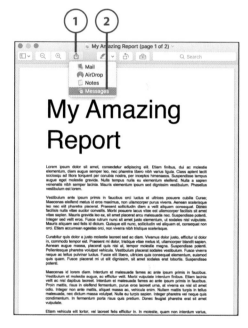

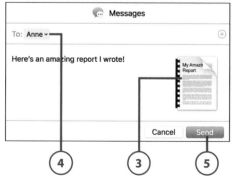

Uploading Files to an Online Service

Using El Capitan, you can now share your files with the world via a number of online services—such as Facebook, Vimeo, and Flickr—without even needing to touch a web browser. Vimeo is a great popular destination for videos on the Internet, so we'll use that as our example.

1. Locate the movie file you want to upload, and click the Share icon.

Before You Upload

To upload a video to the online service of your choice, first make sure you've added an account for the service as described in Chapter 4, "Setting Up iCloud and Internet Accounts."

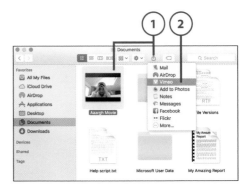

2. Choose the online destination (in this case, Vimeo) from the pop-up menu.

3. Enter a title, description, and a set of keywords (called Tags) to describe the video.

4. Set the video as Personal, if desired. This limits viewing of the video to individuals who you share it with via the Vimeo website. Please note that these settings may vary between the various online services supported in El Capitan.

5. Click Publish.

6. The Movie Export window appears and displays the status of the encoding process.

7. When finished, a link to the video is displayed. Your movie is available online.

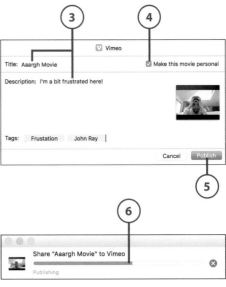

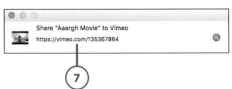

Cutting It Down to Size

To trim a video before sharing it, click the Share icon and choose Edit, Trim from the menu bar. You can move the start and end points of your video clip to wherever you'd like and then trim off the extra.

Sharing Printers

Sharing a printer is a convenient way to provide printing services to your Mac without having to connect any physical wires. With El Capitan, printer sharing just takes a few clicks and then your system acts as if it has a physical printer attached.

Enabling Network Printer Sharing

To share a printer, you must first have the printer connected and configured on another Macintosh (see Chapter 12 for details). After the printer is set up and working, follow these steps to make it available over a local network:

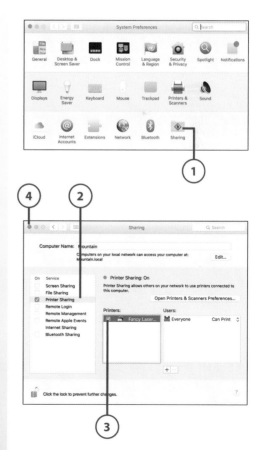

1. In the System Preferences window, click the Sharing icon.

2. Click the checkbox in front of the Printer Sharing service.

3. Within the Printers list, click the checkboxes in front of each printer you want to share. The printers are immediately made available to everyone on your network.

4. Close the System Preferences, or continue setting sharing preferences.

Setting Printer Sharing Permissions

Any shared printer is initially available to anyone with a computer connected to your network. To restrict access to specific user accounts on your computer, do the following:

1. In the System Preferences window, click the Sharing icon.

2. Click the label for the Printer Sharing service.

3. Highlight the name of the shared printer that you want to configure.

4. Click the + button to select a user that can print to your printer. (Use – to remove access for a user you added previously.)

5. A window is displayed to select a user. Choose the user or group and click Select.

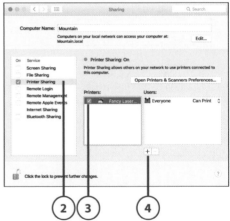

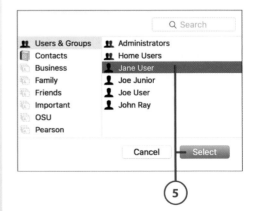

No Access for Everyone

The Everyone group can't be removed from the Users list. To remove access for Everyone, the group must be toggled to No Access.

6. Toggle the pop-up menu beside the Everyone group to No Access to keep everyone except the listed individuals from being able to access the printer.

7. Close the System Preferences.

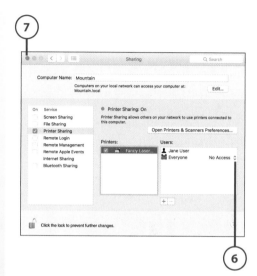

Accessing a Network Printer

To access a printer that is being shared by another Mac, first make sure that both computers are on and connected to the same network and then follow these steps:

1. Choose File, Print from the menu bar within an application of your choice.

2. The Printer dialog box appears. Click the Printer drop-down menu to see the options.

3. If you haven't used the shared printer before, select the printer from the Nearby Printers section of the drop-down menu.

4. El Capitan automatically connects your Mac to the printer and configures it. This might require El Capitan to connect to the Internet to download drivers.

5. Choose the options for the document you are printing and then click Print. The printer behaves exactly as if it is connected directly to your computer. The next time you print, the printer will be available directly in your main printer list.

Printing to Protected Printers

If you set up specific user accounts that can access the printer, you are prompted for a username and password the first time you print. You can, at that time, choose to save the printer connection information to your keychain, which eliminates the need to authenticate for subsequent use.

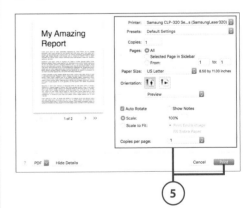

Sharing an Optical Drive

If you're using a DVD-less Mac (which is most of them!) you can use another Macintosh on your network to share a CD or DVD inserted into its drive. This gives you the ability to install software and access files even if you don't have a physical drive connected.

Enabling DVD Sharing

From a Macintosh with a DVD drive available, follow these steps to turn on optical drive sharing:

1. In the System Preferences window, click the Sharing icon.

2. Click the checkbox in front of the DVD or CD Sharing service.

3. Click the Ask Me Before Allowing Others to Use My DVD Drive checkbox to prompt you when other people attempt to access your optical drive.

4. Close the System Preferences.

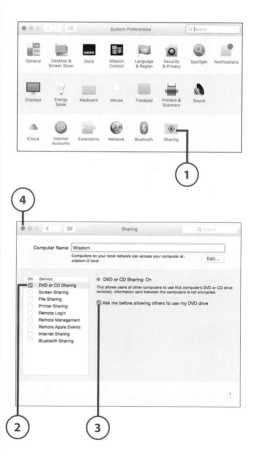

Accessing a Shared Optical Drive

To access a shared optical drive from your DVD-free Mac, do the following:

1. Open a new Finder window and make sure the Devices section in the Finder sidebar is expanded.

2. Click the Remote Disc item in the Devices sidebar area.

3. Double-click the computer that is sharing the DVD you want to use.

4. If the DVD is not immediately visible, click Ask to Use to prompt the host computer that you'd like to use its drive.

5. After access has been granted, the available DVD or CD is listed. Double-click the DVD or CD to begin using it.

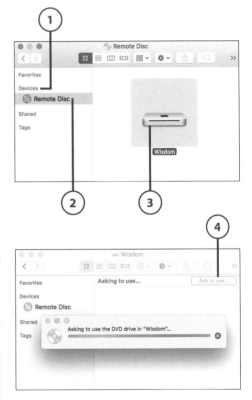

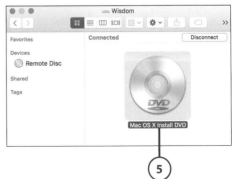

>>>Go Further

CAN I ACCESS A SHARED OPTICAL DRIVE EVEN IF MY MAC *HAS* A DVD DRIVE?

Yes, but not without a few changes. You need to open the Terminal application (found in the Utilities folder in the Applications folder) and then type in the following two lines to enable optical drive sharing:

defaults write com.apple.NetworkBrowser EnableODiskBrowsing -bool true

defaults write com.apple.NetworkBrowser ODSSupported -bool true

Reboot your computer after entering these commands.

Sharing Your Mac Screen (New!)

Chapter 8, "Managing Who, Where, When, and What," includes instructions on how to share your Macintosh's screen using Messages, but there are many instances where you might want to access another Mac's display without having to start a chat.

Built into El Capitan is a standards-based screen-sharing system. Using screen sharing, you can access your Mac's display from anywhere on your local network or, in some cases, from anywhere in the world. El Capitan even has the ability to share a computer's "screen" even if someone else is using the computer. The screen sharing software can now automatically create a virtual screen that you can see and use while the person sitting in front of the computer continues to see their own desktop!

Enabling Screen Sharing

To configure another Mac so that you can access its screen from your Mac, you initially need direct access to the computer:

1. In the System Preferences window, click the Sharing icon.

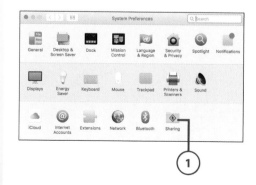

2. Click the checkbox in front of the Screen Sharing service.

3. A URL that you can use to connect to your computer is displayed on the right side of the sharing pane.

4. Close the System Preferences, or continue setting sharing preferences.

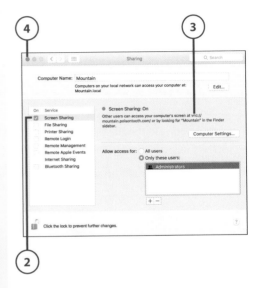

Setting Screen Sharing Permissions

After screen sharing is enabled, choose who can access the display. Initially, only administrative users can view your screen.

1. In the System Preferences window, click the Sharing icon.

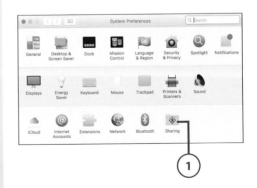

2. Click the Screen Sharing service label.

3. Choose whether All Users on the computer can access its screen, or click Only These Users to restrict access to specific individuals or groups.

4. Use the + button to choose a user or group that should be granted access, or use − to remove a user or group that you had previously added.

5. A window for selecting a user displays. Choose the user or group and click Select.

6. For additional control, click the Computer Settings button.

7. In the dialog box that appears, click Anyone May Request Permission to Control Screen to allow anyone to access the display if the person sitting in front of the computer grants them access.

8. To provide access to your Mac's screen using a standard VNC (Virtual Network Computing) client, click the VNC Viewers May Control Screen with Password checkbox and provide a password that grants access to those users.

9. Click OK.

10. Close the System Preferences.

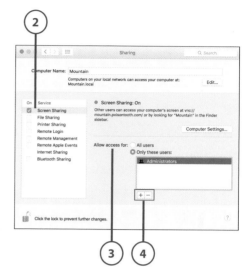

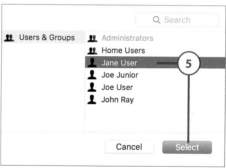

VNC Is Everywhere

There are VNC clients available for Windows, Linux, and even platform-independent Java. If you want to access your Mac's screen from another operating system, check out TightVNC (www.tightvnc.com).

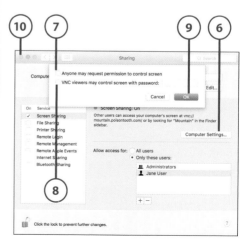

Accessing the Screen of a Local Mac

To access the shared screen of a Mac on your local network, make sure that your Mac is connected to the network and then follow these steps:

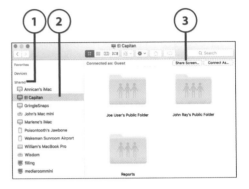

1. Open a new Finder window and make sure the Shared sidebar section heading is expanded.

2. Click the computer whose screen you want to access.

3. Click Share Screen in the upper-right corner of the Finder window.

4. Enter your username and password on the remote system, if prompted.

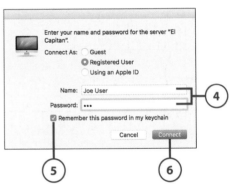

5. Click Remember This Password in My Keychain to store the password and enable password-less connections in the future.

6. Click Connect to begin using the remote display.

7. If another person is using the computer, you can ask to share the display with them, or connect to a new virtual display. Click whichever approach you prefer and click Connect.

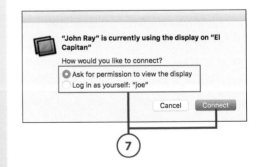

8. The remote display is shown in a window on your Mac.

9. Choose View, Show Toolbar to access a few customization options.

10. Toggle between controlling and observing with the Control Mode icons in the toolbar.

11. Use the Scaling Mode icon to view the screen fullsize or shrink it to fit your window.

12. Use the Clipboard icon to choose how to transfer your clipboard to and from the remote system, or simply share the clipboard.

13. Drag files to and from the remote system to transfer them to (and from!) your computer.

14. Close the window when you're finished using the remote system.

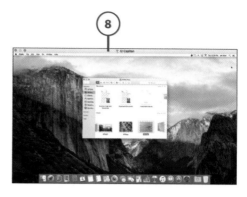

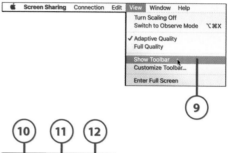

Capture the Moment

If you'd like to take screenshots of the remote system, you can add a screenshot button to the toolbar by choosing View, Customize Toolbar from the menu bar. You can also take a screenshot directly by choosing Connection, Save Screen Capture As.

Accessing Remote Computers and Non-Macs

If you can't browse to a computer to access its screen, or you need to connect to a non-Macintosh computer, you can do so using almost the same process as you used to connect to a remote file share:

1. When you're sharing a screen on your Mac, El Capitan provides you with a URL that can be used to access your screen, even if you can't browse to it on the network.

2. Choose Go, Connect to Server from the Finder menu bar.

3. Enter the screen-sharing URL in the Server Address field. Alternatively, if you only have an IP address (such as 192.168.1.100), prefix the IP address with vnc:// to create a properly formed URL (for example, vnc://192.168.1.100).

4. Click + if you want to add the server to the list of favorite servers.

5. Click Connect to connect to the remote server's screen.

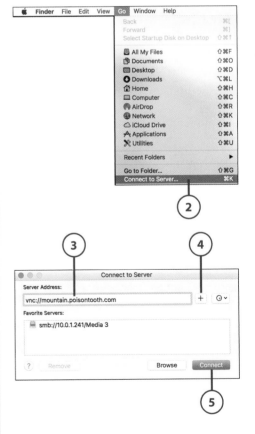

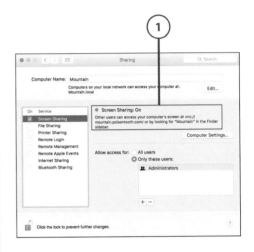

6. Enter a username (and/or password), if prompted, and click Connect.

7. The remote display is shown in a window on your Mac.

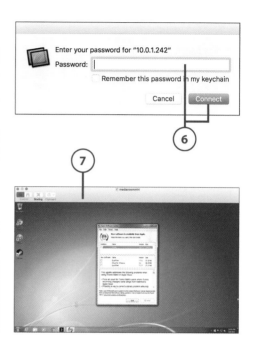

VNC for Windows/Linux

To connect to a Windows or Linux computer, you need to first install a VNC server (Virtual Network Computing) on the computer whose display you want to share. TightVNC (www.tightvnc.com) is an entirely free Open Source option that works on both Windows and Linux platforms.

>>>Go Further
THERE ARE A LOT OF PLACES LIKE HOME

The Shared portion of the sidebar shows you the computers on your local network. This is great for accessing things around you, but what about accessing your computer at home or from work?

You could use the address of your home computer to access it remotely, but you'd need to remember the address and have your home network configured correctly.

Instead, you can simply enable the iCloud service "Back to My Mac" (see Chapter 4 for details). Once enabled, this free service makes all your computers visible to one another wherever you have an Internet connection. You won't be able to tell the difference (network-wise) from being at home or being on a remote (well-connected) island.

Sharing Your Internet Connection

Your Mac is a perfect Internet-sharing platform because it includes both Ethernet and wireless network connections. You can, in a matter of minutes, create a wireless network using just your computer and a cable or DSL modem.

Sharing Your Connection

To share your connection with other Macs, PCs, or devices, you'll need a minimum of two network interfaces on your system—such as Ethernet and WiFi. Assuming you meet that qualification, you can share one network interface to the other by following these steps:

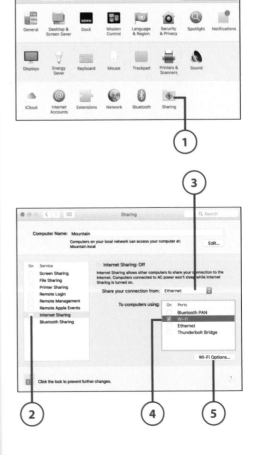

1. In the System Preferences window, click the Sharing icon.

2. Click the Internet Sharing service label. (Note: The checkbox is initially disabled!)

3. Use the Share Your Connection From drop-down menu to choose how you are connected to the Internet (Ethernet, Airport, iPhone, and so on).

4. Within the To Computers Using list, click the checkboxes in front of each of the interfaces where the connection should be shared.

5. If you're sharing a connection over your Wi-Fi card, a Wi-Fi Options button appears. Click this button to configure how your computer presents itself wirelessly.

6. Set the name of the wireless network you are creating.

7. Leave the channel set to the default.

8. If you want to enable password protection for the network, choose WPA2 Personal from the Security drop-down, and then provide a password.

9. Click OK to save your settings.

10. Click the checkbox in front of the Internet Sharing service.

11. Close the System Preferences.

12. Connect to the new wireless network from other computers as described in Chapter 3. You should set the other computers to configure themselves automatically rather than manually configuring the network (not shown).

Keep a Switch Handy

If you're sharing your connection over Ethernet, you need to connect a switch to your Mac's Ethernet port and then connect the other computer systems/devices to the switch.

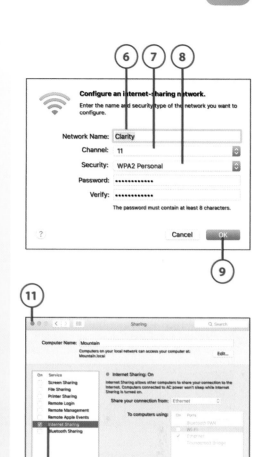

Connect to Twitter and Facebook.

Chat with friends and family in FaceTime.

Post updates and tweets throughout El Capitan.

In this chapter, you learn how to use your Mac to be social online, including:

→ Configuring instant messaging in Messages
→ Conducting video, audio, and screen-sharing chats
→ Messaging across computers and iOS devices
→ Posting Tweets and Facebook updates

Being Social with Messages, FaceTime, Twitter, and Facebook

In addition to providing methods of sending and consuming content, the Internet (and El Capitan) gives us new ways to be social. Using the tools built into OS X, you can send instant messages, conduct video chats, send tweets, and keep in touch with Facebook.

In this chapter, you find out how to use many of the features of Messages, FaceTime, and El Capitan social networking options. These will help you stay on top of current events in your friends' lives and interact with people around the world—without driving up your phone bill.

Instant Messaging with Messages (New!)

When email isn't conversational enough, instant messaging can take over. Your Mac comes with a first-rate instant messaging application called Messages (found in the Applications folder). You can use Messages for text messaging, audio conferencing, video conferencing, and even screen-sharing. If you have an iCloud, Google Hangouts, Jabber, or AIM (AOL Instant Messenger) account, you're ready to go.

There are two ways to use Messages, although both are integrated (somewhat poorly) into the same interface. First, you can use Apple's iMessage protocol to send and receive messages on all your iOS devices and Macs simultaneously. Using this approach, you can start a conversation on Messages on your iPad and then pick it up immediately on your Mac just by starting El Capitan's Messages app. Best of all, after you enable an iMessage account, you don't even have to *start* Messages to receive notifications. As long as your Mac is online, you will receive your iMessages.

The second way to use Messages is with a traditional instant messaging account, such as AIM, Yahoo! Messenger, or Google's Hangouts. The process is pretty similar, regardless of your approach, and when you've started a messaging session, you'll be using the same interface regardless.

To keep things straight in your mind, remember that if I talk about using an iMessage account or sending an iMessage, I'm referring to Apple's Mac and iOS messaging system. I'll be as specific as possible as I describe the features in Messages.

Adding Accounts to Messages

Apple simplifies the process of configuring Messages by emailing you to create an iMessage account *and* a traditional account the first time you run the app. After that, however, I recommend that you manage your accounts in different locations.

Configuring Your Account During Startup

Unlike other accounts, to configure iMessage within Messages, you need to use the application itself. The easiest way to configure Messages with an iMessage account is to do so during the first run, like this:

1. Start Messages from the Dock, Launchpad, or Applications folder.

2. Enter the Apple ID (and password) you want to use with the iMessage protocol.

3. Click Sign In.

4. By default, the email address associated with your Apple ID can receive iMessages. Uncheck addresses to remove them. To add other addresses, edit your account settings after this initial setup.

5. Choose whether you want your contacts to view when you read messages sent using the iMessage protocol.

6. Click Done to begin using Messages.

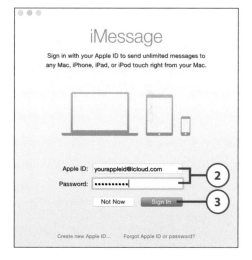

Editing Your iMessage Account Settings

To manage an iMessage account after you've first started the Messages application, you need to use the Messages preferences. Follow these steps to manage your settings:

1. Choose Messages, Preferences from the menu bar.

2. Click the Accounts toolbar icon.

3. Select the iMessage account entry.

4. Use the Enable This Account checkbox to enable or disable the account.

5. Check Send Read Receipts if you want your contacts to see when you've read their messages.

6. Click Add Email to add a new account that can receive iMessages.

7. Close the preferences when finished.

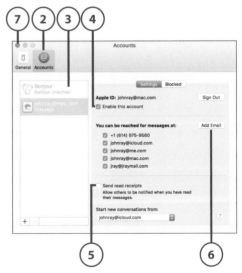

Adding a Traditional IM Account to Messages

If you want to configure IM after running Messages for the first time, I recommend using the central Internet Accounts Preferences panel. You need to know your account type, username, and password before continuing.

1. Open the Internet Accounts System Preferences panel.

2. Choose the online service that provides your IM account by clicking its name on the right. If your service only provides IM and not mail or calendaring, click Add Other Account to directly configure an IM account.

3. If you chose Add Other Account, select Messages Account.

Multiple IM Accounts? No Problem!

Adding multiple IM accounts to Messages is no problem. The Messages buddy list window combines your buddy lists into a single consolidated list.

4. Fill in the requested information in the setup wizard that appears.

5. Click Sign In.

6. Close the System Preferences window.

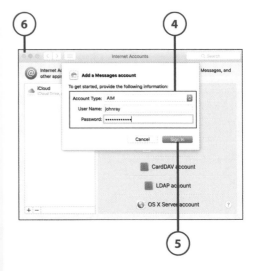

Logging into (and out of) Your IM Account

When Messages has an account configured, you're ready to start Messages and begin chatting immediately. To manually log out of or into your IM accounts, you simply need to set your status.

1. Click the status message in the lower-left corner of the Messages window.

2. Choose Offline to log out.

3. Choose any other status to log back into your IM account.

4. Choose Invisible to log in but hide your availability from other people.

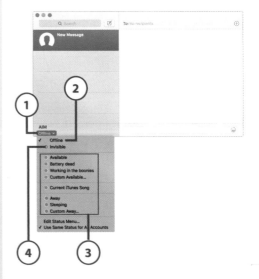

One Mood, One Status

If you configure multiple instant messaging accounts, you'll see a special option appear in the status menu: Use Same Status for All Accounts. Choosing this ensures that whatever status you choose is reflected on all of the accounts in use.

>>>*Go Further*

ADDING A MESSAGES STATUS MENU

To add a Messages status menu to your menu bar, open the Messages Preferences and click Show Status in Menu Bar within the General settings. This gives you the ability to log in and out of your IM accounts when Messages isn't running. Remember, however, that you can't log out of your iMessage account; it is always active unless you explicitly deactivate it in the Messages preferences.

Configuring Your IM Identity

If you're using traditional IM services (AIM, Yahoo!, and so on), you should customize your identity to better represent your online presence. With Messages, it's simple to set custom status messages and pictures to reflect your current mood.

Setting the Messages Picture

Because your Mac has a camera built in, you can swap your IM picture whenever you want. Just smile and click, and instantly your buddies see a new image.

1. Choose Window, Buddies to open the IM buddy list.

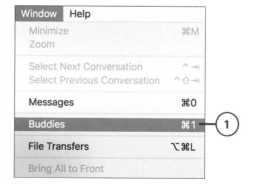

2. Click the picture in the upper-right corner of the Messages buddy list.

3. Choose from a Recent picture, iPhoto Faces, iCloud Photo Stream, Photos linked to your IM account, Default IM pictures, or click Camera to use your Mac's camera.

4. When Camera is selected, click the camera icon to take a new picture.

5. Set cropping and size for the picture by dragging it within the preview window and adjusting the zoom slider.

6. Apply effects, if desired, using the Effects button.

7. Click Done to start using the new picture.

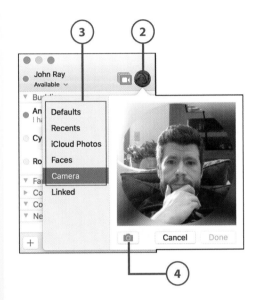

Configuring Custom Status Messages

Your status message can convey your state of mind, ask a question, or present some other information to your buddies. To configure a new status message, follow these steps:

1. Click the status pop-up menu either in your buddy list or in the main messages window.

2. Choose Edit Status Menu.

3. Click + or – under the Available or Away lists to add or remove status messages.

4. Click OK to save your status message settings.

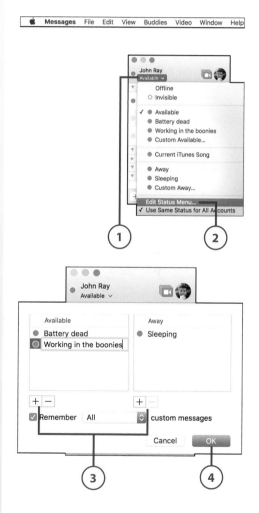

Managing Your IM Buddy List

Sending iMessages to your friends on Macs and iOS devices requires that you know their iMessage address or have it listed in your Contacts application. If you're using an IM account, however, you need to make sure that your buddy list is kept up-to-date with the people you want to chat with.

As you probably know, a buddy list contains all the people you want to chat with (and possibly some you don't). With each buddy is a display of his status (Away, Available, Idle, and so on) and an icon to indicate his chat capability.

Cross-Platform Video Conferencing

Messages can carry out cross-platform A/V chats with Windows users using AIM, Google Talk, or Yahoo!.

Adding Buddies

To initiate an IM chat with someone, you must first add her to your buddy list.

1. Click the + button at the bottom of the buddy list.

2. Choose Add Buddy.

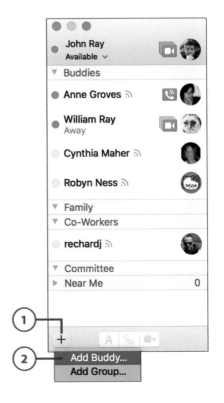

3. If you have a contact card for the person you want to add, click the disclosure arrow in the lower-right corner of the window to display your contacts, and then find and click the person's name.

4. Enter your buddy's screen name (Account Name).

5. Enter a first and last name for your addition, and choose a group, if any are available. Think of groups as a "folder" for your buddy.

6. Click Add.

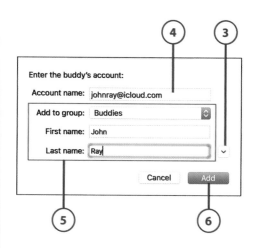

Adding Groups

As your IM buddy list grows, you might want to consider organizing your buddies into groups, such as friends, family, coworkers, and so on. Adding new groups is similar to adding new buddies.

1. Make sure View, Use Groups is selected in the Messages menu bar.

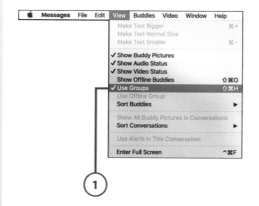

2. Click the + button at the bottom of the buddy list.

3. Choose Add Group.

4. Enter a name for the new group.

5. Click Add.

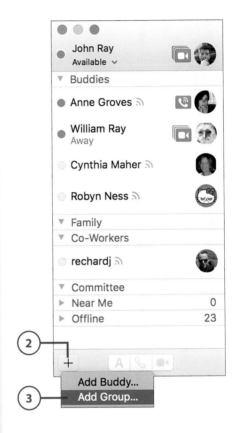

6. Drag buddies within the buddy list into the group where you want them to appear.

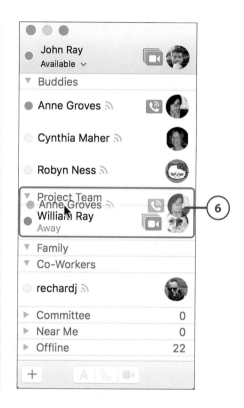

Recent Buddies

By default, a group called Recent Buddies is added to your buddy list after you start chatting with people. This group contains all the new contacts you've communicated with recently. You can disable this group within the Messages IM account settings.

Communicating with IM and iMessage

Messages, through an iMessage account, can communicate with your friends and colleagues using text and file attachments, such as images—or you can even share your screen. iMessage accounts also work with FaceTime (discussed in the next section) to initiate voice and video calls.

When using IM accounts, Messages supports a similar range of features. If you have both an iMessage and an AIM account, for example, you can video conference with your friends across Mac and Windows platforms.

Responding to an Incoming Chat via Notification Center

After you've configured Messages and given your iMessage address screen name to your buddies, chances are, you'll start getting a few messages. To respond to an incoming chat request, follow these steps:

1. If you're in another application with no windows open, the Messages icon updates with a count of the messages you have waiting and a notification appears.

2. Click the notification to reply.

3. Type a reply and press Return.

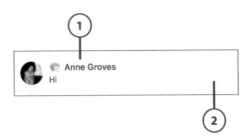

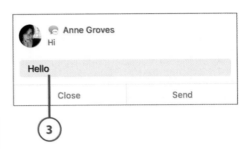

Responding to an Incoming Chat in Messages

Notification Center is useful for quick replies. For a full chat experience, however, you'll want to use Messages itself.

1. Open Messages and make sure the main window is visible. If it isn't, choose Window, Messages from the menu bar.

2. The Messages window shows all your current and new conversations.

3. To accept a conversation request, just click the entry in the list on the left and begin chatting.

4. When you're finished chatting, close the Messages window.

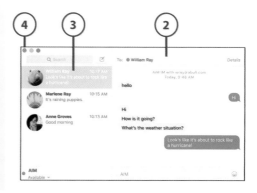

>>>Go Further

ADIOS, BUDDY!

When you're done talking to someone (or don't want to talk to them at all), hover over their name on the left of the Messages window to show an X that will close the conversation. If you find yourself constantly bugged by someone, check out the Blocked and/or Privacy settings available for your IM account by choosing Messages, Preferences from the Menu bar, and then clicking the Accounts icon in the toolbar. Depending on the type of account you're using, you should be able to block the offending individual.

Starting a Chat in Messages

To initiate an IM or iMessage chat with one or more buddies, make sure the Messages window is visible (Window, Messages) and follow these steps:

1. Click the New Chat button.

2. Click the + button to choose from a list of your contacts (useful for iMessaging) or your IM buddy list.

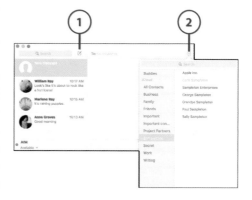

3. Alternatively, begin typing in the To field. Messages autocompletes as you type and shows you the different accounts you can use to communicate with someone. Click the contact (and communications method) you want.

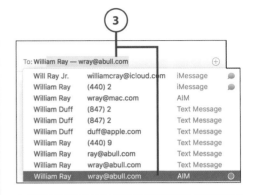

Double-Click to Chat

If you're viewing your buddy list, you can also initiate an IM chat by double-clicking a buddy or clicking his name and then clicking the A (for text chat) button at the bottom of the buddy list.

4. Type to your friend, press Return, and wait for a response.

Consolidate or Separate Messages

Messages automatically consolidates your chats into a single window. To move a chat to a separate window, double-click one of the conversations in the Messages window. It becomes its own standalone chat window.

>>>Go Further
IOS 9, EL CAPITAN, AND SMS

If you've connected your iOS 9 device and El Capitan (as described in Chapter 12, "Using El Capitan with Your iDevices"), you'll be able to select a contact's phone number and send him or her text messages through your iPhone! You'll even see incoming text messages appear directly in your Messages window.

Starting a Chat via Notification Center

El Capitan includes the ability to send a message via Notification Center—even if Messages isn't running. To use this nifty feature, follow these steps:

1. Open Notification Center.

2. Click the Messages (speech bubble) icon in the Notification Center pane—it is located in a widget called Social.

3. In the window that appears, type the name of a contact to message. Notification Center will auto-complete the name as you type.

4. Enter your message below the To: line.

5. Click Send to transmit the message.

Using Voice or Video for Chatting

A/V chats require significantly more bandwidth than text chats. Messages automatically senses the capabilities of your machine and Internet connection, and that of the people involved in your conversations. Messages does not allow chats unless it thinks they will be successful. Using Messages, you can chat with up to 3 other people via video and 10 via voice-only, depending on your connection and assuming that they have microphone- or camera-enabled systems. Unfortunately, not all chat programs are created equal—some of your contacts might not be able to use video; others may only use Facetime or AIM—it all depends on the software that they're using.

Starting a Voice or Video Chat

When creating a voice or video chat, regardless of your system capabilities or those of your chat partners, Messages shows only the relevant options.

1. Begin a chat with the individuals you want to include in an audio or video session.

2. Click the Details link in the upper-right corner of the chat window.

3. You see icons for the available voice (a phone) and video (a camera) chat options listed. Choose one.

4. A menu showing available video/audio chat methods is shown. Here, you can only see one. If a user has both FaceTime and an iPhone, for example, you might see more. Pick the communication method you want.

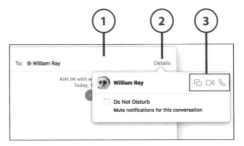

5. Your audio/video chat begins. A FaceTime audio chat is shown here.

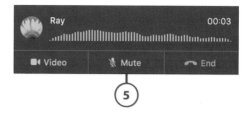

Be Heard with a Headset
If you find yourself using video or audio chat frequently, you might want to invest in a microphone or headset. To change the Messages microphone and set up a headset, open the Audio/Video section of the Messages preferences.

Silence Your Enemies (or Friends!)
When you click the Details link for someone, you see a checkbox labeled Do Not Disturb. If you check the box, you will not be alerted if the person tries to contact you. No beeps, no rings, nothing.

It's Not All Good

Where Did My Multiway Video Chats Go?

Remember when Apple promoted multiway video chats? I do. Unfortunately, that feature is only available when signed into AIM and can be accessed using the camera icon within the AIM buddy list (Window, Buddies). Select the individuals you want to chat with by Command+clicking their names and then click the camera icon.

Sharing Your Files and Screen

In addition to being a great communications tool, Messages can serve as a collaboration platform. If you've ever found yourself in the position of having to talk through a document over a long distance or troubleshoot technical problems remotely, you'll appreciate the ability to transfer files or share your buddy's screen.

Transferring Files over Messages

Messages provides a convenient mechanism for sending files while chatting. You can send individual files or even entire folders just by dragging them into Messages.

1. Find the file or folder that you want to share.

2. To transfer to an online buddy you aren't currently chatting with, drag the file to her name in your buddy list (IM only).

3. To transfer a file within an active chat session, drag the file to the chat window. Files such as images are displayed inline in the chat and can be previewed without opening the file.

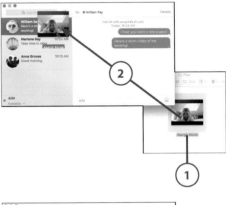

Confirming File Transfers

If someone attempts to transfer a file to you over Messages, you must click the download within the chat window to accept the file. By default, all transferred files are saved in the Downloads directory.

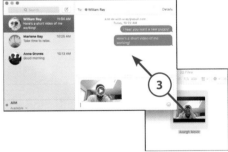

Starting a Screen-Sharing Session

A unique feature of Messages is the capability to share someone else's screen. Using this tool, you can control the other person's computer as if you were sitting directly in front of it.

1. Begin a chat with the individuals you want to include in a screen-sharing session.
2. Click the Details link in the upper-right corner of the screen.
3. Click the Screen Sharing icon (overlapping rectangles).
4. Choose whether you want to request access to your buddy's screen or if you want to share your screen.

5. After the request is accepted, you (or your buddy) have access to the remote screen. You can interact with the desktop as if you were sitting in front of the computer.
6. Close the window to close the session.

>>>*Go Further*

REMOTE SUPPORT VIA MESSAGES

When sharing a screen, Messages also starts a simultaneous audio chat, which makes it easy for you to talk through issues with the remote party. To learn more about the screen sharing utility, be sure to read Chapter 6, "Sharing Files, Devices, and Services."

Video Calls with FaceTime

Similar to an iMessage account in Messages, FaceTime is an always-running video chat service that bridges your iOS devices and your Macs. FaceTime starts automatically if someone places a FaceTime call, and it simultaneously rings on as many Macs, iPhones, and iPads as you want.

Zero Configuration

As with iMessage, FaceTime does not require configuration beyond providing an email address that your friends can "call."

To place a call with FaceTime, you need to have the address or phone number of a FaceTime-compatible contact in your address book. In other words, make sure your family and friends have an iOS device or a Mac and have configured FaceTime. You also need to be sure you've stored their contact information in the Contacts application. (See Chapter 8, "Managing Who, Where, When, and What," for more information.)

Setting Up FaceTime

The first time FaceTime starts, you need to provide it with an Apple ID for registration. After the initial ID is provided, you can associate as many email addresses as you want with a given install. Follow these steps to add FaceTime addresses:

1. Open FaceTime from the Dock, Launchpad, or Applications folder.

2. Enter your Apple ID and password.

3. Click Sign In.

4. FaceTime logs in, and you're ready for calls.

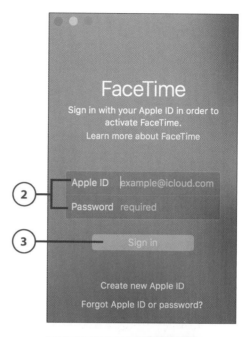

Placing Calls from the Contacts List

When you've got yourself a few equipped friends, follow these steps to call them over FaceTime:

1. Click the + button at the top of the FaceTime window, or begin typing a name.

2. Browse your contacts. When you find the person you want to call, click her name.

3. The contact appears in the Face-Time window with a phone and camera icon to the right. Click the camera icon to initiate a video chat, or the phone icon to start a voice-only chat.

4. If the call is connected, you are able to see and talk to the other person. Otherwise, skip to step 7.

5. Use the button at the bottom-right corner of the window to mute the call, or use the button at the bottom-left corner to go full screen.

6. Click End to hang up when you are finished talking.

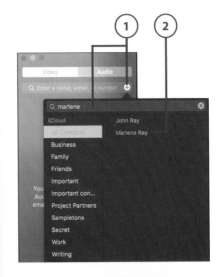

7. If the call does not connect, you're given the options of cancelling the call or calling back (redial).

See Your Surroundings

By default, the FaceTime camera takes a portrait image. If you want to see more of your surroundings, you can rotate to landscape mode by choosing Video, Use Landscape (Command+R) from the menu bar.

Receiving a FaceTime Call

If you've ever received a call on an iPhone, you'll be right at home receiving FaceTime calls on your Mac:

1. When an incoming call registers, FaceTime displays a notification— no need to start the application.

2. Click Decline to ignore the call.

3. Click Accept to begin talking.

4. Click and hold Decline to reply with Messages or to remind yourself to call back.

5. Click Reply with Message to send an instant message to your caller, rather than start a video chat.

Did I Miss a Call?

If you're wondering whether someone tried to contact you while you were away, the FaceTime icon shows a count of your missed calls. You can find out details about the missed calls by accessing the call list, our next task.

Accessing Your Call List

FaceTime keeps a list of all incoming and outgoing calls, even if you aren't around your computer when a call comes, so that you can check later to see who called.

1. Click the Video button at the top of the FaceTime window for video calls or Audio for voice-only calls.

2. All incoming and outgoing calls are shown. Missed calls display in red.

3. Click an entry to place a call.

4. Click the "i" icon at the right side of an entry to view that person's address book information and a full call history.

Disabling FaceTime

FaceTime is great, but as with a phone, sometimes you want to just ignore it. If you're having one of those days, you can disable FaceTime on your Mac so that it won't ring if someone tries to call.

1. Choose Turn FaceTime Off (Command+K) from the FaceTime menu.

2. FaceTime is now disabled on your Mac (not shown).

>>>Go Further
REMEMBER DO NOT DISTURB!

Turning on Do Not Disturb (see Chapter 1, "Managing Your Desktop") keeps FaceTime from "ringing" your machine. You can effectively use Do Not Disturb to silence FaceTime for short periods of time, if you prefer that approach.

Updating Account Information FaceTime Preferences

If you've registered several FaceTime accounts and want them all to ring on your Mac, you need to edit the preferences to list all the email addresses you have. To do this, follow these steps:

1. Open the FaceTime Preferences by choosing FaceTime, Preferences from the menu.

2. Click Add Email to add an alternative email account.

Verifying Your Email

If you have not registered that address with Apple, you need to look for an email with a clickable link for verifying your address. Repeat this step for as many addresses as you want to use with your FaceTime installation.

3. Use the Start New Calls From menu to pick the address or phone number to use as your caller ID.

4. Use the Ringtone dropdown to set the sound that plays for incoming calls.

5. Click the Blocked button at the top of the window to manage the FaceTime "block" list. These are people who are ignored if they try to call you via FaceTime.

6. Use the + and – buttons to add and remove individuals from the block list.

7. Close the preferences when done.

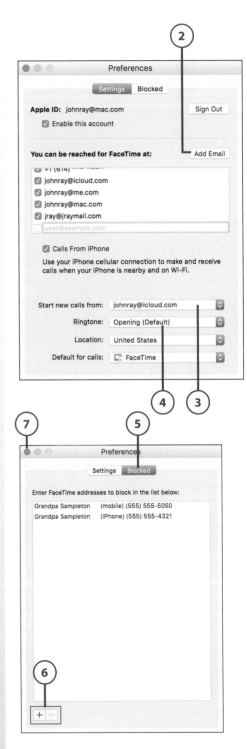

Using the El Capitan Twitter and Facebook Posting Support

El Capitan has baked-in Twitter support to make sending tweets as easy as clicking a button in many of your favorite applications. Facebook users can also get in on the fun by posting to their wall and photo albums in the same way. This section looks at how you can enable Twitter and Facebook support throughout OS X and how to make use of them.

Enabling Twitter

To see the tweeting options in El Capitan, you must first enable Twitter. To do this, follow these steps:

1. Open the Internet Accounts System Preferences panel.

2. Click the Twitter service link on the right.

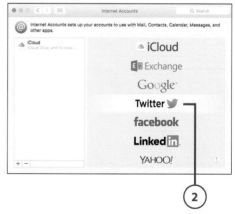

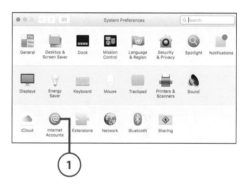

3. Enter your Twitter username and password.

4. Click Next.

5. Read the service notices and then click Sign In.

6. Check Notifications to receive alerts in Notification Center when you have new Twitter messages or mentions.

7. Check Share Menu to add a Sharing Extension to El Capitan, enabling you to tweet from almost any app with a Share menu.

8. On the Summary screen, click Update Contacts to pull Twitter usernames and photos into your system-wide Contacts list.

9. Close the System Preferences.

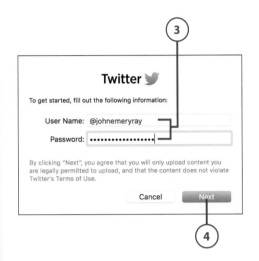

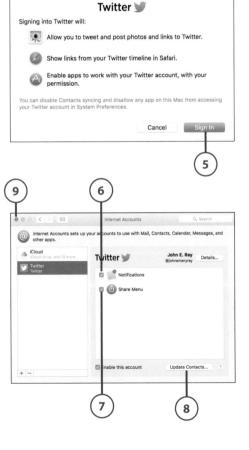

Enabling Facebook

To enable El Capitan to post Facebook updates, follow these steps:

1. Open the Internet Accounts System Preferences panel.

2. Click the Facebook service link on the right.

3. Enter your Facebook username and password.

4. Click Next.

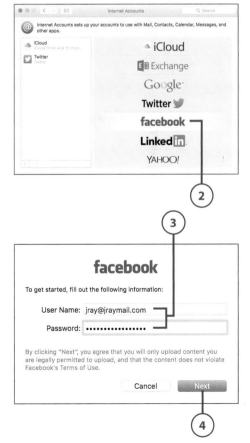

5. Read the Facebook conditions and click Sign In.

6. Click the Contacts checkbox to add Facebook friends to your address book.

7. Click Calendars to tie Facebook calendar into the Calendars application.

8. Check Notifications to receive alerts in Notification Center when you have new Facebook messages.

9. Check Share Menu to enable posting from almost any app with a Share menu.

10. Click the Update Contacts button to pull Facebook photos into your system-wide Contacts list.

11. Close the System Preferences.

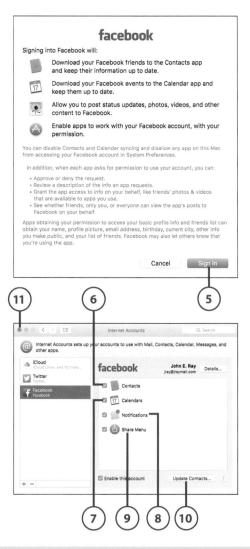

>>>Go Further
WAIT, THERE'S MORE!

If you've opened the Internet Accounts panel, you've probably noticed that there are account options for more than just Twitter and Facebook. LinkedIn, Vimeo, and others are available for you to add. Why aren't they covered here? Because they work identically to Facebook and Twitter. If you can activate one then you can activate them all!

Posting from the Finder and Other Apps

You can send tweets and post Facebook updates from any application that has been updated to support El Capitan's social networking implementation. For example, suppose you want to post a photo from the Finder. To compose the update, do the following:

1. Select or open an image (if you want to attach an image to the tweet or Facebook update).

2. Click the Share Sheet button.

3. Choose Twitter or Facebook from the drop-down menu. (This example uses Twitter.)

4. A composition window appears with the attachment (if any) in the upper-right corner. Enter your tweet/update here.

5. Click the Add Location button to add your current location to the post.

6. Click Post.

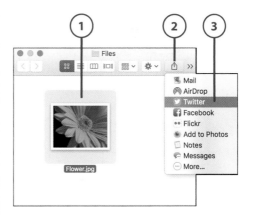

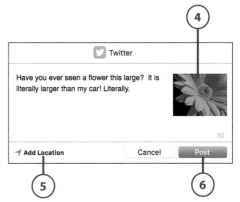

Posting via Notification Center

El Capitan also has the ability to post updates via Notification Center. To use this nifty feature, follow these steps:

1. Open Notification Center.

2. Click the Today button.

3. Click the Twitter or Facebook sharing buttons at the top of the pane (within the Social widget).

4. In the window that appears, type the message to post.

5. Click Post.

No Buttons, No Problem

If you don't see buttons for your social networking sites inside the Notification Center's Today view, make sure that you've added accounts (as described in this chapter) and that the Social widget is active in the Today section of the Extensions System Preferences panel (see Chapter 10, "Installing and Managing Applications and Extensions on Your Mac," for details).

>>>*Go Further*

BEING SOCIAL IS A TWO-WAY STREET

You know how to post to Facebook and Twitter from El Capitan, but that's only part of social networking; you also need to be able to read posts that others send to you. To receive updates from your friends and followers on Facebook and Twitter, configure the Notification Center, as described in Chapter 1. Apple has included Notification Center settings for Twitter and Facebook that let you receive and view updates right on your desktop. Of course, you'll still want a browser handy to access all the features of these popular sites, but OS X has you covered for the basics.

Use Calendar
to schedule
appointments.

Plan your next
vacation with Maps.

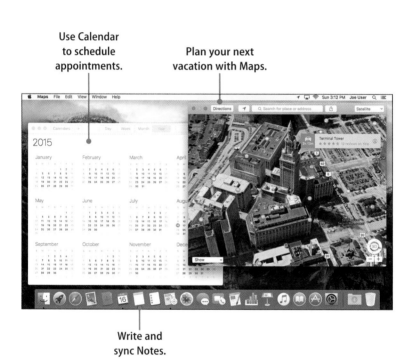

Write and
sync Notes.

In this chapter, you learn how to use your Mac to manage everything from contacts and meetings to road trips.

→ Adding contacts to Contacts
→ Organizing contacts into groups
→ Finding your way with Maps
→ Creating calendars in Calendar
→ Adding appointments to calendars
→ Scheduling meetings
→ Making lists in Reminders
→ Keeping your thoughts in order with Notes

Managing Who, Where, When, and What

One of the joys of owning a Mac is that it is productive "out of the box." You can integrate with enterprise calendaring and address book systems, plan meetings, even get directions—all using the built-in utilities. El Capitan makes these tools accessible to everyone, regardless of skill level. If you've ever been intimidated by Microsoft Outlook, don't worry—El Capitan makes you just as productive without needing an encyclopedic reference book.

In this chapter, you get the hang of the basics of the Contacts, Maps, Calendar, Reminders, and Notes apps. This suite of tools helps us keep our digital lives in tune with our real lives, and does so in a simple and elegant way.

>>>Go Further
THE INVISIBLE, EVER-PRESENT, ICLOUD

The apps in this chapter share a unique characteristic that can be a bit confusing to new users—where they store their information. If you've never set up iCloud, Exchange, or a Google account on your computer, you probably aren't connected to any form of network storage. In this case, the data created in each application is stored locally on your Mac.

In practice, however, it's pretty difficult to get through setting up a Mac with El Capitan *without* establishing a free iCloud account. If you've established an iCloud account (see Chapter 4, "Setting Up iCloud and Internet Accounts," for details), chances are that the information in the applications discussed in this chapter is synced with an iCloud server.

What makes this confusing is that the applications provide very little in terms of visual cues to show that you are using iCloud services for your data. The good news is that it really is transparent, and using iCloud means you can access this information from a web browser wherever you are! If you aren't sure if you're using iCloud, now is a good time to jump back to Chapter 4 so you can ensure you're making the best use of this important suite of El Capitan utilities.

Managing Contacts

Many of the applications you use on your Mac send information to, or receive information from, other people. El Capitan offers a central contact database that you can access in Mail, Calendar, Messages, FaceTime, and other programs. Appropriately enough, you manage this database through an application called Contacts (found in the Applications folder).

Contacts acts as a digital Rolodex, pulling together personal and business contacts. With it you can also connect to enterprise directory servers for accessing centralized company personnel listings. The Contacts application is similar to many other El Capitan applications, providing a drill-down view from a group list, to a contact list, and, finally, to contact details.

Search

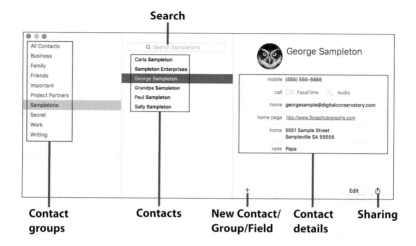

Contact groups | Contacts | New Contact/ Group/Field | Contact details | Sharing

Adding Groups

When you first start Contacts, there is a single pseudo-group available: All Contacts. The group displays any contact available in Contacts. To make the most efficient use of Contacts, you should add groups for the different types of contacts you use—businesses, coworkers, family, friends, doctors, and so on. Like Mail, Contacts can use rules to create Smart Groups.

Emailing to a Group

Contacts groups are more than just organizational tools; they also add functionality to applications that support them. After you've defined a group, you can use it in Mail as your message recipient, effectively sending the email to everyone in the group!

Creating a Group

To create a new group, decide what you'd like it to be called, and then follow these steps:

1. Open Contacts from the Dock, Launchpad, or Applications folder.

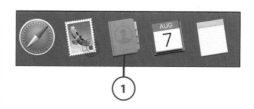

2. Click and hold the + button at the bottom of the Contacts window.

3. Choose New Group.

4. A new "untitled group" is added. Type a name for the group.

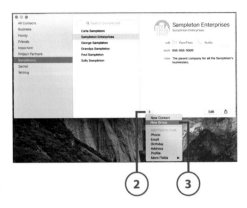

Creating a Smart Group

If you'd like to use search criteria to define your Contacts groups, you're in luck! Contacts supports Smart Groups, capable of pulling contacts together from multiple different groups and even network accounts:

1. Choose File, New Smart Group from the menu bar.

2. Enter a name for the new Smart Group.

3. Use the first drop-down menu from the selection lines to choose a contact attribute.

4. Use the second drop-down menu to set criteria.

5. Enter the value to use in the comparison in the text field at the end of the selection line.

6. Use the + and – buttons to add or remove additional selection criteria.

7. Click OK when you're satisfied with your group definition.

8. The new group is added and automatically shows the contacts based on the criteria you defined.

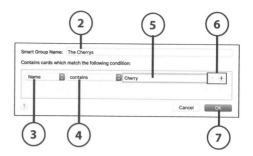

Adding Contacts

The bulk of what you'll do with Contacts is entering contacts. When it comes to people, one size contact does not fit all. For your family, you might want to store email addresses, instant messaging screen names, and birthdays. But for business contacts, you might only be interested in an address and a phone number. Contacts adapts to the information that you want to store.

Creating a New Contact

To create a new contact, gather all
the information you have available
for the person, then do the following:

1. Click the group name that the
   contact should be added to.

2. Click the + button at the bottom
   of the window.

3. Choose New Contact from the
   pop-up menu.

4. A new No Name contact is added,
   and the empty contact details
   display. Use the fields in the detail
   view to enter information for the
   contact.

5. Click Company to classify the
   entry as a business rather than a
   personal contact.

6. Set the context for the card's
   fields (for example, choose home,
   work, or cell for a phone number)
   using the pop-up menu in front of
   each field.

7. If you'd like to store additional
   information for the contact, click
   and hold the + button again,
   choose More Fields, and choose
   the type of field to add.

8. Click the Done button at the bottom of the contact details to save
   changes to the contact.

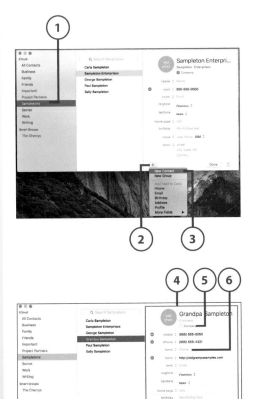

Moving and Editing Contacts

If you find that you've filed your contact in the wrong group, just drag and drop the contact name into another group. You can re-edit contact details at any time by selecting them and clicking the edit button below the details pane.

Setting a Contact Image

Contact images can help you visually identify individuals in your Contacts and are even displayed in Mail or shown on your iOS device if you sync Contacts. To set an image for a contact, complete these steps:

1. Find and select the contact that you want to associate with an image.

2. Click the picture within the card details.

3. Click the Camera label to take a new picture, or see step 4 to use an existing picture.

4. Alternatively, use the Defaults, iCloud Photos, and Faces options to select from default OS X images, iCloud-stored photos, or iPhoto Faces.

5. Set cropping and size for the picture by dragging it within the image window and adjusting the zoom slider.

6. Apply effects, if desired, using the Effects button.

7. Click Done to finalize the contact's custom image.

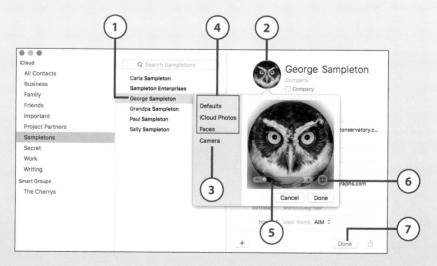

Auto Information Gathering

El Capitan helps you keep your contacts as information-rich as possible by finding and presenting data that it thinks is relevant to a contact. For example, you may see fields displayed that you never explicitly added to a contact, but that your system found in email. To explicitly add or remove this information from a contact, follow these steps:

1. Look for fields with an "i" icon beside them. These have been automatically added.

2. Click the i to show details about where the data was gathered.

3. Choose Keep to store the field permanently or Remove to delete the association.

Creating "My" Card

Many system applications and utilities need to identify information about you. To tell Contacts who you are, enter a new contact for yourself, and then follow these steps:

1. Find and select your name in the Contacts.

2. Choose Card, Make This My Card from the menu bar.

The Importance of Me
You need a functional "My" card to fully use Calendar, so be sure to set this if you have any intention of using Calendar.

Editing the Contact Template

If you find that you constantly need to add new fields to contacts, you might want to consider modifying the default contact template. Changing the default gives you a starting place for all future contacts.

1. Choose Contacts, Preferences from the menu bar.

2. Click the Template icon in the Preferences toolbar.

3. Use the Add Field drop-down menu to add additional fields to the contact template.

4. Click the double arrows to open the pop-up menus in front of each field to set the context for fields displayed in the template.

5. Close the Contacts Preferences window when you're finished.

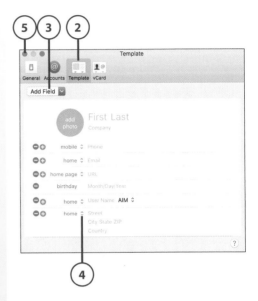

Searching Contacts

When you aren't sure of an exact name, or where you filed a contact, you can quickly search across all your groups and contact data.

1. Click the name of the address group to search.

2. Type into the search field.

3. As you type, the contact list is filtered to show only matching contacts.

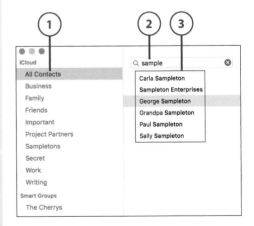

Detecting and Merging Duplicates

Over time you might find that you've created several Contacts entries for a single person. To identify and merge duplicate cards, follow these steps:

1. Choose Card, Look for Duplicates from the menu bar.

2. Contacts analyzes your contacts and presents you with the option to merge identified duplicates.

3. Click Merge to fix the duplicates.

Merging Cards
If you manually identify two or more cards that need to be merged, select the cards, and then choose Card, Merge Selected Cards from the Contacts menu bar.

Using iCloud and Server-Based Contacts

Contacts isn't just limited to keeping information on your Mac; it can also synchronize with Google, Yahoo! contacts, and connect to enterprise directory servers such as Exchange, standard LDAP servers, as well as Apple's iCloud service. You can even pull contact data from social networking sites such as Twitter and Facebook. Using a central server means that changes and updates are available immediately for everyone who is connected.

If you've already configured iCloud (see Chapter 4), you're probably already storing your contacts "in the cloud."

Connecting to iCloud Contacts Syncing

To connect to iCloud, or verify that your Contacts app is using iCloud to store and sync contacts across your devices, follow these steps.

1. Click the System Preferences icon on the Dock and then click iCloud.

2. Check the box beside Contacts.

3. Close the System Preferences. Your Contacts application is now connected to iCloud.

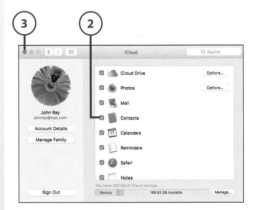

Connecting to Other Contact Servers

Although iCloud is consumer-friendly, many organizations provide central enterprise contact directories that you can access via Contacts.

To configure non-iCloud server-based contacts, follow these steps:

1. Click the System Preferences icon on the Dock and then click Internet Accounts.

2. Choose the service providing contact information from the list on the right. Alternatively, click Add Other Account (at the bottom of the list) to add LDAP, CardDAV, or OS X Server accounts.

3. The account creation window appears. Use the fields in the window to configure your account information.

4. Click Sign In or Continue (the button name depends on your service provider) to walk through the account setup wizard.

5. If you're setting up a service that provides more than just contacts (such as Exchange), you are prompted to automatically set up corresponding email accounts and calendars.

6. Click Done to configure your Mac to connect to the server.

7. Close the System Preferences.

Settings, Settings, Everywhere!

Apple includes the ability to add contact servers directly within the Contacts app's Preferences (the same goes for the Calendar app, which we'll cover next). If you happen to stumble upon these, you can use them (it's the same as using the Internet Accounts Preferences panel), but I'd suggest using the central preferences to be consistent.

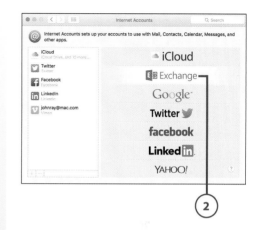

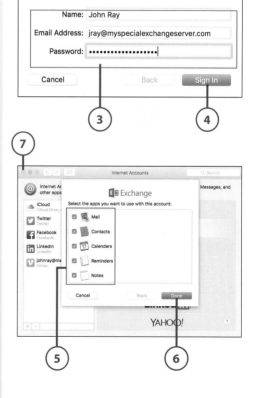

8. The new server appears in the Contacts group list. You can click to select groups within it, and from there, create new groups if desired.

Sharing Contacts via Email, Messages, and AirDrop

To share a contact via email, messages, or AirDrop, you can use an El Capitan Share button. For detailed information on Share buttons, refer to Chapter 6, "Sharing Files, Devices, and Services." For now, be aware that the basic process works like this:

1. Navigate to a contact that you want to share.

2. Click the Share button to show the sharing options.

3. Choose the method of sharing that you'd like to use.

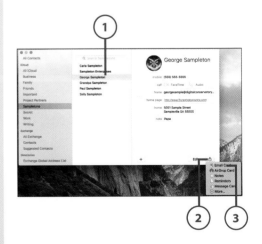

4. Your choice launches the appro-
    priate supporting application and
    attaches the note for sending.

>>>*Go Further*
EXPORTING AND IMPORTING VCARDS

In addition to sharing contacts, you can also export the contact information
directly to a vCard. These are small files that store all the information for one
or more contact entries. Just highlight the entries in Contacts, and then drag
them to your desktop. A vCard file is created with all of the contact data.

To import a vCard, reverse the process. Drag a received vCard into Contacts (or
double-click it in the Finder), and it is imported automatically.

Printing Addresses

When you need to use actual
paper for your communica-
tions, Contacts provides several useful print options for
printing your contacts onto
envelopes or labels.

1. Select individual contacts or con-
    tact groups to print.

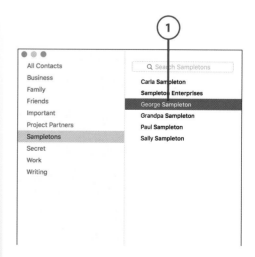

2. Choose File, Print from the menu bar.

3. Click the Hide/Show Details button so that the full print dialog window appears.

4. Use the Style pop-up menu to select an output format (Mailing Labels, Envelopes, and so on).

5. Set any of the additional configuration options for the style you've chosen.

6. Click Print to output the contact information in the selected style.

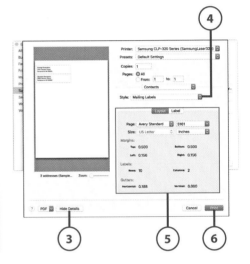

Finding Your Way with Maps (New!)

El Capitan continues the tradition of OS X in providing great software for managing your who, when, and what—but it now can help you with the *where*. OS X uses Maps, a simple, fun, and fast way to access mapping information on your Mac.

Starting and Navigating Maps

To start using Maps, you need an active Internet connection and your Wi-Fi needs to be enabled if you want your system to automatically locate your current position. To get started, follow these steps:

1. Start Maps from the Applications folder, Dock, or Launchpad.

2. After a few seconds, a basic map loads in standard view.

3. You can pan the map by clicking and dragging—or by dragging two fingers on a trackpad.

4. Use the +/– buttons to zoom in and out.

5. Click and drag within the compass to rotate the entire view.

Using Map Views

If you've ever used Google Maps (or any other online mapping service) you'll be right at home with Maps. There are a variety of different views that you can access—from the Maps toolbar and Show menu.

Choosing a View Mode

Like your maps flat, like a book? Want to see photography of a given area? How about a combination? Using Maps, you can have all of this, just by clicking a button.

1. Click the Map button to show a traditional "atlas"-style map with roads, points of interest, and so on.

2. Click Transit to show public transit routes, rather than roads.

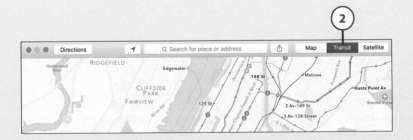

3. Click Satellite to show the area using satellite photography.

4. Use the Show menu in the lower left to add labels. This is similar to Google Maps and will show a combination of satellite photography with overlaid roads and points of interest.

Viewing Maps with 3D Flyover

In addition to the standard map views, you can also look at many large cities in full 3D. To see the map in 3D, follow these instructions:

1. Navigate to a point you want to view in 3D.

2. Click the 3D button in the compass to toggle the display to 3D.

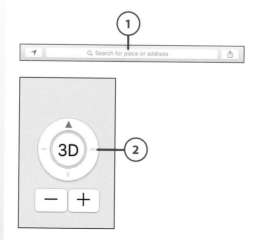

3. Switch to Satellite mode to view a nearly photo-realistic image of the location.

Tilting Your 3D World

While viewing a map in 3D, you can click and drag up and down in the compass to change the amount of "tilt" with which the map is displayed. You can also hold Option and click and drag anywhere on the map to tilt the view.

>>>Go Further
TAKING A VIRTUAL TOUR

When viewing some 3D locations (try *Golden Gate Bridge*, for example), you'll notice a message at the bottom of the window that reads 3D Flyover Tour with a Start button beside it. Click Start to see an animated tour of the location. Click End to stop the tour and return to the normal map.

It's Not All Good

No 3D for You!

If you switch your view to 3D and it looks decidedly "flat," it's because 3D data doesn't yet exist for your location. There's not much to do about this but wait until Apple acquires the right information for your area.

Finding Places

How good would a map be if you couldn't find things on it? Using Apple Maps, you can quickly locate your position, companies, points of interest, people, and so on.

Finding Yourself

Without needing to be a Zen guru, Apple Maps can help you find yourself in the world. Although not as precise as GPS, your El Capitan computer can use Wi-Fi to find its general location (usually within a few blocks). To use this feature, follow these steps:

1. While viewing any map, click the arrow icon at the left of the Search field.

2. The map zooms in, placing a blue dot on your location.

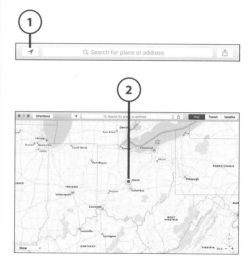

Closer Please

Don't worry—the map does zoom closer than shown in this example. I manually zoomed out to reduce the amount of competing clutter on the screen.

Finding Contact Entries

Although finding yourself can be handy, finding others is likely more useful. To locate any address (personal or business) stored within the Contacts application, complete the following:

1. Click the Search field in the Maps toolbar.

2. Click the Favorites entry at the top of the list that appears.

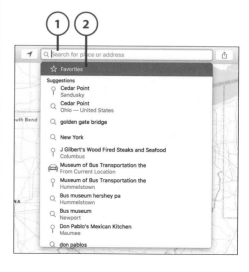

3. Choose an entry in the Address Book and click it.

4. Click the address for the entry that you want to view.

5. The map zooms in and highlights the chosen address.

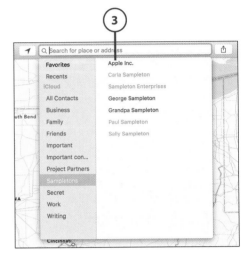

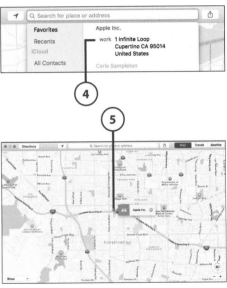

Searching the Map

If the place you want to locate isn't in your Address Book, you can just search for it.

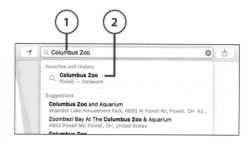

1. Type into the search field at the top of the Maps window.

2. As you type, potential matching searches appear below. Choose one, or press return when finished typing.

3. The search results are displayed on the left.

4. Click one you want to view.

5. The chosen location is highlighted on the map.

Working with Points of Interest

You've seen how to find places, but how about finding out *about* places? Maps can help you with that as well. You may be surprised at how much Maps can do for you!

Seeing Point of Interest Details

There's more to a location than just a marker on a map. To see more detail for any point on the map, follow these instructions:

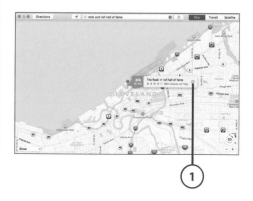

1. Find a location on the map that you want to view. Click the i icon.

2. The location window expands to show a photo and additional information.

3. Click the Directions button to open the directions pane, showing how to reach the location.

4. Click Add to Favorites (or heart button) to add a bookmark to the location.

5. Click Add to Contacts to add a new contact to your Address Book for the location.

6. Click Report an Issue if there is an error in the listing.

7. Click More Info on Yelp link to view Yelp reviews of the location (if available).

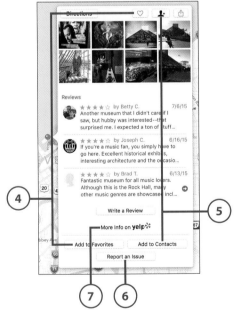

Making Your Own Point of Interest

Sometimes Apple Maps won't have the information that you want. Apple, for example, doesn't know your favorite fishing hole, or in which tree you hid the ransom money. To accommodate your activities, you can create your own points on the map by following these steps:

1. Right-click on the map where you want a point to be located.

2. Choose Drop Pin from the pop-up menu that appears.

3. A new point of interest window appears that you can interact with like any other point.

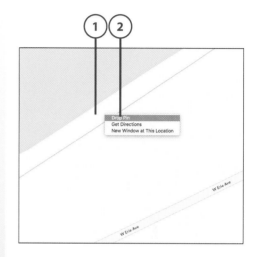

Sharing a Point of Interest

If you find yourself viewing something on your Mac and want to see it on your iOS device, no problem. You can use the Share button to share a location via email, or just send it directly to your phone or iPad. To do this, just follow these steps:

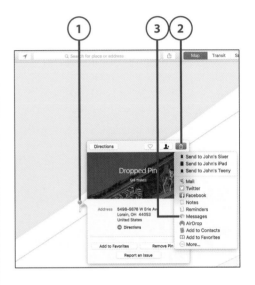

1. Locate the point of interest you want to use.

2. Click the Share button.

3. Choose the method or device that you want to use to share.

Share Your Anywheres, Anytime

You can share what you are looking at in the Maps window at any time by using the Share button in the Maps window.

Traveling with Maps

The last trick that Maps has up its sleeve is the ability to view turn-by-turn directions, transit instructions—and even the traffic that you'll encounter if you follow them. Let's start by looking at directions.

Getting Directions

To get directions from point A to point B, you only need to click. Follow these steps to get where you need to be:

1. Click the Directions button to show the directions panel on the left.

2. Enter an address or location in the Start field (or leave it blank to use your current location).

3. Enter an address or location in the End field.

4. Use the Drive, Transit, and Walk buttons to choose between driving, public transit, and walking directions.

5. Quickly swap the start and end fields by clicking the squiggly line to the right of the fields.

6. If multiple paths are shown, click the path you want to take.

7. The turn-by-turn instructions are shown on the left.

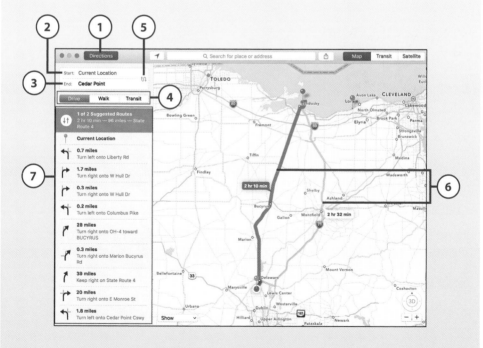

8. Click an individual step of the directions to show a close-up of your route—including lane guidance.

Share the Path!
Remember, using the Share button at the top of the Maps window, you can share your location and complete route with your iOS device.

Showing Traffic Indicators

If you're wondering about the traffic on your favorite road, Maps has you covered. Use this simple process to see when it's safe to leave your house.

1. Navigate to the road you want to check for traffic conditions.

2. Use the Show menu in the lower left to add Traffic.

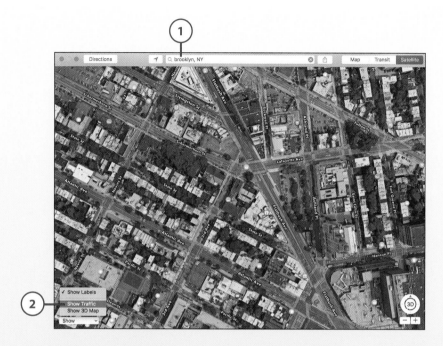

3. Orange and red dotted lines indicate slow or stopped traffic.

Working with Schedules in Calendar (New!)

Much of our lives revolve around adhering to a schedule. Calendars, in whatever form we use them, keep us informed of upcoming appointments, holidays, birthdays, and anniversaries. Your Mac can serve as your scheduling work center. The Calendar application (found in the Applications folder) is a fast and well-connected way to keep your life in order.

Calendar's general operation is similar to other El Capitan applications. Clicking the Calendar button displays a list of calendars you have access to. Selecting a calendar in the calendar list displays the content of the calendar to the right. Double-clicking a calendar entry shows the details of the entry. The four buttons at the top (Day, Week, Month, Year) coupled with the View menu control the appearance of the calendars.

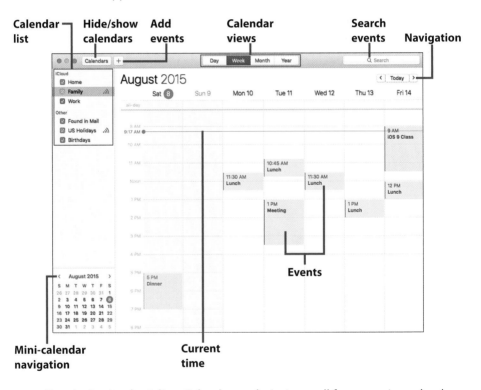

Despite its simple styling, Calendar works just as well for managing calendars located on your Mac as it can interacting with Exchange, iCloud, Facebook, Google, and other standards-based enterprise calendaring systems.

Adding Calendars

The first step in using Calendar is to create the calendars that you use to store your events. Two calendars are already created: Home and Work. If you've established an iCloud account and turned on Calendar syncing, these are iCloud-based calendars. If not, they are stored locally on your Mac. Use these default calendars or create new calendars, depending on how you want to categorize your events.

Creating New Calendars

To create a new calendar (locally or on a server), follow these instructions:

1. Open the Calendar application from the Dock, Launchpad, or Applications folder.

2. Click the Calendars button to show the list of calendars (if they are hidden) on your Mac.

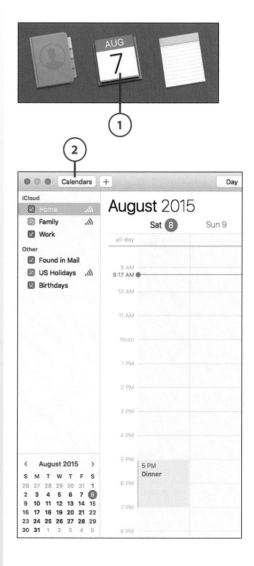

3. Click File, New Calendar from the main menu bar. You might have to choose iCloud (or another calendar provider) if you've already set up a calendar account.

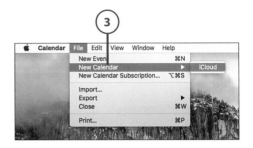

4. A new Untitled calendar is added at the bottom of the calendar list. Type to replace Untitled with whatever name you'd like.

5. Verify that the checkbox next to the calendar is selected so that the calendar entries are visible.

>>>Go Further
LOCAL VERSUS NETWORK CALENDARS

The Calendar application can work with calendars located directly on your Mac (local) as well as calendars located on a server, such as iCloud. Depending on how your system is set up, the menus in the Calendar application may change slightly. For example, if you are using calendars hosted on multiple network servers (iCloud and your office's Exchange calendar server, for instance), you'll notice that when you choose to create a new calendar, you are given the option of choosing which server should hold it. Only if no server accounts are available will the On My Mac (locally) option be visible.

Additionally, Calendar supports the notion of local calendar groups (go to File, New Calendar Group) when working with local calendars. Using calendar groups, you can organize clusters of calendars and enable or disable all of them at once. The bad news? As soon as you use iCloud or another network service, this option completely vanishes. Because Apple is obviously weaning us off this feature, we're omitting it from this edition.

Connecting to iCloud and Server-Based Calendars

Server-based calendars are stored on a central network location rather than on your Mac. You can access and modify network calendars on multiple computers. Many businesses use Exchange Server, for example, to provide shared calendars and scheduling. Apple's iCloud service provides free shared calendaring that you can use across your Mac and iOS devices. Another option, Google Calendar, is also free and can be used on virtually any desktop or mobile device.

Connecting to iCloud Calendar Syncing

iCloud is the easiest and fastest way to create shared network calendars on all your devices. To use iCloud to store your calendars, follow these steps:

1. Click the System Preferences icon on the Dock and then click iCloud.

2. Check the box beside Calendars.

3. You might be prompted to merge any existing calendars with your iCloud calendars. Click Merge to move their information to iCloud (not shown).

4. Close the System Preferences window.

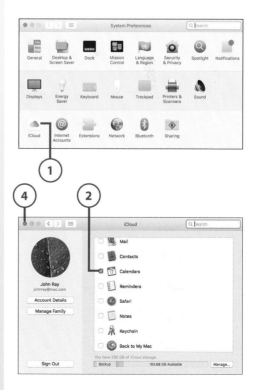

Connecting to Other Calendar Servers

As you'd expect, calendar services are configured through the Mail, Contacts, and Calendars panel, as you've become accustomed to seeing.

1. Click the System Preferences icon on the Dock and then click Internet Accounts.

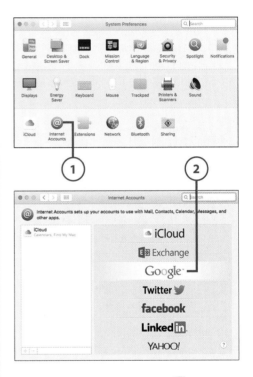

Gathering Info

Most server-hosted calendars are associated, in some way, with an email account. To configure a server-based calendar, you probably only need an email account and password. If you know, however, that your calendar is hosted somewhere else, you should collect the server name in addition to your username and password before proceeding.

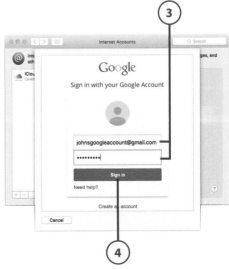

2. Choose the service providing the calendar information from the list on the right. Alternatively, click Add Other Account (at the bottom of the list) to manually add a CalDAV account. If you aren't sure, ask your ISP or network administrator.

3. The account creation window appears. Use the fields in the window to configure your account information.

4. Click Sign In or Continue (the button name depends on your service provider) to walk through the account setup wizard.

5. If you're setting up a service that provides more than just calendars (such as Exchange, Yahoo!, or Gmail), you are prompted to automatically set up corresponding email accounts and contact servers. Be sure to choose Calendars and Reminders (not shown/visible).

6. Click Done.

7. Close the System Preferences when finished.

8. The calendar list displays a new section with any calendars that are located on the server.

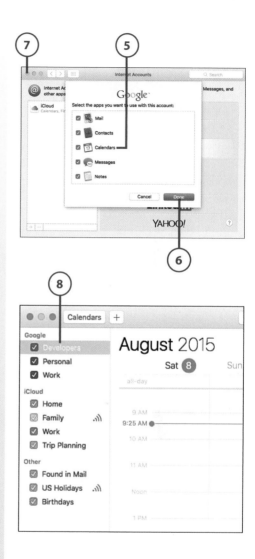

Subscribing to a Public Shared Calendar

Another calendar type is a shared calendar. These read-only Internet-published calendars are available for TV show schedules, holidays, sports team game dates, and other useful information. To subscribe to a shared calendar, copy the URL for the calendar and then follow these steps:

1. Choose File, New Calendar Subscription from the Calendar menu bar.

2. Enter the URL for the calendar you are subscribing to.

3. Click Subscribe. If prompted, enter a login name and password to access the calendar, and then click OK to continue.

4. Set a name, color, and storage location for the calendar.

5. If there are any embedded Alerts or Attachments in the calendar (this depends entirely on the person making the calendar available), you may want to strip them out. Click the Remove checkboxes to make sure you get only calendar data.

6. To enable the calendar to automatically update, choose an Auto-refresh time.

7. Click OK.

8. Depending on whether you're connected to a network calendar (like iCloud), the shared calendar appears either under your main calendar list or in a section called Other.

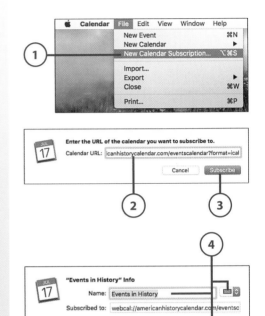

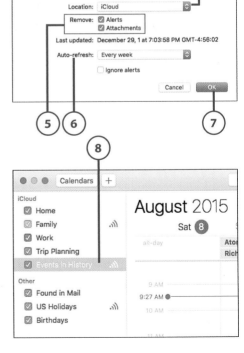

>>>*Go Further*

IT'S YOUR BIRTHDAY OR A HOLIDAY (OR SOMEONE JUST SENT YOU AN EMAIL)!

By default, Calendar shows three other calendars, even if you haven't added any. The first is the "Found in Mail" calendar—displaying events that Mail *thinks* it found in your email messages. The US Holidays calendar displays holidays in the United States. There is a third special calendar added by default—Birthdays—that displays birthdays for the individuals in your Contacts (address book) application.

Viewing Calendars

After you've set up one or more calendars in Calendar, you can view their contents. To view a calendar in the calendar list, follow these steps.

1. Click the checkbox in front of the calendars you want to view.

2. Use the Day, Week, Month, and Year buttons to narrow or expand your calendar view.

3. Use the arrows to move forward or backward by day, week, month, or year, depending on the current view. You can always navigate by month using the arrows by the mini-calendar in the lower-left corner.

4. Click Today to jump to today's date.

Working with Events

What good is a calendar if you don't have the ability to add events? In Calendar, events can be anything you'd like—birthdays, outings, reminders, anything—as long as they are associated with a date. If you'd like to include other people in the event, you can even send out invitations that are compatible with other calendaring systems, such as Exchange.

Creating a New Event

Events can hold a large number of attributes that describe what the events are, when they are, where they are located, and so on. All you need to know to create an event, though, is the date and a name for the event:

1. Navigate to the day on which the event takes place.

2. Switch to Day or Week view.

3. Click and drag from the start time to the end time to create the event. The default event name, New Event, is highlighted automatically.

4. Type a name and location for the event.

5. Click the drop-down in the upper-right corner of the event information to choose which calendar should hold the event.

Double-Click to Add

You can add an event in the month view of the calendar by double-clicking a day. This method, however, does not let you define the start and end time of the event initially, so you need to edit it later to add that information.

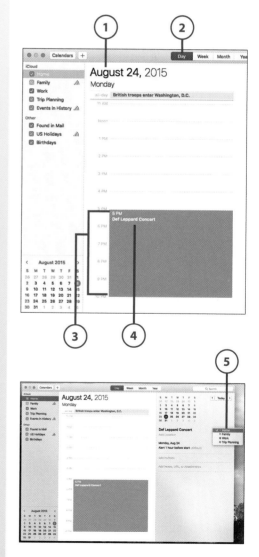

Using the Quick Event Feature

The Calendar application also supports a simple way of creating events without any calendar navigation at all. Quick Event provides simple, plain-text entry of new events directly from the Calendar toolbar. To use this feature, follow these steps:

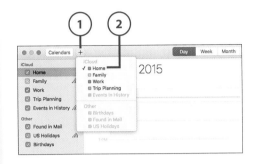

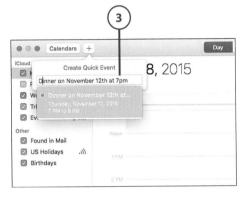

1. Click and hold the + icon in the Calendar toolbar.

2. Choose the calendar that should contain the new event.

3. In the Create Quick Event field that appears, type a description of the event, such as "Dinner on November 12th at 7pm," and press return.

4. A new event is added and opened for additional editing.

Editing Event Information

To edit the information for an event that you've created, first find the event on the calendar where you added it, and then follow these steps:

1. Find and double-click the event you want to edit.

2. An event summary window appears.

3. Click any of the available fields to change values such as start or end times, location, notes, and so on.

4. Click off of the event when you are finished editing. Your changes will now be visible in the Day view's summary pane or when you click on the event again.

Browse and Schedule

Need to browse your calendar while editing an event? No problem. To turn the edit event pop-over window into a separate window, just click near the top and drag off of the calendar.

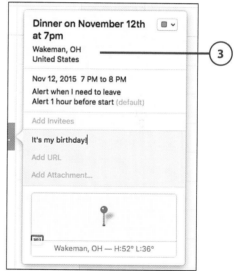

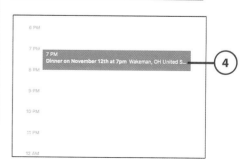

It's Not All Good

Where Are All of My Event Attributes?!

When you see the edit event pop-over window, you might ask yourself, "Where in the world are all the fields I need?" El Capitan collapses these into the different sections shown in the pop-over window. For example, if you want to see settings for receiving alerts prior to an event, just click the date—it will expand to show all the date and time related options. Be sure to click around to find all the different fields you can edit for an event.

Sending Event Invitations

Calendar can work directly with Mail to send invitations for your events. When the invitees respond, their attendance status is updated directly in Calendar. Use the previous task to find and start editing an event, and then follow these steps to send invitations for that event:

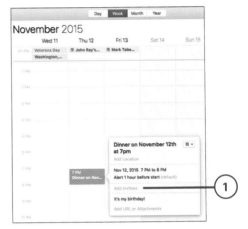

1. Click the Add Invitees link.

2. Enter email addresses in the field that appears, just as you would in Mail, pressing return after each one. Add as many as you'd like.

Checking Availability

If supported by your calendar server (such as Exchange), you can view an individual's availability for events by selecting an event and then choosing Window, Availability Panel from the menu bar.

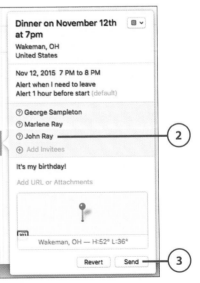

3. Click Send to send the invitations.

4. An icon appears in the upper-right corner of the event to show that invitations have been sent. A question mark indicates that responses haven't been received from all invitees.

Setting Optional Attendees and Resending Invitations

After you've added an invitee to an event, you can click the name in the event summary or edit screen to show a drop-down menu that enables you to flag the person as an optional attendee or to re-send an invitation.

Accepting Invitations

You can easily add to your calendar invitations that you receive. Even though invitations are sent through email, El Capitan's Mail program works with Calendar to automatically transfer the invitations to the Calendar Notifications area where you can act on them.

1. When a new invitation arrives, the Calendar application icon updates to show the count of invitations in the Dock.

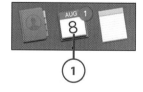

2. The event is shown with diagonal lines through it in the Calendar to indicate it has not yet been added.

3. Click the Notification button to show the notification panel in Calendar. This is only visible when invitations are pending.

4. Use the Maybe, Decline, and Accept buttons to respond to the invitation.

5. Declined invitations are removed from your calendar; accepted and tentative invitations are added.

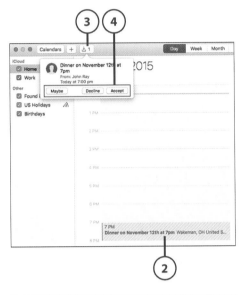

Accepting Invitations through Notification Center

When event invitations come in, you can quickly access them through notifications:

1. When a new invitation arrives, a notification appears.

2. Click Accept to accept the invitation without opening the Calendar app.

Confirming "Found in Mail" Invitations

When someone sends you an email with text like "Hey, wanna grab lunch Tuesday at 1pm?" Mail automatically parses the text to help you add an event. You can view these suggested events into "real" events by doing the following:

1. Open the email in the Mail application.

2. Click the add link to the right of the identified event.

3. Edit whatever details you want in the window that appears.

4. Click Add To Calendar to add the event to the calendar.

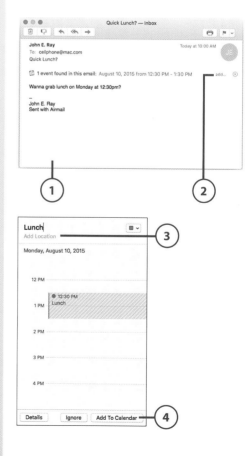

5. If you're already in the Calendar app, you can find these auto-magically identified events visible under the Found in Mail calendar, where you can edit and move them around like any other event.

Changing Your Event Status

If you change your mind about an event, you can edit it in Calendar and change the My Status field to Accept, Maybe, or Decline.

Searching Events

If you're a heavy scheduler, or have dozens of enterprise calendars to manage, sometimes it's useful to be able to quickly search for events, which is a breeze in Calendar.

1. Make sure the checkboxes are selected for the calendars you want to search.

2. Enter your search terms in the Search field.

3. As you type, search options are displayed; pick the best option from the drop-down list or just press Return.

4. The results of the search are displayed in a pane at the right of the Calendar window. Click an entry to jump to that event.

5. Click the X in the search field to hide the search results.

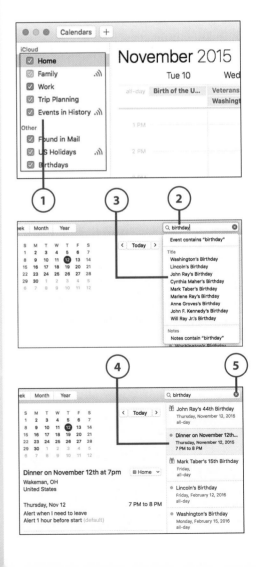

Printing Calendars

Despite our best efforts, sometimes we can't take our Macs (or even our iPads and iPhones) everywhere. When you need your calendar information in paper form, Calendar does an amazing job of printing calendar and itinerary views.

1. Choose File, Print from the Calendar menu bar item.

2. Set the view you want to print.

3. Set a time range for the calendar being printed.

4. Click the checkboxes beside each calendar to print.

5. Select which options should be added to the printed page.

6. Click Continue, which takes you to available printing options; after selecting options, you are ready to print.

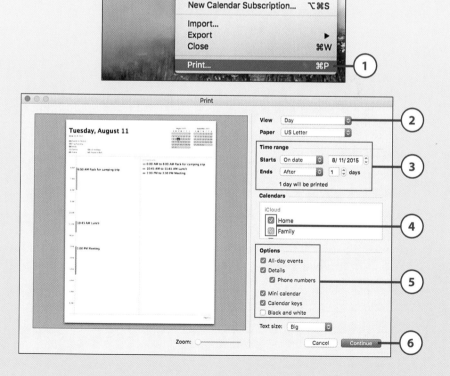

Remembering with Reminders

Beyond simple events that happen on a given date, day-to-day life often requires that you keep track of multiple to-do lists in your head—from home repairs that need to be done to birthday shopping lists to grocery store visits. Using the Reminders app, you can create your own digital to-do lists and even make them contextually aware of your location—prompting you with reminders that apply only at home or the office.

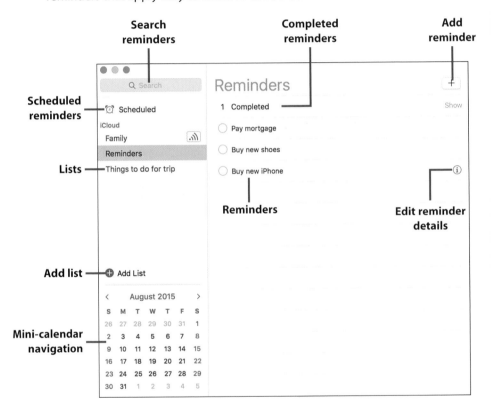

Reminders are organized into lists of related items. You can have as many lists as you want, but you need to have at least a single list to contain reminders at any given point in time. By default, you start with a single list called Reminders, but you can add as many as you'd like.

Creating a List

To create a new reminder list, follow these steps:

1. Open Reminders from the Dock, Launchpad, or Applications folder.

2. If the Lists aren't visible, choose Show Sidebar from the View menu.

3. Click the + Add List button near the bottom of the Reminders window.

4. A new list appears with the name selected. Type a new name and press return. The list is added and ready to be used.

Nothing Is Set in Stone

To rename a list, click its name in the left column in Reminders—it immediately becomes editable. Delete lists by clicking to select them and then pressing your Delete key.

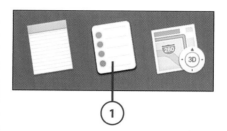

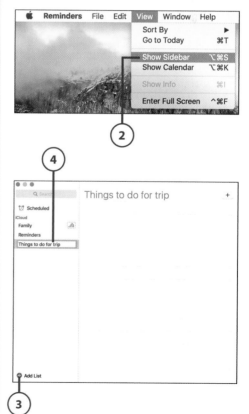

Adding a Reminder

After you've created a list, you'll want to fill it with individual reminders. To create a new reminder within a list, complete the following actions:

1. Click to select the list you want to add a reminder to.

2. Click the + button in the upper-right corner of the Reminders window.

3. The cursor moves to a new line in the reminder list. Type the name for your reminder.

4. Press return to add additional reminders, or click on an empty line to end editing.

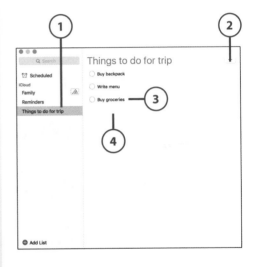

Setting Reminder Attributes, Including Location

A reminder can be more than just a title in a list—it can contain a date, a location, a repeating schedule, and more. Set the attributes for a reminder by doing the following:

1. Hover your pointer over a reminder item. An i icon appears near the right side of the reminder.

2. Click the i to show the reminder settings.

3. Use the title field to change the name of the reminder.

4. Click the On a Day checkbox to set a specific date/time for the reminder.

5. Use the date/time field to configure when the reminder is shown.

6. Use the Repeat drop-down list to set a repetition schedule.

7. Click the At a Location checkbox to receive the reminder when leaving or arriving at a given location.

8. Use the drop-down list/field to choose a contact's address, or enter a new address to be used in conjunction with the location-aware reminders.

9. Set whether the reminder occurs when arriving or leaving.

10. Set a priority for the reminder using the priority pop-up menu.

11. Use the Note field to set any additional notes related to the reminder.

12. Click Done to save the reminder.

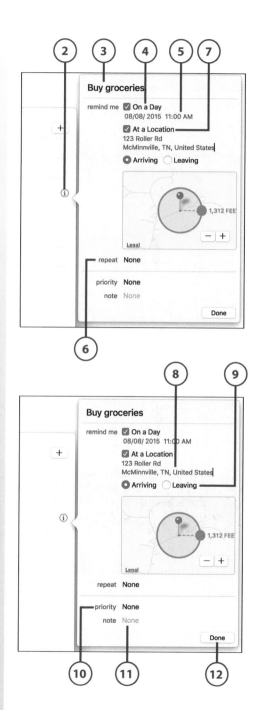

Location Reminders Require Your Location!

The first time you use reminders based on a location, you might be prompted to enable Location services. Click Open Privacy Preferences when prompted, or follow the instructions in Chapter 14, "Securing and Protecting Your Mac."

Completing Reminders

When you're done with a reminder, you'll want to indicate that it is completed. To set the completion status of a reminder, follow these steps:

1. Click the list that contains the reminder you want to complete.

2. Click the checkbox to the left of the reminder.

3. The reminder moves to a Completed section of the list, which you access by clicking Show.

Don't Want to Do It? Just Delete It!

To delete a reminder or a reminder list (rather than having to actually follow through on it), just highlight it and press your Delete key.

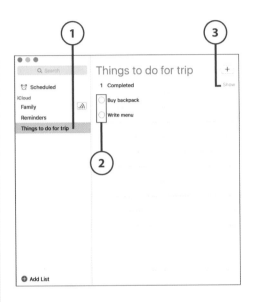

Finding Reminders

Because reminders can be created across many different lists and many different dates, it's helpful to be able to quickly search your lists to figure out what you are supposed to be remembering, and when you should be remembering it. Thankfully, Reminders makes it easy to search all your lists and all your reminder dates very quickly.

Viewing Reminders by Date

If you've set dates for reminders, it's easy to see what reminders are associated with what dates (across all your lists) using the built-in mini-calendar in the Reminders application:

1. Show the mini-calendar (if hidden), by choosing Show Calendar from the View menu.

2. Use the forward and backward arrows to navigate the calendar.

3. Click an individual date to show reminders associated with that day.

4. Choose View, Go to Today from the menu bar to quickly jump to the current date.

All Scheduled Reminders, All in One Place

To show all the scheduled reminders in all your lists, click the Scheduled item that appears at the top of the sidebar. This entry is only visible when scheduled reminders have been added.

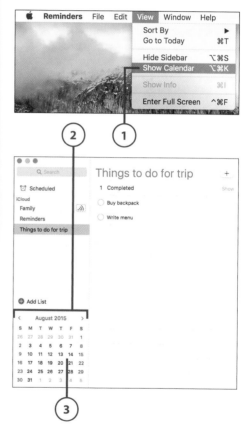

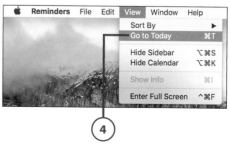

Searching Reminders

To search for reminders across all of
your lists, follow these steps:

1. Type a search term in the Search
    field at the top of the sidebar.

2. The results are shown, organized
    by list, on the right side of the
    window.

3. Click the X in the search field to
    clear the results.

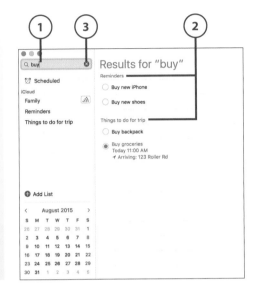

Using iCloud and Server-Based Reminders

As you might have noticed, reminders are very similar to Calendar entries.
They're so similar, in fact, that they use the same server connections to manage their information. To learn how to configure Reminders to use an iCloud
account, follow the instructions in "Connecting to iCloud Calendar Syncing" earlier in this chapter. Similarly, to connect to a different server for your
reminders (Exchange or Google, for instance), follow the instructions in "Connecting to Other Calendar Servers."

Choosing Servers When Creating a New List

If you are connected to several different servers that each provide Reminder
storage, you can choose which one a new reminder list is created on by clicking
and holding the + icon in the bottom-right corner when you create a new list.

Keeping Track with Notes (New!)

Calendars and reminders capture much of our hectic schedules, but life can also be less structured—with new information and ideas coming at us from a dozen different directions. To keep us from losing our idea for "the next big thing," El Capitan includes a full-featured note-taking application—Notes. Like the other apps in this chapter, Notes is also iCloud/server-connected, meaning that no matter where you take your notes, they'll be seamlessly accessible across all your devices.

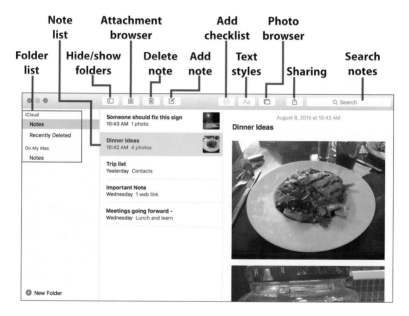

Thoughts and ideas are rarely truly random. Chances are, you take notes about things you want to do at home, at work, with the kids, and so on. To create a sense of order, you'll want to start your OS X note-taking by setting up some folders for yourself.

Adding Folders

By default, notes are added to a
default folder called Notes. To add a
new folder of notes, do the following:

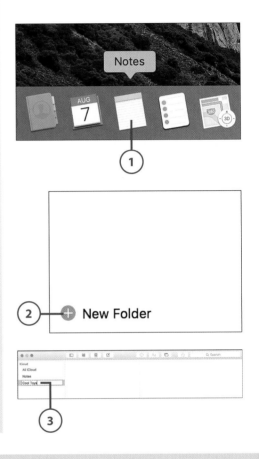

1. Open Notes using the icon in the
   Dock, Launchpad, or Applications
   folder.

2. Choose New Folder at the bottom
   of the folder list.

3. A new folder appears with its
   name selected and editable. Type
   a new name for the folder and
   press return to save it.

>>>Go Further
DELETE TO DELETE

Deleting a folder in Notes is the same as deleting a List in Reminders. Click to
select its name, and then press the Delete key.

The exception to this is the "All" folders (All On My Mac, All iCloud), which
can't be removed. They contain all the notes stored on that device and appear
after you have created multiple note folders.

Adding Notes

The most important aspect of using the Notes application is also the easiest—adding notes. To add a new note, follow these steps:

1. Select the folder that should contain the note.

2. Click the Compose icon.

3. A New Note title appears at the top of the list, and the text entry cursor appears in the content area, ready to edit.

4. Type your note as you see fit.

5. The top line of the note automatically becomes the title for the note in the column to the left of the content.

6. If you decide you don't want a note, select it and press the Delete key to remove it (not shown).

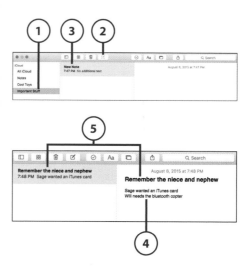

Prettify Your Most Mundane Notes

Your notes don't have to be plain text—you can add formatting, checklists, and more. Follow these steps to make your notes even better:

1. Edit a new or existing note by selecting it, then clicking the note body.

2. Click the Checklist icon to begin inserting a checklist.

3. Each line is a new checklist item. Press Return twice to end the list.

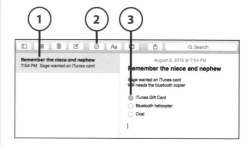

4. Use the style button to choose between different styles for the note text.

5. To insert an image, either drag it from the Finder into the note body, or select the photo browser button.

6. Drag from the photo browser into the note body.

7. In addition to images, you can drag documents from the finder to store them with the note.

Any Font You'd Like, Any Way You'd Like It

You aren't stuck with *just* the styles Apple picks for you. Use the Format menu to choose indentation, justification, and font options as well.

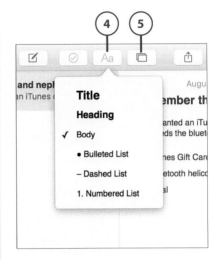

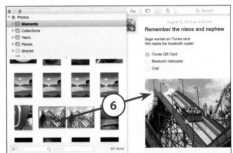

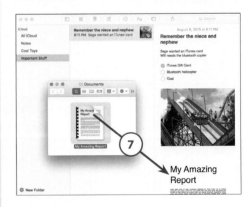

Adding Notes from Other Applications

You aren't limited to adding notes just from memory. You can use the Share menu in many other apps to add a new note or append to an existing note:

1. Use an application that employs the share menu. For example, assume I want to store a map location within a note.

2. Click the Share icon.

3. Choose Notes.

4. Enter text for the note, if desired.

5. Use the Choose Note pop-up menu to select an existing note, or create a new note.

6. Click Save.

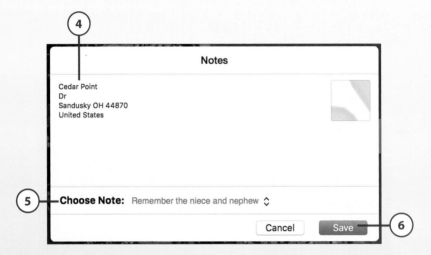

7. The location (or other information) is added to the note as a double-clickable attachment.

Moving Notes Between Folders

If you've created notes in one folder that you later want to move to another, this is easily accomplished with a simple drag and drop. Do the following to move notes between folders:

1. Click a note title to select it. Hold the Command key to select multiple notes at a time.

2. Click and drag from the selected note to a folder in the folder list. The notes are immediately transferred to the folder.

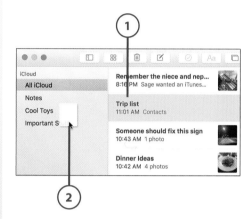

Searching and Displaying Notes

Notes can contain quite a bit of information, and after you've amassed a library of hundreds of notes, you might find yourself trying to track down a single tiny bit of information within a note. To search the available notes (in all note folders), just follow these steps:

1. Choose a folder of notes to search or view, or All Notes to access all folders.

2. Type a search term in the search field to filter the notes being displayed (if desired).

3. The results are shown in the center column of the window.

4. Attachments (if any) are displayed below the notes.

5. Click a result to show that note's content to the right of the search results.

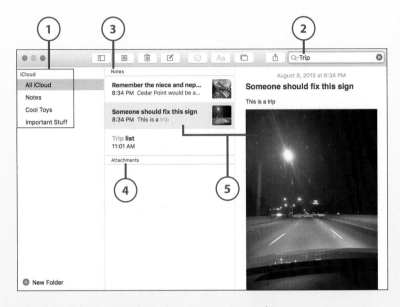

6. Double-click a note's title to show it in a new window.

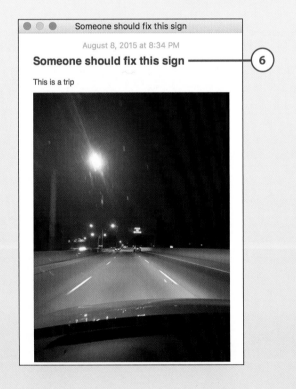

Showing Attachments

If you keep lots of documents with your notes, you'll be happy to hear there's any easy way to find and browse them—in one place. Access the attachment browser by following these steps.

1. Click the attachment browser button.

2. Choose the type of attachment you want to view.

3. The results are shown in the window.

4. Right-click a file and choose Go to Note to see the note that contains the attachment.

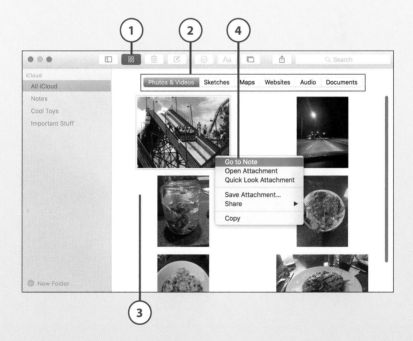

Sharing Notes via Email and Messages

To share a note via email or Messages, you can use a El Capitan Share button. For detailed information on the process, refer to Chapter 6. The basic process works like this:

1. Navigate to a note you want to share.

2. Click the Share button to show the sharing options.

3. Choose the method of sharing that you'd like to use.

4. Your choice launches the appropriate supporting application and attaches the note for sending.

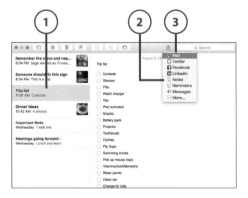

Using iCloud and Server-Based Notes

Notes, like the other utilities in this chapter, are stored, by default, on an available server account—iCloud, if configured. To set up or verify an existing server setup for your notes, you can use the instructions in the next two sections.

Connecting to iCloud Note Syncing

If you've already established an iCloud account, connecting Notes to iCloud is just a matter of clicking the right checkbox. If you do not have an iCloud account, you should review Chapter 4 for information on setting one up.

1. Click the System Preferences icon on the Dock and then click iCloud.

2. Check the box beside Notes.

3. Close the System Preferences. Your Notes application is now connected to iCloud.

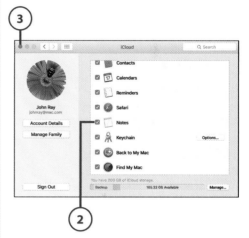

Connecting to Other Note Servers

As you've probably guessed, Exchange servers and Google accounts can also provide shared note storage. To use one of these servers to share notes between your computers or devices, follow these steps:

1. Click the System Preferences icon on the Dock and then click Internet Accounts.

2. Choose the service providing note storage from the list on the right.

3. The account creation window appears. Use the fields in the window to configure your account information.

4. Click Sign In or Continue to proceed.

5. If you're setting up a service that provides more than just calendars (such as Exchange, Yahoo!, or Gmail), you are prompted to automatically set up corresponding email accounts and contact servers. Be sure to click the checkbox beside Notes.

6. Click Done.

7. Close the System Preferences when finished.

Your Utilities, Everywhere

Wish you had access to the suite of utilities described in this chapter wherever you may be? You do! You can access Calendars, Contacts, Notes, and Reminders using Apple's iCloud web service. Just sign in at http://www.icloud.com/ to use Apple's meticulously crafted and stunningly beautiful web versions of these useful tools.

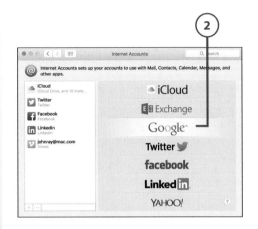

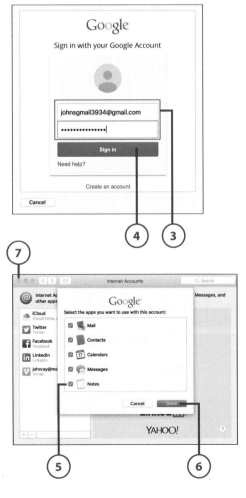

>>>*Go Further*

CHOOSE A FOLDER TO SET YOUR SERVER

If you have multiple servers set up, the process of creating a new folder is a bit ambiguous as to what server it will be created on. To force the folder to be created on a specific server, first make sure the Notes folder list is visible and then click a folder name on the server you want to use. Subsequent *new* folders will be created on that server.

It's Not All Good

Gone for Good. Everywhere.

Even though the applications in this chapter are frequently configured to use servers (much like Mail), it doesn't mean that they work with information in the same way as Mail. In email, when you delete a message, it typically gets moved to your email's trash folder—where it can be recovered.

In Calendar and Reminders, deleting an event, reminder, or note is permanent. What's more, if you're using iCloud, it will be removed from all of your devices—virtually simultaneously.

The exception to this is the Notes application. Notes automatically puts any deleted notes into a Recently Deleted folder where you can recover the note, if needed.

Purchase and read
books in iBooks.

Challenge your friends
in Game Center.

Enjoy movies, music,
and more in iTunes.

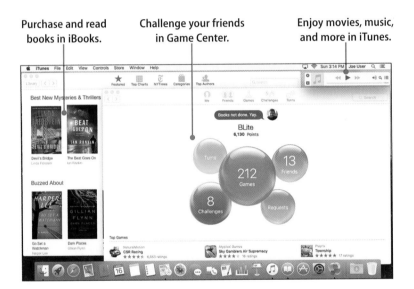

In this chapter, you discover how to use digital music and video to turn your Mac into a big-screen entertainment center, including:

→ Buying digital media using iTunes
→ Syncing your iOS device with iTunes
→ Keeping a cloud library with iTunes Match
→ Using Apple Music
→ Purchasing books with the iBooks Store
→ Reading with iBooks
→ Social gaming with Game Center

Entertainment on the (Big) Little Screen

In case you hadn't noticed, your Mac has a gorgeous screen. The LED IPS display provides excellent color reproduction and amazing depth—at HDTV resolutions or higher. Why bother sitting in front of the TV when your Mac does so much more? Using iTunes (and the new Apple Music service), you can build a library of thousands of songs, TV shows, and movies.

In addition to iTunes, your Mac also includes software to browse, purchase, and read thousands of the best-selling books. If challenging your friends is more your style, Game Center gives you a full social gaming platform, just a click away.

Creating a Media Library in iTunes (New!)

Apple's iTunes enables you to manage and play digital media files, including song tracks you import from CD, content you purchase from the iTunes Store, or podcasts you subscribe to online.

You can also create and sync playlists with your iDevices or share them with other iTunes users on your local network.

Running iTunes for the First Time

The first time you launch iTunes, you won't have anything in your music library. Follow these steps to complete the setup process:

1. Open iTunes from the Dock, Launchpad, or by locating its application icon in the Applications folder.

2. Click Agree after reviewing the iTunes Software License Agreement.

3. The Welcome window, with video tutorials for various tasks, appears. Click Take a Quick Tour if you'd like to see video demonstrations of iTunes in action.

4. If you're okay with iTunes sharing information about your library in order to see artist information, album covers, and other niceties, click Agree; otherwise click No Thanks.

5. Click Scan for Media to search your account for any music files you might already have. These are copied to the iTunes folder, inside your Music folder. (This option might not appear if you have a previous version of iTunes already installed.)

6. To immediately start searching the iTunes Store, click the iTunes Store button in the top center of the window.

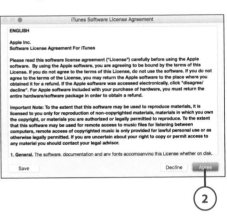

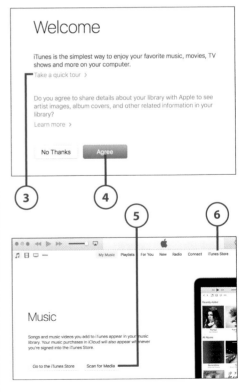

Finding Your Way Around iTunes

First, here is a quick tour of the iTunes controls to acquaint you with the basics. The default view in iTunes is the Library view.

1. The icons on the left side of the iTunes toolbar enable you to choose between Music, Movies, TV Shows, and other content (represented initially by three dots).

2. In the top center of the window are icons for choosing the source of your media, such as your library (My Music), playlists you've created, Music iTunes thinks you'll like (For You), New music, iTunes Radio, Connect (for interacting with your favorite artists), and, of course, the iTunes Store.

3. On the right is a drop-down menu that enables you to choose how your library is displayed (by song, album, artist, genre, and so on). The options change depending on the type of library you have selected.

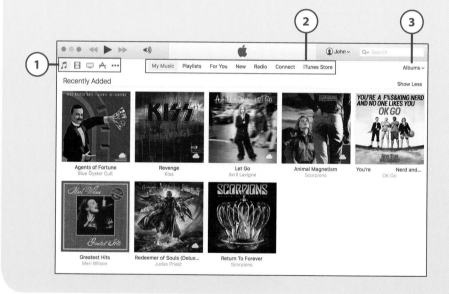

Interacting with Your Library

After choosing a content type and a viewing organization, your screen shifts to one of many different displays of your media library. The interface encourages exploration. The album view for music, for example, has these features:

1. Double-clicking an item (song, album, and so on) begins playback.

2. Clicking an album opens an expanded view of the contents.

3. Positioning your cursor over an item displays an ellipsis (…) that opens a menu that enables you to jump between different media organizations, add the item to your playback list, create an iTunes Radio Station, or show the iTunes Store for the artist.

4. Clicking Show in iTunes Store shows additional items you can purchase related to the chosen media. If iTunes cannot find related content within the store, you do not see this option.

5. Click the heart icon for songs and albums you like. This helps Apple create its suggestions for your musical interests.

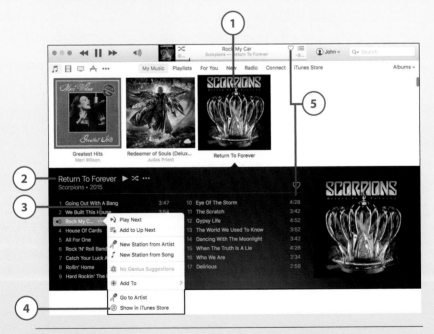

Not in the Store

You can always toggle whether or not iTunes shares information about your library using the Store settings within the iTunes preferences. Be aware that if you choose not to share, certain iTunes features will not be available to you—such as In the Store links that help you locate additional music by your favorite artist.

Controlling Playback

Along the top of the window are controls for all your playback needs:

1. Move back, forward, play, and pause your media playback.

2. Adjust your speaker volume.

3. Choose a device, such as an Apple TV or AirPort Express, to output your sound.

4. View the playback progress.

5. Set playback to shuffle.

6. Set a favorite.

7. View the next song that will be played or the songs that already have been played.

8. Search all your media or the iTunes Store.

9. Show active iTunes downloads.

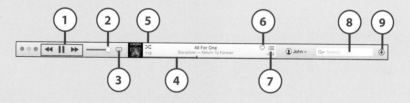

Building Your Media Library

Apple offers plenty of content for you on the iTunes store. Everything from music to movies, podcasts, music videos, and TV shows. With just a few clicks, you can go from a Saturday night with nothing to watch to a movie night with the latest blockbuster releases.

>>>Go Further
USING YOUR PURCHASES

You can authorize up to five computers to play songs purchased on a single account. To do this, choose Store, Authorize Computer and enter your Apple ID. (Remember to deauthorize computers that no longer need access, which frees up openings for new computers to be added.) You can also take advantage of Family Sharing to share downloads with family members who have been designated in the iCloud Family Sharing setup, discussed in Chapter 10, "Installing and Managing Applications and Extensions on Your Mac."

Purchasing Digital Media on the iTunes Store

To purchase media from the iTunes Store, follow these steps:

1. Click the iTunes Store link in the top center of the window (or use the In the Store link when viewing media) to connect to the iTunes Store.

2. Click Sign In. If Sign In doesn't appear, skip to step 5.

3. Enter your Apple ID and password in the Sign In dialog box.

4. Click Sign In.

Redeem Your Gift Cards

If you have an iTunes gift card to redeem, click the toolbar link with your Apple ID (visible after signing into the iTunes Store) and then choose Redeem from the menu that appears. On the subsequent screen you can type in your gift card number or click Use Camera to scan the card with your FaceTime HD camera.

---

5. When you're logged in, your Apple ID appears in place of the Sign In button.

6. Use the links and scrolling content views to browse available media—just as you would a web page.

7. Click the Play button that appears as you move your cursor over a song to play a preview.

8. To make a purchase, click the Price button that appears beside items. In the case of music, you can buy individual songs or albums.

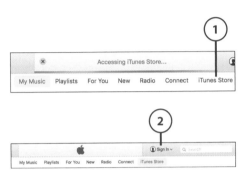

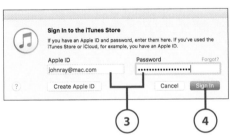

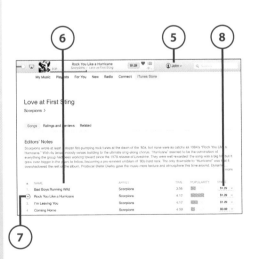

9. When you're asked to confirm that you want to buy the selection, click the Buy button. Your selection is downloaded and added to your library under the Purchased playlist.

10. Click the download button (down arrow) to view all the current downloads taking place.

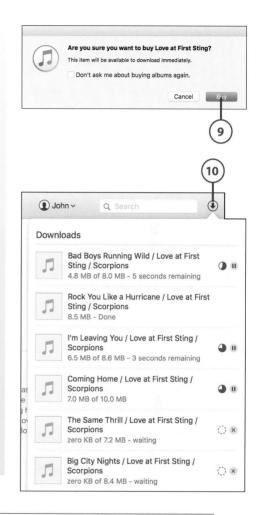

The Rental Countdown

When you choose to rent a movie, you have 30 days to watch it and 24 hours from the time you start watching it to finish it. Rented movies appear in your library just as other files do.

>>>Go Further

IMPORTING FROM CD

Although Apple has dropped optical drives from virtually all of its shipping Macs, you can still use iTunes to import from a CD. To do this (if you have an optical drive), just insert the CD; iTunes launches and prompts you to import. It's as simple as that.

Additionally, when you import an audio CD, iTunes connects to a music database, identifies your disc, and applies information such as title, artist, and genre to each track. Album artwork might also be available if the album is part of the iTunes Store.

If iTunes doesn't find your CD in the database, you can edit the track information yourself by selecting it and choosing File, Get Info. Select several tracks at a time to update all the shared information and save yourself some typing.

Using Genius Recommendations

Genius Recommendations attempt to predict what new and existing media you might enjoy based on the current items in your library. Follow these steps to enable and peruse Genius Recommendations:

1. Choose Account, Turn On Genius from the menu bar.

2. Click the Turn On Genius button on the screen that appears. (If you're already signed in with your Apple ID, you won't see this or the next step.)

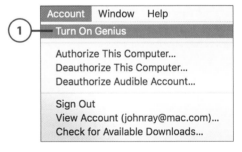

3. Enter your Apple ID and password (if prompted) and click Sign In.

4. Check the box to agree to the terms of service and click Agree (not shown).

5. A screen announcing Turning On Genius appears while the contents of your library are analyzed and personalized results are prepared.

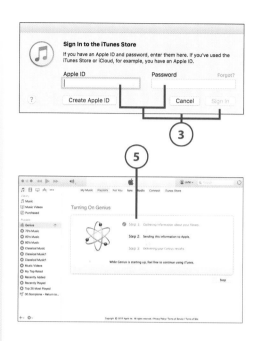

Gathering Data

Three stages are displayed while this occurs: gathering information, sending information, and delivering Genius results.

6. Select a song in your library.

7. Click the disclosure ellipsis beside a song or album to view recommendations in your existing library.

8. Choose Start Genius to begin playing a playlist of songs similar to the currently selected song.

9. Pick Create Genius Playlist to create and save a new playlist based on the current song. The new playlist is saved and visible within the Playlists view category.

10. Click Genius Suggestions to list the songs that Genius thinks are similar to the chosen song.

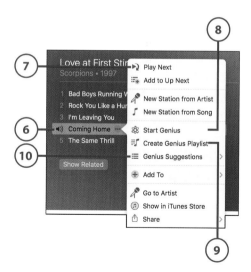

11. Pick from the genius recommendation list to jump to any song.

Downloading Podcasts

Podcasts are a series of digital broadcasts, either audio or video, that you can subscribe to for regular updates. You can locate and subscribe to a variety of podcasts (most of them free) in the iTunes Store by following these steps:

1. Click iTunes Store to open the store.

2. Click the icon with three dots (on the left), and then choose Podcasts from the menu that appears.

3. Click an item to see details and a list of available episodes.

4. Click the Subscribe button to download the most recent episode and all future episodes of this podcast. The podcasts are downloaded to your iTunes library.

Not Listening? Unsubscribe

iTunes checks for updates as long as you are subscribed; if you change your mind about following a podcast, select it in the list and click the Unsubscribe button displayed at the top of the list of individual podcasts.

5. Click Subscribe when you're asked to confirm that you want to subscribe.

6. Exit the store and select the My Podcasts item in the center of the iTunes toolbar.

7. Choose the podcast from the list on the left.

8. Select an episode and click the Play control button to listen.

9. Access a list of all Recent podcast updates using the Recent Updates selection.

10. View all unplayed podcast episodes by clicking the Unplayed Episodes item.

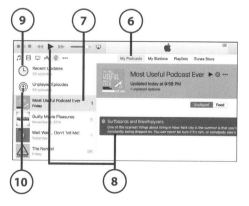

Oldies But Goodies

Episodes produced prior to your subscription appear when you click the Feed button located above the Podcast list. Click the cloud icon to download any old episodes not stored on your Mac.

>>>Go Further
FREE EDUCATION WITH ITUNES U

If you're looking for educational materials, iTunes U is the place to go. Here, dozens of schools publish free course material that is yours for the downloading. Audio, video—it's all here, and subjects from business management to programming are available. iTunes U lessons work identically to podcasts, but are downloaded from the iTunes U section of the iTunes Store and are managed in the iTunes U media category.

Quick Searches

Your iTunes library can grow large quite quickly with so many sources from which to draw. Fortunately, it's easy to search your library to find just what you're looking for:

1. Click inside the Search box at the upper right of the iTunes window and begin typing a search term. As you type, a pop-over window appears showing potential matches.

2. Make sure that My Library is selected.

3. Choose an item in the results to jump to it within your library.

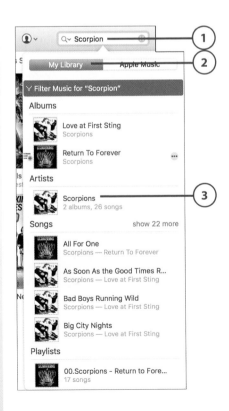

Setting a Search Filter

To filter your search results further,
do the following:

1. Click beside the magnifying glass
    in the search field.

2. Uncheck the Search Entire Library
    item to search only the type of
    media you are currently viewing.

3. Choose the filter option you want
    to apply (Song, Album, Artist,
    Composer, and so on).

4. Perform the search as described
    in the section "Quick Searches."

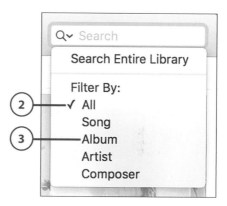

Using Playlists

Playlists help you organize your music and media into themes to suit your
mood. You can define your own playlists, set search criteria to automatically
cluster certain artists or genres, or have iTunes use the Genius profile it created from your library to generate lists for you.

Creating Playlists

To define a playlist of songs you choose, follow these steps:

1. With Music media selected, click the Playlists item in the upper center of the window.

2. Click the plus button at the bottom of the list of playlists on the left. (There are several
    playlists provided by default.) Choose New Playlist.

3. Enter a name for the new playlist and then press Enter.

4. Click Edit Playlist in the upper right to add songs to the playlist.

5. The screen refreshes with your music library on the left and the playlist on the right. Browse your music library as you normally would.

6. Drag songs, albums, or artists to the playlist column on the right.

7. When finished adding songs, click Done.

Playlist Organization

If you add so many playlists that you feel the need to put them in folders to keep track of them, choose New Playlist Folder when clicking the same plus button you used to add a playlist.

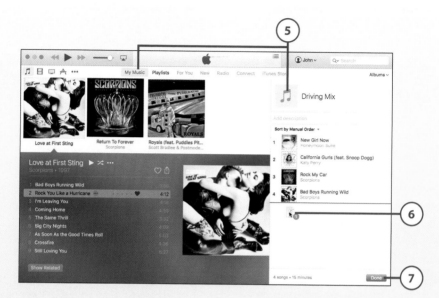

Defining Smart Playlists

To set criteria that iTunes can use to make a playlist for you, follow these steps:

1. Within the Music media section, click the Playlists item in the upper center of the iTunes window.

2. Click the plus button at the bottom of the list of playlists on the left. (There are several playlists provided by default.)

3. Choose New Smart Playlist.

4. In the Smart Playlist window, set your search criteria.

Setting Criteria

Options include obvious choices, such as artist, album, or rating, as well as more obscure settings, such as bit rate (which relates to sound quality). You can also set a limit on the number of songs and allow live updates, which creates a list that changes as your library changes.

5. One option that might not make immediate sense is Match Only Checked Items. This only matches songs that have checkmarks. If you view your library as a list, you can check/uncheck beside each song. This refers to that checkmark.

6. Click OK when you're done setting search criteria. Your Smart Playlist appears under the Playlists.

7. Enter a Name for the new Smart Playlist, and then press Return.

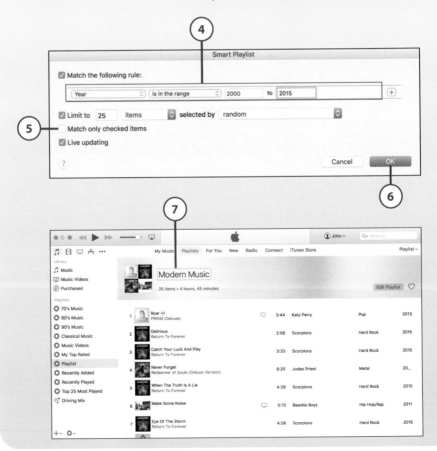

Genius at Work

Refer back to "Using Genius Recommendations" to have iTunes generate a play-list for you based on a song, album, or artist of your choice.

Accessing Playlists

To access, edit, or play back the media in your playlist, follow these steps:

1. Within the Music media section, click the Playlists item in the upper center of the iTunes window.

2. Click the playlist you want to use from the list on the left.

3. Click Edit Playlist to modify the playlist (or Edit for Smart Playlists).

4. Click Play/Pause to begin (or stop) playback. Here, Pause is shown.

5. Click Shuffle to randomize the playback order.

Using the Mini Player

After you've set up your media library and decided on the songs you want to play, chances are you don't want to keep the huge iTunes window around. To use the mini player, follow these steps:

1. Choose Window, Switch to Mini-Player (or Window, MiniPlayer to leave the main iTunes window visible as well). Alternatively, click in the upper left corner of the playback information area.

2. The mini player appears and displays the currently playing song.

3. Move your cursor over the window to show standard playback controls.

4. Click the list icon to show upcoming songs or your playback history.

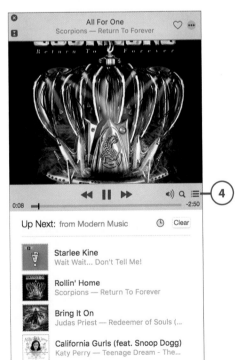

5. Use the magnifying glass to search for songs directly from the mini player.

6. Click the ellipsis to show a contextual menu for rating the song, showing genius suggestions, and so on.

7. Click the >< icon to collapse the window even further!

8. Click X to close the mini player.

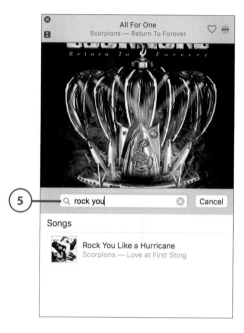

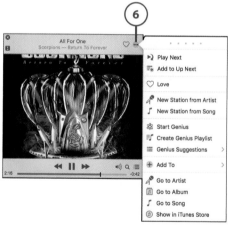

Using iTunes Radio

If you find yourself wanting to just listen to good music, iTunes now includes iTunes Radio. iTunes Radio offers both curated (Beats 1) and automatically created stations that literally play *anything* you want. Be your own DJ!

We Interrupt This Song…

iTunes Radio is a great service, but it is supported by ads that play between songs. If you want ad-free music, just subscribe to iTunes Match or Apple Music (discussed a bit later in this chapter), and your music won't be interrupted.

To start listening to iTunes radio, you need an active Internet connection. Beyond that, you're just a few clicks away from your favorite artists and songs.

Listening to iTunes Radio

Follow these steps to listen to one of the many ready-to-play Featured stations available:

1. Make sure you have selected Music from the icons on the left side of the iTunes toolbar.

2. Click the Radio button near the center of the iTunes toolbar.

3. Scroll left and right in the list of Featured or Recently Played stations until you find something you'd like to listen to.

4. Click Play to begin playing iTunes Radio.

5. Click the Star to display options for liking or disliking a song.

6. Click the Fast Forward button to skip to the next song (you can only do this six times in a 60-minute period).

7. Click the Price (displayed to the right of the song information) to purchase the track being played.

Creating Your Own iTunes Radio Station

After you've had a taste of the featured stations, you'll likely want to create your own.

1. Find and expand an artist or album that you want to use as the basis for a station.

2. Click the ellipsis by the item you like.

3. Choose New Station from Artist.

4. The new station appears and begins playing.

More Than Music

iTunes Radio features more than just music! If you'd like to listen to comedy broadcasts, I recommend Bob Newhart.

>>>Go Further
YOUR RADIO, ANYWHERE

Any iTunes Radio station that you create will be available on any Mac or iOS device where you've signed into your iTunes account. It even works with your iPod/iPhone-compatible car audio system!

Fine-Tuning Your iTunes Radio Station

Not only can you build your own station, featuring your favorite song or artist, but you can fine tune the station for your mood. Follow these steps to tune your radio station:

1. Play the station that you want to modify.

2. Click the ellipsis in the playback area.

3. Click Play More Like This if you like the song.

4. Click Never Play This Song if you never want to hear a song again.

5. Create brand new stations based on the song or artist.

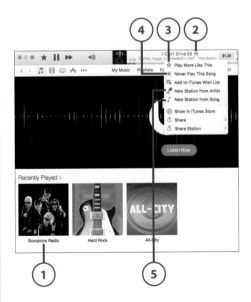

Answering the "What Was That Song?" Question

If you've ever heard a song and wondered what it was, you'll be happy to hear that *can't* happen on iTunes Radio. If you hear something and want to see what it was, follow these steps:

1. Click the list icon beside the playing song information.

2. A pop-over window displays the recently played songs on all your stations.

3. Click the price to purchase any song you've heard.

Station Specifics

To focus on the recent songs on a specific station, click the station to open it and display the recently played songs.

Sharing Your Good Taste

Radio stations are meant to be shared. After you've crafted the perfect station, you can easily share it with your friends by following these steps:

1. Click the ellipsis beside a song in the playback area.

2. Click the Share Station item.

3. Choose a method for sending the station to your friend.

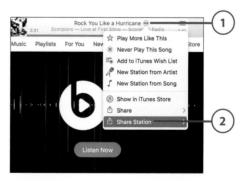

Using Apple Music

iTunes Radio is only so useful—you can't listen to *anything* you want, just things that Apple chooses to play. Things get *much* more interesting when you subscribe to Apple Music ($9.99 a month, or $15 for a 5-person family per month). Apple Music lets you play virtually any song in the massive iTunes library (with some notable exceptions, like the Beatles) without buying it. You can get started using Apple Music with a free 3-month trial, giving you plenty of time to determine if it's something you want to keep.

Subscribing to Apple Music

To subscribe to Apple Music, follow these steps:

1. Choose Apple Music from the iTunes Account menu.

2. Click the Start Free Trial Link.

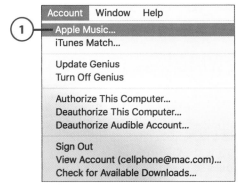

3. A screen appears to gather your music preferences. Click the circles of the genres you like, once for a little, click twice if you like them a lot.

4. Hover over a genre and click the X if you don't like it at all.

5. Click Next.

6. Click the artists you like. Click twice on the ones you love.

7. Hover over an artist to reveal an X. Click the X to remove the artist.

8. Click Done to begin using Apple Music.

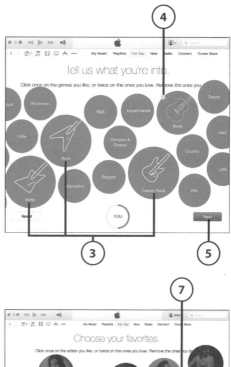

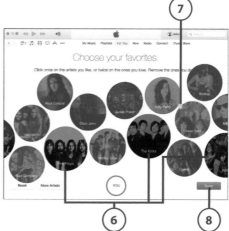

Resetting Your Preferences

Music tastes evolve over time. To reset your initial "likes" (or to add new genres and artists), click the account icon in the iTunes Toolbar and then pick Choose Artists For You.

Adding Songs to Your Library

Once you've subscribed to Apple Music, you can search for and instantly add songs to your library—no purchasing required.

1. Make sure My Music is selected.

2. Search for an artist or song (or even a playlist) you think you might like.

3. Click Apple Music at the top of the search results.

4. Choose a result to display.

5. Drill down to an album or song you want to add to your library.

Disappearing Pricing

You'll notice that the prices disappear in your iTunes Radio stations after joining Apple Music. Just click the ellipsis beside the current playing song and choose Add to My Music. Done!

---

6. Click the ellipsis beside the item.

7. Choose Add to My Music. The item is now part of your library—free to play, download, include in playlists, and so on for as long as you subscribe to Apple Music.

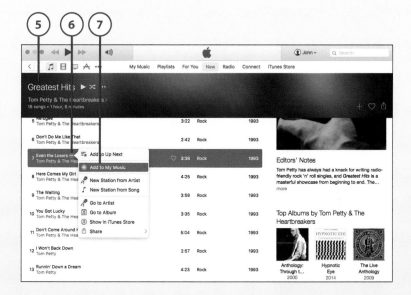

Everywhere You Want It

Even though Apple Music songs are tied to a subscription service, you can use them on your iOS devices and download songs for offline playback just like any other song.

Using Apple Music Recommendations

Apple Music also works to help you discover new music. As you play songs and click the heart (Love It) icon, you teach iTunes what you do and don't like.

To see what Apple Music suggests for you, follow these steps:

1. Click the For You source area.

2. Click Play on any recommended album or Playlist to begin listening.

Connecting with Artists

With the introduction of Apple Music, Apple is also trying to create a social "connection" platform for artists to reach out to listeners. To access the "Connect" platform, do the following:

1. Click the Connect link.

2. Artist posts are shown in chronological order. When you purchase music, the artists are automatically added.

3. Some artists may post playable links to new music, videos, or interviews.

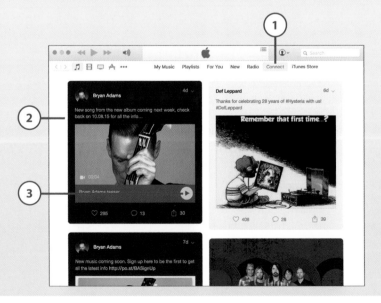

Following New Artists

To follow a new artist without making a purchase, complete these steps:

1. Search or browse for an artist as described in this chapter.

2. On the artist page, click the Follow button.

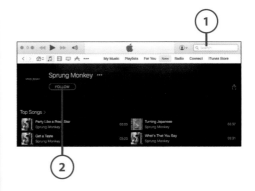

Managing Followed Artists

To manage the artists you're following (and unfollow the ones you've stopped listening to), just click along:

1. Click the Account icon in the iTunes toolbar.

2. Choose the @Following item.

3. A page appears showing the artists you're following. Click the Following button to toggle your following status (that is, to unfollow them).

Syncing Media Between Devices

iTunes is more than a virtual filing cabinet for storing music and media files. It also syncs with iPods, iPhones, and other computers on your network so you never have to be without those items, even when you're away from your Mac.

Syncing Purchases

By enabling syncing of purchases in iTunes, you ensure that your purchases are downloaded to other copies of iTunes that are signed in with your Apple ID.

Follow these steps to turn on purchase syncing:

1. Open the Preferences from the iTunes menu.

2. Click the Store button at the top of the Preferences window.

3. Click the checkboxes in front of Music, TV Shows, Movies, and Apps (or any combination of these) to download any purchase made on another Mac (or even your iOS device) to your iTunes library automatically.

4. Click OK to close Preferences.

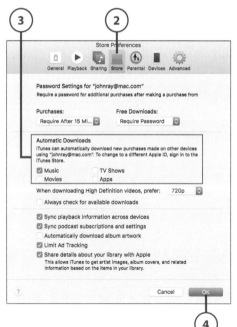

Syncing Your Media with Your iPod, iPad, or iPhone

iTunes was designed to be used with iPods, iPhones, and iPads, which makes syncing your Library between devices a cinch. Follow these steps to transfer content from your Mac to your iPod, iPhone, or iPad:

1. Connect your iOS device to your Mac using the supplied USB cable. iTunes detects the device and begins synchronizing. Click the device button in the iTunes toolbar to open information about the connected device.

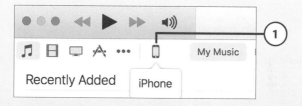

First-Time Connections

If the device has not been connected before, iTunes guides you through a short registration process.

2. View the Summary screen, which shows the name, capacity, software version, serial number, and any updates available to your device.

3. Choose Sync over Wi-Fi to sync without your USB cable in the future!

Syncing to a New Mac

If your device was previously synced with another Mac, you have the option to Erase and Sync or transfer purchases to your new Mac.

4. To conserve space on your device, open the different Media categories, and, on each, select which items to sync.

5. Click Apply to sync your device. The status of the sync appears at the top of the window. Do not disconnect your device until syncing is completed.

6. When the sync completes, click Eject and unplug your device and cable.

Cable-Free Bliss

After you've enabled Wi-Fi syncing, you can start a sync any time your iPhone, iPad, or iPod is on the same network as your iTunes library. Just open the Settings app on your iOS device and navigate to General, iTunes Wi-Fi Sync.

>>>*Go Further*
EVERYTHING EVERYWHERE!

If you've chosen to automatically download media purchases to your iOS device, chances are you will rarely even need to sync directly with iTunes because iCloud will keep everything up-to-date on its own!

Even better, with the latest releases of iOS, you don't even need to sync. Just start listening to music or watching your favorite videos and they'll be streamed straight to your device.

Sharing Media Between Home Computers

Home Sharing enables you to browse up to five computers on your local network and import music to your own library. In addition, it enables you to stream media to your iOS device when it is connected to your home network.

1. Choose File, Home Sharing, Turn On Home Sharing from the menu.

2. Sign in with your Apple ID by entering your username and password.

3. Click Turn On Home Sharing.

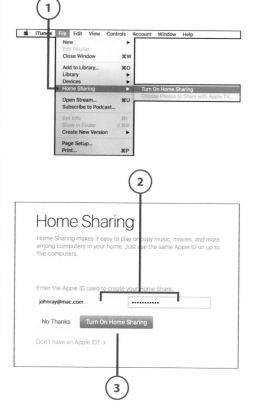

4. Click Done when the confirmation page appears. Repeat these steps for all the other computers in your home, connecting with the same Apple ID.

5. Use the Home Sharing icon (a house) to display a menu and choose the shared library you want to peruse.

6. Interact with the songs and media as if they were local to your computer.

7. Click Settings to enable auto-download of items in the remote library.

8. Use the Import button to copy any selected item to your library.

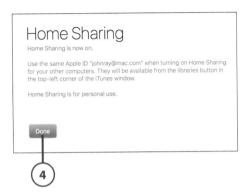

Home Sharing

Home Sharing is now on.

Use the same Apple ID "johnray@mac.com" when turning on Home Sharing for your other computers. They will be available from the libraries button in the top-left corner of the iTunes window.

Home Sharing is for personal use.

Done

④

⑤

⑥

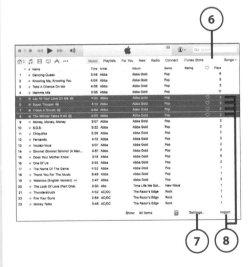

⑦ ⑧

Keeping an iCloud Library with iTunes Match

All songs, movies, and TV shows that you purchase through iTunes are available on any of your computers, as long as you're signed into iTunes with your Apple ID. These are referred to as being "stored in iCloud." Although this is fine and dandy, what about all the media you have that you *didn't* purchase through iTunes?

For that, you have Music Match. Music Match keeps your entire iTunes music library in Apple's iCloud service and makes it available to all your devices, including the Apple TV. What's more, it replaces poorer quality recordings you may have in your library with the best Apple has to offer.

How is this different from Apple Music? Good question. The answer is that iTunes Match music is for what you *own*. This is your personal, *purchased*, music library in the cloud—not music that you're playing thanks to a monthly fee.

It's Not All Good

Pay to Play

iTunes Match isn't free. It costs $25 per year and matches up to 25,000 songs that you didn't purchase from iTunes. Any song purchased through iTunes doesn't count toward the total song limit.

Activating iTunes Match

To sign up for iTunes Match, follow these simple steps:

1. Choose iTunes Match from the Account menu.

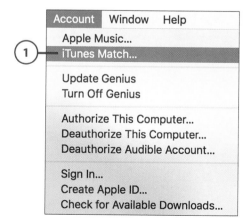

2. Click the Subscribe button to join the iTunes Match service, or click Add the Computer (not shown) if you're already a subscriber.

3. Enter your Apple ID and password.

4. Click Subscribe.

5. Click Add This Computer when prompted

6. The iTunes Match process runs, analyzing your library and adding your music to iTunes Match in iCloud. You can continue to use iTunes during this process (not shown).

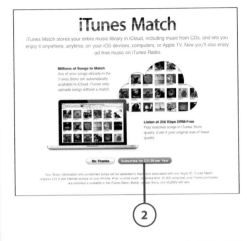

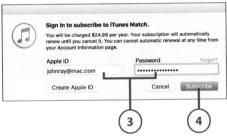

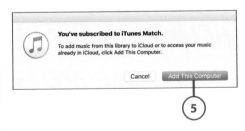

Accessing Purchases in iCloud

After you've activated iTunes Match on a computer or iOS device, all your songs, movies, and TV shows appear—whether they're located in iCloud or stored locally. To access your media, simply follow these steps:

1. Browse your library. Media items available for download from iCloud (but not stored locally) are shown with a cloud and a download arrow. Items that are stored locally have no cloud icon.

2. You can select and play any item. As long as you are connected to the network, iTunes will stream your media selection.

3. Click the cloud/arrow icon to download a local copy of the item.

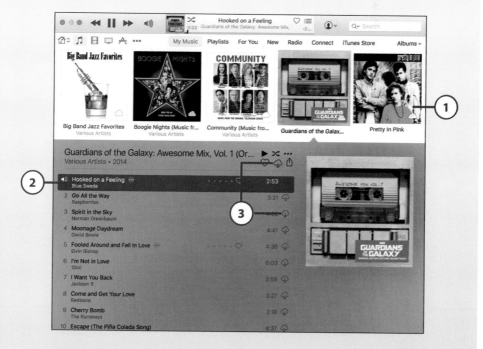

Music Matching Only

Note that there is no "video matching" within iTunes Match. Although your purchases will be available on all your devices, iTunes will not find and match movie and TV show downloads that occur outside of iTunes.

>>>Go Further

MEDIA CENTER EXTRAORDINAIRE

Once upon a time, OS X included a media center application called Front Row. Front Row provided a TV-ready interface for browsing and playing your iTunes Media. When Apple discontinued this feature, it left a void that several Open Source projects quickly filled.

The most Mac-like and feature-rich of these projects is Plex (www.plex.tv). Using Plex, you can create a media center system that plays *any* format of video or audio, looks great on a TV, accesses Internet video, streams to iOS devices, shares with friends, and much more. For free. If you're a media junkie, Plex is definitely the way to go.

Reading Your iBooks

If music, TV, and movies aren't your cup of tea, then perhaps a book will do. El Capitan supports full integration with Apple's iBooks Store and enables you to shop for new titles and read them on your gorgeous Mac display. The iBooks application is *very* similar to iTunes, so make sure you're comfortable with shopping for content on iTunes before continuing.

For many users, your first experience with iBooks came on your iPhone or iPad. That's fine, but it means that you might need to authorize your computer before you can read your previous book purchases. Let's walk through the steps of starting iBooks for the first time and then authorizing your Mac to read previous purchases.

Starting iBooks

Before you can start using iBooks, you need to walk through the setup wizard and log in with your Apple ID. Follow these steps to get ready to read:

1. Open iBooks from the Applications folder, Dock, or Launchpad.

2. Click Get Started.

3. Go to the iBooks Store to log into the iBooks Store with your Apple ID.

4. Enter your Apple ID and password information and click Sign In.

5. You're taken to the iBooks store.

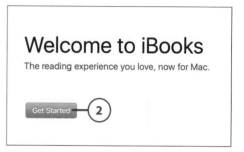

Welcome to iBooks

The reading experience you love, now for Mac.

Get Started

There are no books in your iBooks library.

Visit the iBooks Store to download the latest bestselling books and your favorite classics. Books you download are available in iBooks on your Mac, iPhone, and iPad.

Go to the iBooks Store

Sign in to download from the iBooks Store.

If you have an Apple ID and password, enter them here. If you've used the iTunes Store or iCloud, for example, you have an Apple ID.

Apple ID: johnray@mac.com   Password   Forgot?

Create Apple ID   Cancel   Sign In

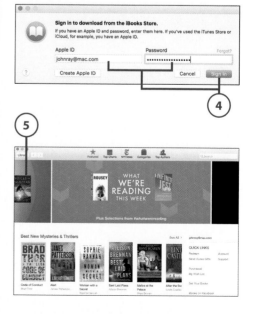

Authorizing Your Mac

If you've previously purchased books on another device and want to read them on your Mac, you probably need to authorize your computer.

1. Choose Authorize This Computer from the Store menu. (If this is not visible, you are already authorized and can skip this task.)

2. Enter your Apple ID and password.

3. Click Authorize.

4. A confirmation message is displayed.

5. Click OK. Your system is now prepared to read previous purchases.

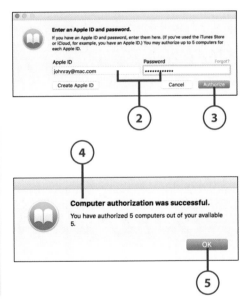

>>>Go Further
HITTING YOUR LIMIT

If you find that you've hit your maximum number of authorized systems (in iBooks or iTunes) you can use the Store menu to deauthorize the computer you're currently using, freeing up a spot. Alternatively, you can choose View My Account from the Store menu to view all authorized computers and a somewhat-hidden option to deauthorize *all* of them. You can only use this mass-deauthorization once a year, however, so use it wisely!

Purchasing Books

When iBooks is up and running, your next step is adding content. This is identical to the iTunes store, so refer to the previous section for a more detailed walkthrough. To use iBooks to purchase new books, follow these basic steps:

1. If you are viewing the iBooks library (you see either books you already own, or a blank screen), visit the iBooks Store by clicking the iBooks Store button in the upper left.

Finding the Button

The button reads "Library" when you're in the iBooks Store and "iBooks Store" when you're in your library.

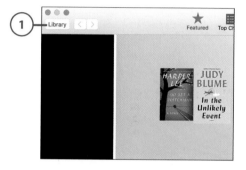

2. The iBooks window refreshes to show an iTunes-like store.

3. Use the toolbar buttons to choose between Featured content, Top Charts, NYTimes best sellers, Categories, and Top Authors.

4. Use the links and pop-up menu on the right-hand side to select between other popular book categories.

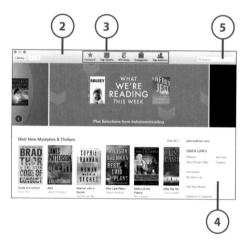

5. Search for books using the search field in the upper-right corner.

6. When you arrive at a title that you want, click the Buy Book button.

7. Enter your Apple ID and Password.

8. Click Buy.

9. Click the Arrow icon in the upper-right corner to show your iBook download status.

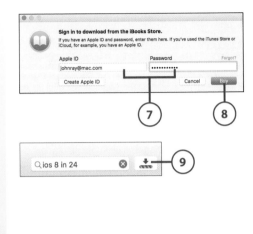

Kindle Me

Not a fan of the iBook Store? If you're a user of Amazon's Kindle eBook service, you'll find everything you need in a download of the Kindle app from the Mac App Store.

Viewing and Arranging Your iBooks Library

After you've made a few purchases, you can browse your virtual library—and even arrange your books into Collections. iBooks is perfectly suited to accommodate both prolific readers and the occasional book browser.

Browsing the iBooks Library

To browse the iBooks library (assuming you've made a purchase or two), just follow along:

1. If you are within the iBooks Store, click the Library button to view your book library.

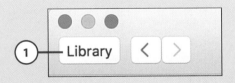

2. Click the All Books button to view all the content in your library.

3. Use the Sort By menu in the upper-right corner to set sorting criteria for the view.

4. Books marked with a cloud icon have not yet been downloaded to your computer. They download automatically when opened.

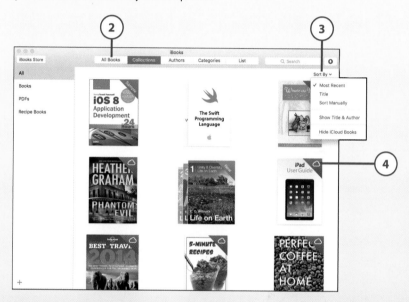

5. Click the Authors tab to view the books by author, with a list of Authors on the left.

6. Click an author's name to show the books written by that individual.

7. Click Categories to show books by category.

8. Click a category in the list on the left to show only the books in that category.

9. Use the List button to quickly view all books in your library and see whether or not they have been downloaded (no cloud icon).

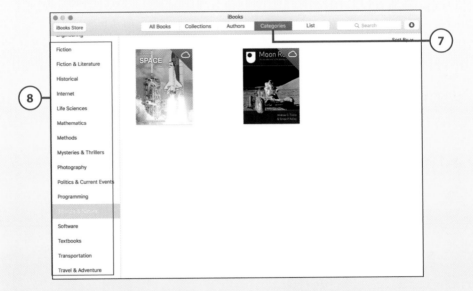

iBooks—It's Not Just for iBooks

You can use iBooks to manage any content in ePub or PDF format. Just drag compatible files into your iBooks library and they'll appear—ready for reading—just as if you had purchased them from the iBooks Store.

Organizing by Collection

In addition to the sections that Apple provides for browsing your library, you can create your own organization with Collections. To view, create, and manage Collections, do the following:

1. Click the Collections tab at the top of the iBooks Window.

2. Click the All collection to see all of your iBooks.

3. Click the Books collection to view all books, regardless of whether they were purchased or manually added.

4. Click PDFs to view all PDF files that were manually added to iBooks.

5. Click the + button at the bottom of the window to add a new category.

6. Name the category by clicking and typing (Recipe Books is used here).

7. Click and drag books from one of the predefined collections (All, Books, PDFs) into the new collection.

8. Collections help you organize your library as you see fit.

9. To remove a Collection, select it and press delete. The content in the collection is not removed (not shown).

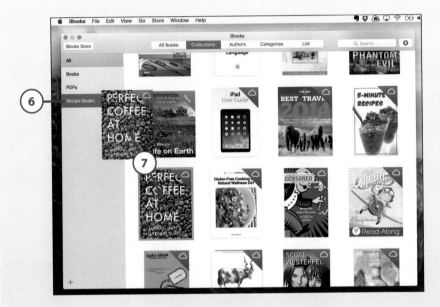

Searching for Searching for Bobby Fischer

If you've amassed a huge iBooks collection and no longer know exactly where your favorite book is, you can quickly search your entire library using the search field in the upper-right corner of the iBooks window.

Reading iBooks

Okay, you can buy books, you can organize them, but can you read them? Yes! iBooks does indeed enable you to read books. Not only can you read your books, but you can also make notes and highlights—and even change the color of your virtual paper!

Reading Basics

To get started reading with your favorite book and your favorite computer, first make sure that you've purchased the book and that it appears in the iBooks library. Then follow these steps:

1. Browse (using whatever method you'd like) to the book you'd like to read.

2. Double-click the title. If it hasn't been downloaded yet, iBooks downloads it.

3. A reading window appears.

4. Position your cursor next to the edges of the screen and click the arrows to move from page to page. Alternatively, swipe with two fingers to move between pages.

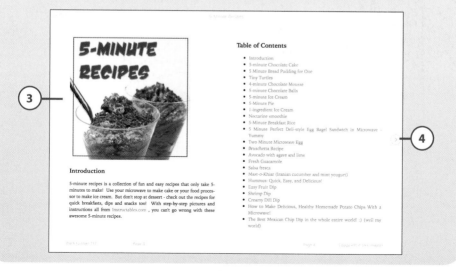

5. Click and drag at the bottom of the page to quickly move through the book.

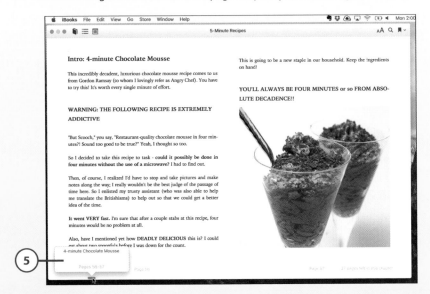

6. Click the list icon to show a table of contents for the book. Click any entry to jump to that page.

7. Click the book icon to return to the main iBooks library window.

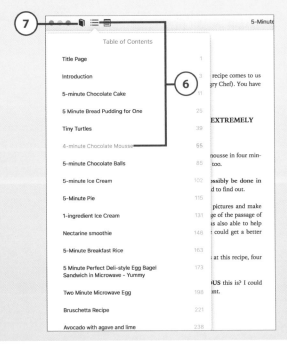

Using Annotations

Have you ever found something in a book that you wish you could easily refer to in the future? With iBooks, it's simple to create comments and highlights while you read—and you won't get yelled at for destroying your books!

1. Browse to a point in a book that you want to annotate.

2. Highlight the text you are interested in.

3. A pop-up window displays that points to your text.

4. Choose a color (or underline) to highlight the text.

5. Choose Add Note to set a note and highlight the text.

6. A note window appears. Type your message and then click outside the box.

7. View all your notes for a given book by clicking the Notes icon (a square box) in the toolbar.

8. The Notes panel lists all notes.

9. Click a note in the list to navigate to that note.

10. Use the magnifying glass icon to search your notes.

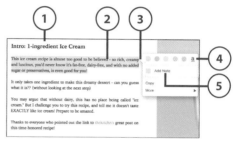

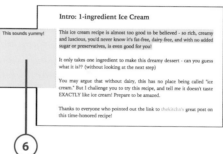

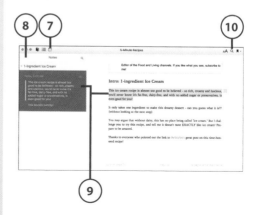

The More Menu

When you select text and bring up the annotation pop-up window, you see a More menu. Selecting More gives you the ability to search the Web/Wikipedia for the highlighted text, post it to social network sites, email it, or even hear it read aloud.

Adding Bookmarks

If you'd prefer to just bookmark content within a book (rather than annotating it), you can use the one-click bookmark tool. Follow these steps to bookmark (and return to) any page:

1. Navigate to the page that you want to bookmark.

2. Click the ribbon icon to toggle a bookmark on and off.

3. Click the down arrow beside the ribbon icon to show the bookmarks that have been set.

4. Select a bookmark to jump to that page.

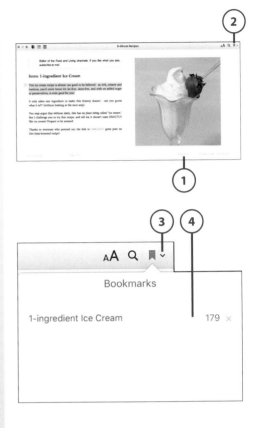

Fine-Tuning Your Display

If the default text size and screen color don't make for a comfortable reading environment, Apple has provided some settings to customize the display. To change your book's appearance while reading, follow these steps:

1. Click the AA icon in the toolbar while reading.

2. Use the buttons at the top to shrink or enlarge the text.

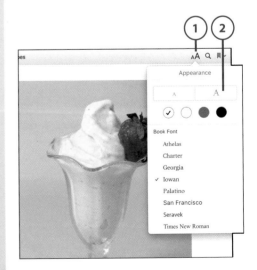

3. Use the White, Sepia, Gray, and Night buttons to set the color of the text and background.

4. Choose a font from the Book font list to set the type style for your book.

5. Click outside the menu to continue reading.

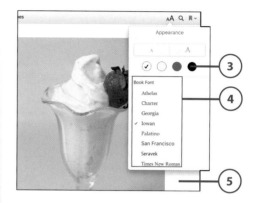

Getting Your Game on with Game Center

If your idea of fun is speeding through exotic locations and talking trash to your friends, Game Center may be your preferred entertainment option. El Capitan features Game Center, a social gaming system similar to Xbox Live and the Playstation Network. With Game Center, you can create lists of friends, compare games and game achievements, discover new games, and launch games that you have installed on your Mac. What's more, Game Center is fully integrated with iOS, so you can keep track of your friends (and frenemies) wherever you are.

Cross-Device Play—Sometimes

You might have heard that the OS X version of Game Center enables you to play games on your Mac against friends on their iPhones and iPads. It's true that this feature is available, but it's on a per-game basis for the developers to enable—it doesn't just start working if you have the same games installed on different devices.

Signing into Game Center

The first step to using Game Center is signing in. This requires an Apple ID, so it's a good idea to have one before starting. If you don't have one, however, it can guide you through the setup.

1. Open Game Center from the Launchpad or Applications folder.

2. Click Create Apple ID to get a new Apple ID, if needed.

3. If prompted, enter your Apple ID and Password in the provided fields.

4. Click Sign In. If this is your first time using Game Center, complete steps 5–8.

5. Enter a Nickname on the screen that appears.

6. Click the Public Profile if you want others to be able to search and find you within Game Center.

7. Click the Use Contacts checkbox if you want Game Center to use your contacts to try to find new friends.

8. Click Continue.

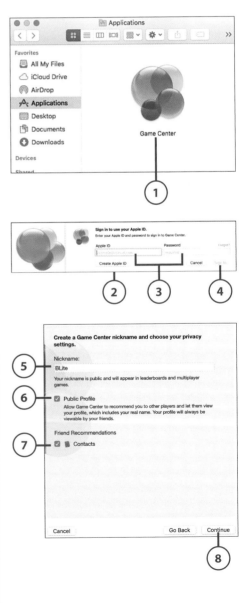

Navigating the Me Screen

After logging into Game Center, you are taken to a screen that describes your account status and provides some additional features.

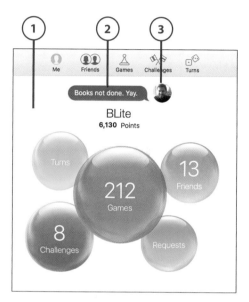

1. A summary of the games you have installed (across all your devices), points you have accumulated, number of friends, pending requests, and challenges is shown in bubbles near the center of the screen.

2. Click the speech bubble by your avatar to set your current status, or what is displayed to your friends in their Game Center.

3. Click your photo to take a new picture of yourself.

Managing Friends and Friend Requests

After getting into Game Center, it's a good idea to start adding and managing friends—otherwise, you'll be lonely. Let's review the process for sending friend requests, reviewing friend recommendations, and responding to requests that have been sent to you.

Sending a Friend Request

How do you get a new friend? By sending a request. To send a friend request to someone you know, follow these steps:

1. Click the Friends button at the top of the Game Center window.

2. Click the + button on the left side of the window.

3. A friend request dialog box appears. Enter the email address for the person you want to add.

4. Type a message to your potential friend.

5. Click Send. A request is sent to your friend, who can respond on her Mac or iOS device.

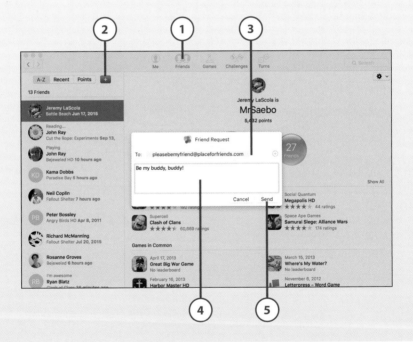

Responding to a Friend Request

When a friend request comes in, you can respond wherever you are by clicking a link in email. You can also respond directly in Game Center.

1. The Requests bubble on the Me screen updates with the number of pending requests. (The Game Center icon also shows this count.) Click the bubble.

2. Choose the friend request you want to view.

3. Click Ignore to ignore the request, or click Accept to make the person your friend.

4. If you clicked Accept, the person is added to your Friends list (not shown).

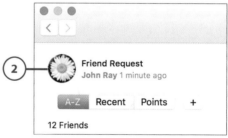

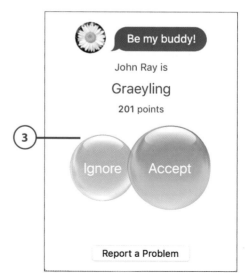

Getting Friend Recommendations

Not sure who you should add as a friend? Game Center can give you recommendations based on your contacts and the games you have installed. To see the recommendations, follow these steps:

1. Click the Friends button.

2. Scroll down the list until you see the Recommendations heading.

3. Click Show All to see all recommendations.

4. Choose an individual from the list to view his information on the right.

5. Click Send Friend Request to send a friend request to the individual.

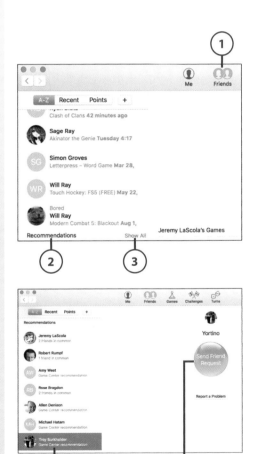

Sizing Up Your Friends

After you have established a few friends, you probably want to see how your gaming skills compare to theirs. Game Center enables you to drill down to view a number of different stats about your friends and their games. To see a few, follow these steps:

1. Click the Friends button.

2. Choose how your friends are sorted using the buttons at the top of the Friends list.

3. Filter your list down to a specific friend using the Search field, if desired.

4. Click an entry in the list to select a friend.

5. A summary of your friend's game-playing activity is shown on the right.

6. Click a game to drill down to more information.

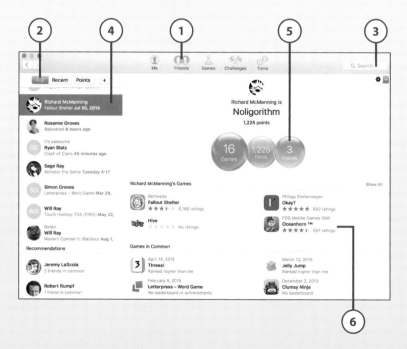

7. The window refreshes to show the scores and achievements that your friends have earned and how you compare.

Lost? Just Go Back

It's easy to drill down to a great detail of information in Game Center. If you ever feel lost, you can use the forward and back arrows in the upper-left corner; they work just like the arrows in a web browser.

Browsing by Game

In the previous step, you located a friend and used her as the starting point for browsing to a game and showing a comparison of activity. You can also take a more game-centric approach.

1. Click the Games button at the top of Game Center.

2. The window refreshes to list all your games across all devices and game recommendations at the top.

3. Search for individual games using the Search Games field.

4. Click a game to view information about it.

5. Use the Achievements button to show your personal achievements in the game.

6. Click Leaderboards to show how you compare against players worldwide.

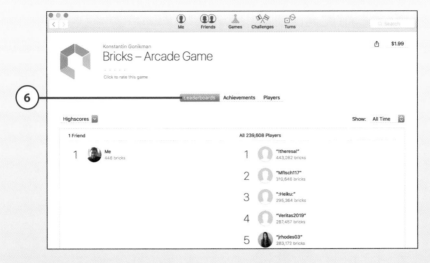

7. Use the Players button to display any friends who have recently played the game.

8. Click the Share button to message your friend and convince her to download the game.

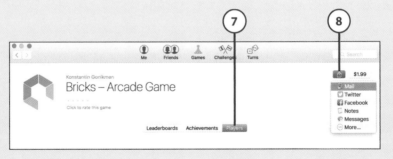

Making and Taking a Challenge

Within Game Center, you can challenge your friends to beat your achievements or game scores. For some games, you can even challenge them to a live match.

To send (or receive) a challenge, follow these steps:

1. Navigate to the game you want to challenge your friend in.

2. Click the achievement (or a score from the leaderboards) that you want to base the challenge around.

3. In the pop-over window, click Challenge Friends.

4. Pick the friends you want to challenge.

5. Click Next.

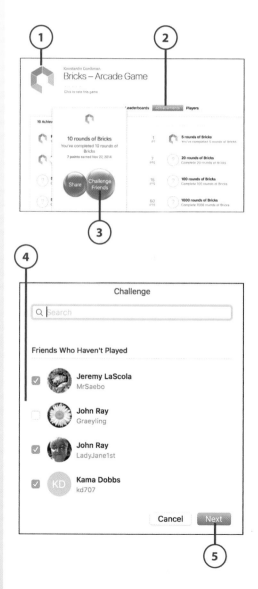

6. Enter a message (if desired) to go with the challenge.

7. Click Send. Your challenge will now be sent, and you'll be notified if your friends meet (or beat!) your results.

8. Click the Challenges button at the top of the Game Center window to view any Challenges your friends have sent you in return. This includes links to buy the game if you don't already own it.

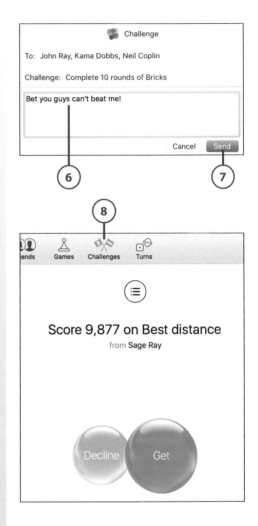

**Download and install
new apps using the
Mac App Store.**

**Use Family Sharing
to share your
purchases.**

In this chapter, you learn how to install applications on your Mac and keep El Capitan up-to-date, including:

→ Browsing the Mac App Store
→ Downloading and managing App Store applications
→ Downloading and installing non–App Store software
→ Working with OS X software distribution formats
→ Setting up Family Sharing of purchases
→ Configuring software updates and auto downloads
→ Managing extensions

Installing and Managing Applications and Extensions on Your Mac

Up to this point in the book, you've been looking at software that came as part of El Capitan. That's a bit limiting, don't you think? There is a wide world of software waiting to enhance your computing experience—including upgrades to El Capitan itself.

Through the use of the Mac App Store and its built-in update mechanism, you can install new applications, new extensions, and widgets, keep them up-to-date, and keep your Mac running smoothly and securely. When that isn't enough, you can turn to thousands of other non-App Store apps that run natively on your Mac.

Mac App Store

Applications make a Mac a Mac. As intangible as it is, a certain "something" about using a Mac application is rarely replicated on a Windows computer.

When you've become accustomed to the day-to-day operation of your Mac, you'll likely want to begin installing third-party software. The easiest place to do this is through the Mac App Store. Like the popular App Store for iOS devices, the Mac App Store is a one-stop shop for thousands of applications and extensions that you can install with point-and-click ease.

Logging into the App Store

To log into the store, follow these steps:

1. Open the App Store application from the Dock, Launchpad, or Applications folder.

Creating an ID

To use the Mac App Store, you need a registered Apple ID—the same account you used to access iCloud in Chapter 4, "Setting Up iCloud and Internet Accounts," will work just fine. If you don't have an ID, you can create one directly in the App Store.

2. The App Store window opens.

3. Click Sign In from the Quick Links on the right side of the page.

4. Provide your Apple ID and password in the form that appears.

5. Click Sign In.

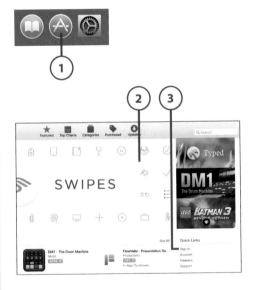

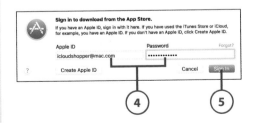

6. Your Login Status and links to
   your account information are
   shown in the Quick Links section.

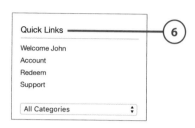

Browsing for Software

Part of the joy of using the App
Store is that browsing is simple and
fun—and, like iTunes and iBooks, it
works in the same manner as a web
browser. As you encounter links
(such as See All), click them to view
more information. You can browse
within a variety of categories that
cover the gamut of what you can do
on your Mac:

1. Follow steps 1–6 of the previous task, "Logging into the App
   Store."

2. Click the Featured icon to browse
   apps tagged by Apple as New and
   Noteworthy or Hot.

3. Click Top Charts to see the apps
   that are currently selling the best
   or being downloaded the most.

4. Click Categories to browse by
   the different types of software
   (games, business, developer, and
   so on).

5. When you see something you're
   interested in, click the icon or
   name.

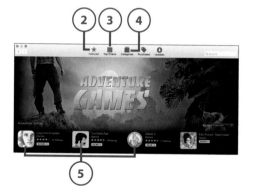

6. A full page of information, including reviews, opens.

7. Use the Forward and Back buttons to move back and forth between pages, just like a web browser.

Quick Links for Faster Browsing

The featured page actually contains more than the new/hot apps. In the column on the right side of the page, you can quickly jump to specific app categories to see Top Paid apps, Top Free apps, Extensions, and more without leaving the page.

Searching for Software

Sometimes you might know the software title you want but do not know where it is located. In these cases, you can simply search the App Store:

1. Follow steps 1–6 of the earlier task, "Logging into the App Store."

2. Type a search term or terms into the field in the upper-right corner. You can use application names, categories (news, for instance), and even author/publisher names.

3. As you type, a list of possible searches appears. Click one if you want to use it; otherwise, press Return to use the search term you've typed.

4. The Search results are displayed.

5. Use the Sort By menu to choose how the results are sorted within the window.

6. Click App Icons or Names to view more information.

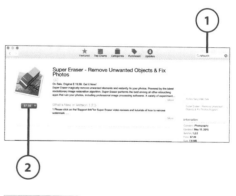

Purchasing Software

When you've decided to purchase software, the process couldn't be simpler. Follow these instructions to download and install software on your Mac:

1. Browse or search for a software title, as described in the previous tasks, "Browsing for Software" and "Searching for Software."

2. From within the search/browse results or the larger information page, click the Price button.

3. The Price button changes to read Buy App. If the title is free, it reads Get. Click the Buy App (or Get) button.

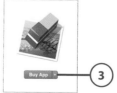

Remember It on Payday!

The right side of the Price button for an app has a downward-pointing arrow. This is actually a separate button that opens a pop-up menu. Use this menu to copy a link to the app or to send an email message to someone (maybe yourself) about the app.

4. Provide your App Store Apple ID and password, if prompted.

5. Click Sign In.

6. The application immediately downloads to your Applications folder and is visible in Launchpad.

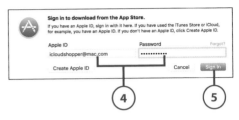

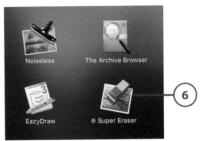

>>>Go Further
SPARKLING NEW APPS

New apps you purchase through the App Store have a blue dot beside their names in Launchpad, helping you see what has been added.

It's Not All Good

I Don't Want It—Make It Go Away!

If the App Store makes it so easy to install things, it certainly makes it easy to delete them, right? Yes and no. The App Store is used for installing, but Launchpad is used to uninstall the apps. Learn about Launchpad in Chapter 2, "Making the Most of Your Screen Space."

Apps That Aren't Apps

You'll notice that I frequently refer to "software" rather than apps. Starting with El Capitan, you can now purchase extensions in addition to apps. Although the process is the same, extensions don't act as apps—they offer features in your existing applications, provide new ways of sharing, and give you simple utilities and controls in the El Capitan Notification Center. We look at how to manage extensions a bit later in this chapter.

Reinstalling Software and Installing Purchases on Other Macs

One of the best things about buying applications through the App Store is that you can install them on other Macs you own. No licensing hassles—just download and go. You can also reinstall software that you may have deleted in the past but want to start using again. To download a title that you (or possibly a family member) have purchased, but that isn't installed, follow steps 1–6 of the "Logging into the App Store" task and then complete these steps:

1. Click the Purchased icon at the top of the App Store window.

2. The Purchases list is displayed, along with a button/label showing the status of each app.

Family Sharing

With Family Sharing in El Capitan, you can even set up a "family" of people who can share purchases among themselves. We explore this a bit later in the chapter.

---

3. Apps labeled as Open are currently installed and up-to-date.

4. Click the Install button to install (or reinstall) an app that you already own.

5. Click the Update button to update a piece of software that is currently installed.

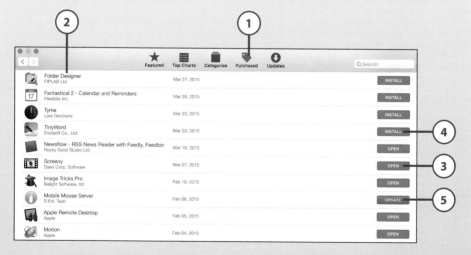

Auto-Install Your Apps!

El Capitan prompts you to turn on automatic downloading of apps that you download on other machines. If you activate this feature, any software you download on one Mac will automatically be downloaded on any other Mac that is logged into the Mac App Store with your account. You can also control this via the App Store preference pane, which you learn about later in this chapter.

Hiding Apps You No Longer Want

I've downloaded a lot of apps; you probably will, too. Unfortunately, these won't all be apps you want to keep updating (or even remember that you purchased). To hide an app from the update list, follow these steps after logging into the App Store.

1. Click the Purchased icon at the top of the App Store window.

2. Right-click the item you want to hide.

3. Choose Hide Purchase to remove the item from the update list.

Find What's Missing

To show the items that you've hidden, choose the Account quick link from the right side of the Mac App Store after following the instructions in the section "Logging into the App Store." Use the Hidden Purchases options to show the hidden apps.

Installing Non–App Store Applications

The App Store is great, but that doesn't mean that it defines the limits of what you can do on your Mac. There are certain restrictions in place on the App Store that make some pieces of software impossible to distribute through that site. There are also thousands of developers who want to sell and market their applications through their own websites.

By default, El Capitan enables you to install and run any software you want—but this can be disabled by an administrator. Read the section "Application Execution Security," in Chapter 14, "Securing and Protecting Your Mac," to learn how to adjust the controls to enable (or disable) software installations on your Mac.

Installing software from non–App Store sources is frequently a matter of browsing the Web in Safari, clicking a download link, and copying the application to your Applications folder.

Getting the Lowdown on the Download

Recall that El Capitan has a Downloads folder that is available in your Dock. Software archives that you download in Safari or most other Mac applications are stored in this location.

Unarchiving Zip Files

A decade ago, almost all Mac applications were distributed in a compressed archive format called SIT (StuffIt). Today the Mac has adopted a standard used on Windows and other platforms called zip files. A zip file can contain one or more compressed files.

To unarchive a zip file and access the contents, follow these steps:

1. Find the file that you want to unarchive.

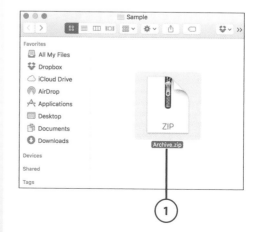

2. Double-click the file. Unarchiving can be virtually instantaneous or can take several seconds, depending on the archive size.

3. The contents of the archive are made available in the same folder where the zip file is located.

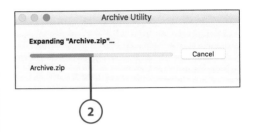

Just StuffIt

If you find that you need to deal with a StuffIt file, you can download StuffIt from http://www.stuffit.com. Despite the decreasing use of the format, it has been actively maintained over the years.

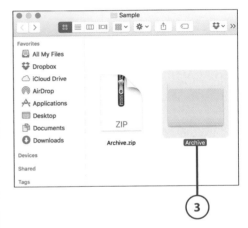

Accessing Disk Images

Sometimes applications are distributed on a disk image, or DMG file. When mounted on your system, DMGs act like a virtual disk drive. Files in a DMG must be copied off the disk image by way of an installer or a simple drag-and-drop process.

To mount and access the contents of a disk image, follow this process:

1. Find the disk image you want to access.

2. Double-click the DMG file. The disk image mounts and appears as a disk in the Finder.

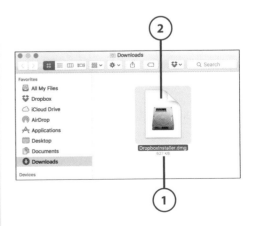

3. Access the files in the disk as you would any other storage device.

4. To eject the disk image, click the Eject icon beside the mounted disk in the Finder sidebar or drag it to the trash.

> ## >>>Go Further
>
> ## WHERE CAN I FIND SOFTWARE FOR MY MAC?
>
> Apple writes great applications for maintaining a mobile lifestyle, but third-party publishers have created utilities that meet or exceed Apple's own efforts.
>
> Many websites track Macintosh applications, but two of the best are MacUpdate (http://www.macupdate.com/) and VersionTracker (http://www.versiontracker.com/).

Sharing Purchases with Family Sharing

El Capitan includes the ability to activate Family Sharing. Family Sharing makes it possible to share music, book, and app purchases among up to five additional accounts. These five individuals (presumably family and/or friends) will have access to your downloads and will be able to download and redownload content that you've purchased on the App Store, iTunes, or the iBook Store.

Each family has an "organizer" who manages purchases. As the organizer, you are responsible for paying for the purchases made by your family.

Setting Up Family Sharing (Organizer)

To set up a new Family Sharing account, open System Preferences and then follow these steps:

1. Open the iCloud Preferences panel.

2. Click the Set Up Family Button.

3. Click Continue on the Intro screen that appears (not shown).

4. Click Continue to acknowledge that you want to be the organizer for your family.

5. Family Sharing prompts for the account to use for purchases. Click Continue to move on or Use a Different Account to enter another Apple ID.

6. Click Continue to acknowledge the payment source you'll be using for purchases. If your account does not have a payment type associated with it, you'll be prompted to enter one.

7. Click the Me line to edit your account information, disable sharing, or begin adding family members, as described in the next section.

8. Click Done to end Family Sharing Setup.

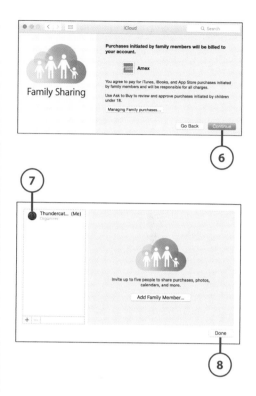

Adding a Family Member

To add a new member to Family Sharing (remember you can have up to five, including yourself), open System Preferences and then complete these steps:

1. Open the iCloud Preferences panel.

2. Click the Manage Family button.

3. Click Add Family Member on the management screen, or click the + button.

4. In the Add a Family Member dialog, use the first radio button and field to select and enter the email for a family member you want to invite.

5. If you'd like to make a new account for a child, click the second radio button to be guided through a new account wizard.

6. Click Continue.

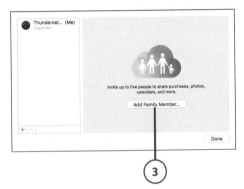

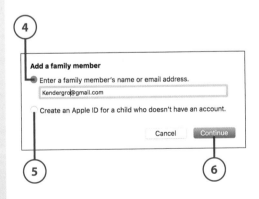

7. Enter the verification information requested.

8. Click Continue to move on.

9. When prompted, you can use the first radio button and field to ask the family member to enter his or her password (on your Mac) to immediately join the family.

10. If your family member would rather accept on his or her own device, select the radio box beside Send an Invitation. This delivers an email with a link for the invitee to join your family.

11. Click Continue to move on.

12. The invitation is sent, and OS X shows the status.

13. Click Done to exit family management.

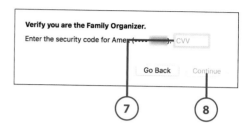

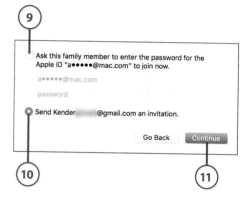

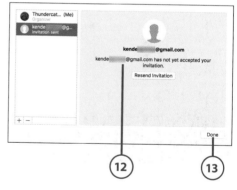

Managing Family Members

To manage your family members and invitees, open System Preferences and then follow along:

1. Open the iCloud Preferences panel.

2. Click the Manage Family button.

3. In the list on the left, click the Organizer line to manage your personal settings.

4. Click individuals whom you've previously invited to resend their invitation.

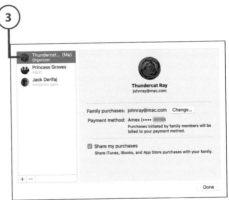

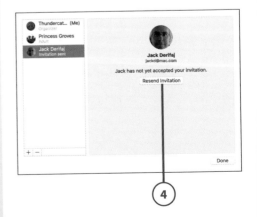

5. Click other members to configure their settings and to choose
   whether they can approve others'
   purchases.

6. Click the – button to entirely
   remove a member. This eliminates his or her ability to use the
   purchased family content.

7. Click Done to finish managing
   your family.

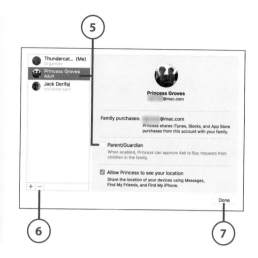

Keeping Your Applications and Operating System Up-to-Date (New!)

Keeping your operating system and applications up-to-date is important
both from the standpoint of maintaining your system security and providing
the best possible user experience.

With El Capitan, you can activate an automatic update process that periodically checks and prompts you with available updates. You can even set all
your Macs to automatically download applications that you've purchased
through the App Store—ensuring a seamless computing experience moving
from system to system.

How Will I Be Notified of an Update?

All El Capitan software update notifications appear in the Notification Center. Using the controls on the notification, you can postpone its install or have it applied immediately. To learn more about the Notification Center, refer to Chapter 1, "Managing Your Desktop."

Configuring Software Updates and Auto Downloads

To configure how your Mac handles software updates and new downloads from Apple, follow these steps:

1. Open the App Store System Preferences panel.

2. Select the Automatically Check for Updates checkbox to have your system periodically look for new software downloads.

3. Check Download Newly Available Updates in the Background to have your system download the update packages while it is idle so that they are available to install when you are ready.

4. Check Install App Updates to keep all your App Store purchases automatically updated.

5. Check Install OS X Updates to ensure your operating system is always on the latest possible version.

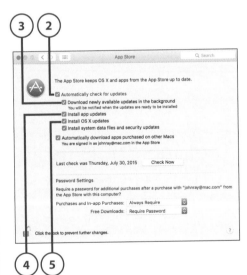

6. Choose Install System Data Files and Security Updates to keep many of the critical OS files automatically updated without any interaction required.

7. If you'd like all your App Store purchases to be downloaded automatically to your Mac, check Automatically Download Apps Purchased on Other Macs.

8. Click Check Now to immediately check for new updates.

9. To configure when passwords are required for downloads, use the Purchases and In-app Purchases and Free Downloads pop-up menus.

10. Close the System Preferences when finished.

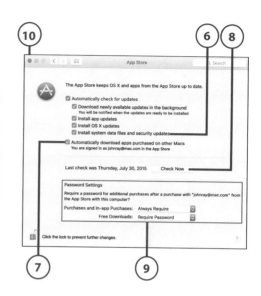

Manually Applying Software Updates

If you're like many people (myself included), you want the latest and greatest without waiting. With the Mac App Store, you can manually update your system as soon as updates become available: El Capitan manages your applications and system updates in a single location.

To check and install application and OS updates, do the following:

1. Open the App Store.

Notification Badges
The App Store icon and App Store menu item under the Apple menu display a counter badge listing the number of updates available to you. Update notifications also appear in the Notification Center.

2. Click the Updates button in the App Store toolbar.

3. All your available app updates are listed.

4. Click the Update All button to update all software at once.

5. Click an individual Update button to update just a single app.

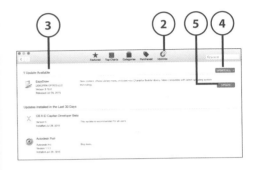

6. Update progress appears in the App Store window, but you don't have to wait to continue using your computer. The updates are automatically installed in the background.

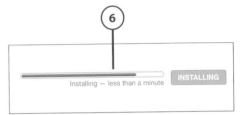

Confirming Updates

Depending on the type of update, you might be asked to give your password and accept any applicable software license agreements before an update is installed. You might also be required to quit running applications or even reboot your Mac for low-level OS updates.

>>>Go Further
MICROMANAGE YOUR UPDATE SCHEDULE

To force your updates to occur at a specific time, click the right side of the Update All button. This displays a drop-down menu that enables you to choose when (in an hour, tomorrow, and so on) updates should be applied.

Managing Extensions

Extensions enable you to customize how your El Capitan system looks and works—without compromising the security. This great feature, however, isn't front and center in the user interface. You've seen how to use built-in extensions in other chapters, but how do you add new ones to your system?

To find extensions, you'll need to read the notes that come with the applications you download from the Mac App Store. Apps may come packaged with extensions, and app updates may even add extensions. Frankly, you probably won't even know when you download an extension—until you go looking for it.

Managing Installed Extensions

After you install an application that adds an extension, you need a way to manage it. The Extensions panel comes in handy here. Follow these steps to keep your extension software in order:

1. Open the Extensions System Preferences panel.

2. Choose a category on the left—from All, Actions, Share Menu, Finder, and Today widgets.

3. Within each category, use the checkboxes to enable or disable an extension. If an option is grayed out, you cannot modify it.

4. Some categories, such as the Share Menu, let you click and drag to reorder where the extensions appear.

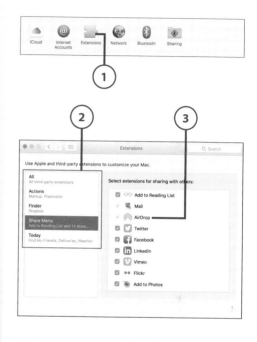

**Optimize your Mac's
built-in hardware in
System Preferences.**

In this chapter, you find out how to make your Mac hardware work at its best for your particular needs, including:

→ Balancing performance and battery efficiency
→ Fine-tuning the keyboard settings
→ Adjusting trackpad and mouse gestures
→ Setting sound input and output
→ Configuring display resolution and color
→ Recording audio and video

Making the Most of Your Mac Hardware

When you purchased your Mac, you bought more than just a "computer"—you bought a power system, monitor, keyboard, track-pad (and maybe a mouse), video camera, microphone, and speakers! On a traditional desktop system, these might all be separate components, but on your Mac, they're part of a tightly integrated package.

To help personalize your Mac, you can adjust many of the settings available for these hardware devices, such as enabling trackpad gestures, setting a system boot and shutdown schedule, setting your microphone up for dictation, and much more. El Capitan even includes a few out-of-the-box tricks such as video, audio, and screen recording that let you take advantage of the built-in FaceTime HD camera (except on the Mac Mini) without needing any additional software.

Energy-Saving Settings

If you're a MacBook owner, chances are you frequently use it just like a desktop computer; battery life is a non-issue. When you're on the go, however, the battery becomes the lifeblood of the system. You need to make sure that you get the performance you need from your system, when you need it. Monitoring the battery life of your computer is necessary to keep you aware of when you need a recharge, as well as whether there are issues occurring with your MacBook's built-in battery.

For non-MacBook users, you don't need to worry about batteries running down, but that doesn't mean you should waste electricity. Configuring settings such as how long the computer waits for input before its energy-saver settings kick in is a good way to make sure you're being an energy-conscious individual.

Monitoring Battery Life and Application Energy Use (MacBook Only)

Follow these steps to use and configure the El Capitan battery status monitor:

1. By default, the battery status is shown in a battery icon in the menu bar. The dark portion of the battery indicates the remaining life of the battery.

2. Click the battery icon to show the amount of time remaining until the battery power is exhausted, or, if the MacBook is plugged in, until the battery is recharged.

3. Review the applications listed in the Apps Using Significant Energy section. If you aren't using these apps, you should quit them to conserve battery life.

4. Use the Show Percentage option to include the percentage of the battery life left directly in the menu bar.

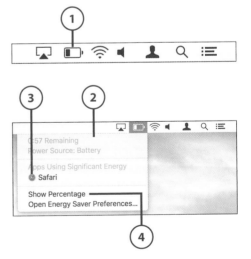

Battery Status

If battery status is not visible in your menu bar, it has been manually removed. You can re-add the icon to the menu bar using the Show battery status in the menu bar option in the Energy Saver System Preference panel.

Battery Condition

If you suspect something might be wrong with your battery, the Battery Status menu will tell you. If you don't see any warnings, you're fine! To force the menu to show the condition of your battery at any time, hold the Option key and open the Battery Status menu.

Configuring Display, Computer, and Hard Disk Sleep

To help improve battery life, El Capitan includes the Energy Saver System Preferences panel.

1. Click the System Preferences icon on the Dock to open it and then click the Energy Saver icon.

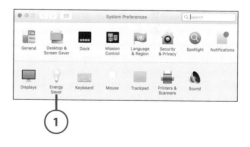

2. Click the Battery button to configure the system for when it is
running on battery power (not
available on desktop Macs). Click
Power Adapter to access the
settings for when it is connected
directly to a power adapter.

3. Drag the sliders, Computer Sleep
and Display Sleep, to set the
period of inactivity after which
your Mac puts itself or its display
into Sleep mode.

4. Select Put Hard Disks to Sleep
When Possible to shut down your
hard drive when it's not in use.
This helps save power but sacri-
fices some speed.

5. Select Slightly Dim the Display
While on Battery Power to have
your display run at a lower brightness level.

6. Select Enable Power Nap While
on Battery Power to have your
Mac wake occasionally for backups and network updates while
sleeping. What your system does
depends on whether it is running
via Battery or Power Adapter.

7. Close the System Preferences.

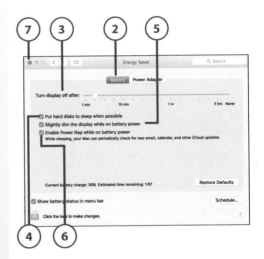

Powered Options

The Power Adapter options include a
few additional settings not available
when running on battery—including
the ability to wake up for network
access and preventing the Mac from
sleeping automatically (such as when
the MacBook display is closed).

Creating a Sleep/Wake Schedule

If you have a daily schedule and want your Mac to follow it, you can configure wake-up and sleep/shutdown times. Follow these steps to set a power schedule for your system.

1. Click the System Preferences icon on the Dock and then click the Energy Saver icon.

2. Click the Schedule button at the bottom of the window.

3. To have your computer start up on a schedule, click the checkbox beside Start Up or Wake.

4. Use the Every Day pop-up menu to set when (weekdays, weekends, and so on) the startup should occur.

5. Set the time for the computer to start up.

6. To configure your computer to go to sleep, shutdown, or restart, click the checkbox in front of the Sleep pop-up menu.

7. Use the Sleep pop-up menu to choose whether your Mac should sleep, shutdown, or restart.

8. Configure the day and time for the shutdown to occur, just as you did with the start options in steps 4 and 5.

9. Click OK.

10. Close the System Preferences.

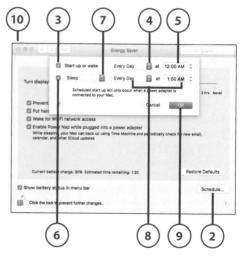

Updating Keyboard and Dictation Settings

Having trouble getting used to your keyboard? Never fear! Using the built-in keyboard settings, you can adjust the keyboard repeat rate, key delay, and even set system-wide shortcuts for trackpad and mouse-free operation.

If you prefer to talk rather than type, El Capitan includes built-in dictation, accessed from anywhere with a single keystroke.

Setting Keyboard Repeat Rate

To choose how frequently the keys on your keyboard repeat, and how long it takes to start repeating, follow these simple steps:

1. Click the System Preferences icon on the Dock and then click the Keyboard icon.

2. Click the Keyboard button at the top of the panel.

3. Use the Key Repeat slider to set how quickly letters appear when you hold down a key on your key-board. Move the slider all the way to the left to turn off repeating.

4. Move the Delay Until Repeat slider to choose how long you must hold down a key before it starts repeating.

5. Close the System Preferences.

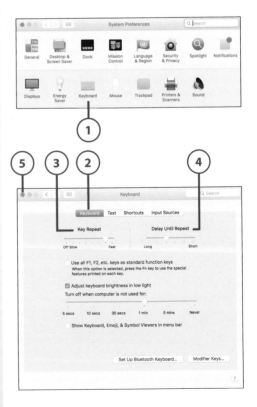

Using Function Keys

You've probably noticed that the top row of keys on your Apple keyboard have special functions, such as dimming the display, changing the volume, and so on. These keys, however, are also function keys that your applications might need. To set the keys to always work as function keys without having to hold down the fn key, click the Use all F1, F2, etc. Keys as Standard Function Keys checkbox.

Changing Keyboard Illumination (MacBook Only)

When it gets dark, your keyboard comes to life, lighting the way for your typing. To activate this function and control how long the lighting stays on, follow these steps:

1. Click the System Preferences icon on the Dock, and then click the Keyboard icon. (Make sure the Keyboard button is chosen in the panel that opens.)

2. Check the Adjust Keyboard Brightness in Low Light to automatically turn on the keyboard backlight when your environment gets dark.

3. Drag the Turn Off slider to choose how long the keyboard remains lit when your computer is idle.

4. Close the System Preferences.

Setting Keyboard Brightness...
from Your Keyboard

You can adjust keyboard brightness using the keyboard dim/bright keys (shared with F5 and F6).

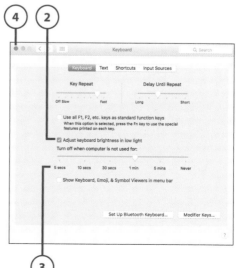

Creating Keyboard Shortcuts

There are times you might find yourself working with your Mac and thinking, "Geez, I wish I could just push a key for that rather than having to mouse around." Using keyboard shortcuts, you can create key commands for almost anything. There are two types of shortcuts supported in El Capitan—traditional shortcuts where you must press a key combination, and text shortcuts where you type a certain string and it is substituted with another. We will start with the latter.

Enabling Text Shortcuts and Spelling Correction

To set a shortcut for frequently typed text, follow these steps.

1. Click the System Preferences icon on the Dock, and then click the Keyboard icon.

2. Click the Text button at the top of the panel.

3. Select the Correct Spelling Automatically checkbox to enable auto-correct across all your applications.

4. Select the Use Smart Quotes and Dashes checkbox to enable straight quotes to automatically be replaced by characters of your choosing.

5. Set the drop-down menus for Double Quotes and Single Quotes to the characters you'd like to appear. The default is for curly quotes to be used.

6. Click the + button at the bottom of the list on the left to create a text replacement shortcut.

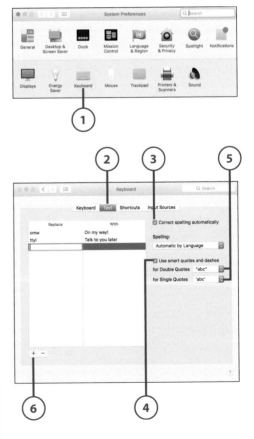

7. Use the left column field to enter the shortcut text you want to type ("brb," for example).

8. Use the right column to enter the full text it should be replaced with ("Be right back").

9. Use the – button to remove any shortcuts you are no longer using.

10. Close the System Preferences.

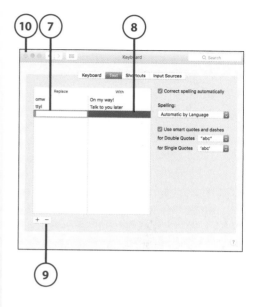

Setting Shortcuts for Existing El Capitan Actions

To set the shortcut for an existing system feature, follow these steps:

1. Click the System Preferences icon on the Dock and then click the Keyboard icon.

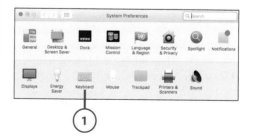

2. Click the Shortcuts button.

3. Choose one of the El Capitan system features from the left pane.

4. Scroll through the list of available actions in the right pane.

5. Click the checkbox in front of an action to enable it.

6. Click to the far right of an action name to edit its shortcut field.

7. Press the keys that you want to assign to the shortcut. If you are setting an F-key (for example, F12) that already has another function, you need to press the Function (fn) key on the keyboard to set the F key as the shortcut.

8. Close the System Preferences after making all of your changes.

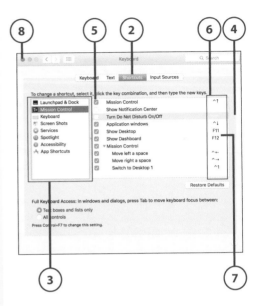

Setting Shortcuts for Arbitrary Applications

To configure a shortcut that works with an arbitrary application, not a built-in feature, do the following:

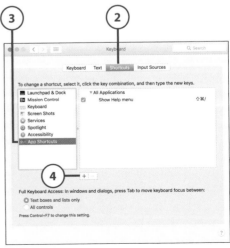

1. Click the System Preferences icon on the Dock, and then click the Keyboard icon.

2. Click the Shortcuts button.

3. Click the App Shortcuts entry in the list on the left side of the window.

4. Click the + button at the bottom of the shortcut list.

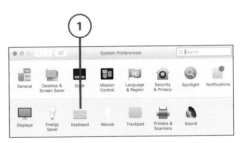

5. In the dialog box that opens, use the Application pop-up menu to choose an application to which you want to assign a shortcut.

6. Enter into the Menu Title field the exact wording of the menu item that you want the keyboard shortcut to invoke.

7. Click into the Keyboard Shortcut field and then press the keys you want to set as the shortcut.

8. Click Add when you're satisfied with your settings.

9. Close the System Preferences.

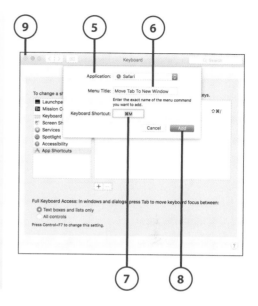

Activating Dictation

If you find that your Mac's keyboard is tiring your fingers, you may want to switch to using the El Capitan dictation feature. This enables you to input text *anywhere* using your voice. The only requirement is that you work in a noise-controlled environment (or have a high-quality headset). In El Capitan, you have the option of voice recognition being performed by Apple's cloud servers or locally on your machine.

Enabling Dictation

To enable dictation support and configure how it is triggered, follow these steps:

1. Click the System Preferences icon on the Dock and then click the Dictation & Speech icon.

2. Click the Dictation button at the top of the panel.

3. Click the On radio button to turn on dictation support.

4. Click Use Enhanced Dictation to enable local (non-iCloud) dictation support. You need about 1.2GB of free space for El Capitan to download additional software.

5. Click the label below the microphone image to set your preferred input mic.

6. Use the Shortcut drop-down menu to configure what key combination will start dictation.

7. Set the language you will be speaking using the Language drop-down menu.

8. Close the System Preferences when finished.

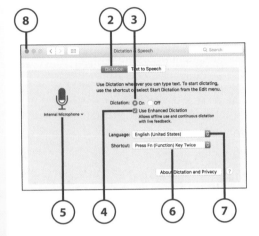

Your Mac Can Talk Back

Your Mac can talk back to you using a variety of different voices. To configure speech feedback, click the Text to Speech button at the top of the Dictation & Speech Preferences panel. This will let you test and choose your favorite speech synthesizer and the rate of speech.

Using Dictation

To use dictation, you must have it enabled (see the preceding task) and have an active Internet connection. If you meet those qualifications, just complete these steps to type with your voice:

1. Position your cursor where you want to dictate.

2. Press the key combination you configured when enabling dictation (not shown).

3. The dictation microphone appears. Begin speaking now—be sure to speak the name of the punctuation symbols you want to insert, such as "period," "comma," and so on.

4. Press any key or click Done to end dictation. After a short pause, the spoken text is inserted into the document.

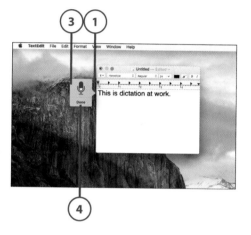

Changing Trackpad and Mouse Options

Whether you're a mouser or a trackpad devotee, Apple's hardware offers precision input in a multitouch package. Although these devices are intuitive for beginners, they can be customized to provide advanced features within El Capitan. Using the Trackpad and Mouse preferences, you can fine-tune the operation of your input device and set up different multifinger gestures in popular applications.

Perfect Pairing

If you've just purchased a new input device and need to connect it, skip ahead to Chapter 13, "Connecting Peripherals to Your Mac," for details on Bluetooth pairing.

Setting the Trackpad Speed and Click Pressure

To choose how quickly your trackpad follows your input, follow these steps:

1. Click the System Preferences icon on the Dock and then click the Trackpad icon.

2. Click the Point & Click button at the top of the window.

3. Choose how quickly the cursor moves by dragging the Tracking Speed slider.

4. If you have a new Force Touch trackpad, use the Click Pressure and Force Click and Haptic Feedback options to configure how hard you have to click and whether a "force click" (pushing extra hard) registers with El Capitan.

5. Close the System Preferences.

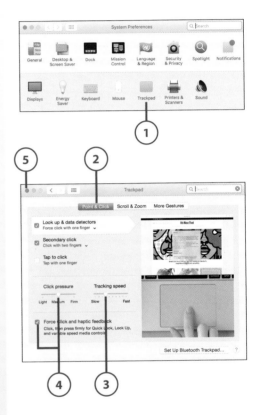

Controlling Trackpad Gestures

Apple trackpads can take advantage of a wide range of different two-, three-, and even four-finger motions to control your applications.

1. Click the System Preferences icon on the Dock and then click the Trackpad icon.

2. Use the Point & Click settings to configure click and drag options and dictionary look-ups.

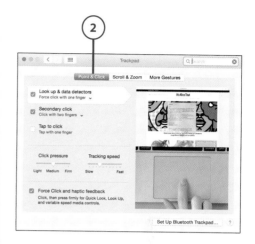

3. Use the Scroll & Zoom settings section to control scrolling, rotation, and pinching gestures.

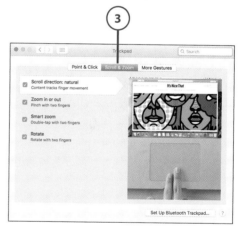

4. The More Gestures settings control advanced features, such as whether swiping to the left or right moves forward or backward in Safari and how Mission Control is activated.

5. Many settings contain a drop-down menu to fine-tune the gesture.

6. As you mouse over a particular setting, a video demonstrating the action appears in the right side of the window.

7. Close the System Preferences.

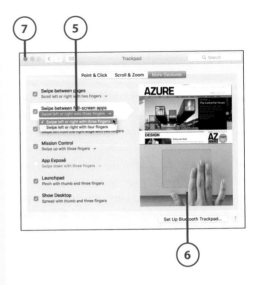

Configuring the Magic Mouse Speed

The Apple Magic Mouse is a multi-touch trackpad and mouse in one. Although it doesn't support nearly as many gestures as the trackpad, it's still a capable device. To configure the Magic Mouse tracking speed, follow these steps:

1. Click the System Preferences icon on the Dock and then and click the Mouse icon.

2. Click the Point & Click button at the top of the window.

3. Choose how quickly the cursor moves by dragging the Tracking slider.

4. Close the System Preferences.

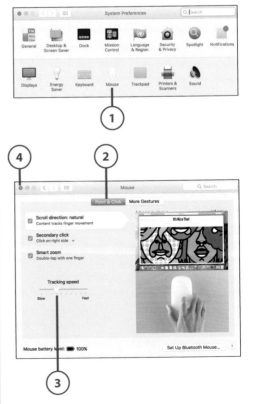

Configuring Magic Mouse Gestures

To set up the different single and two-finger gestures supported on the Magic Mouse, complete the following:

1. Click the System Preferences icon on the Dock and then click the Mouse icon.

2. Use the Point & Click settings to configure click, scrolling, and zooming.

3. The More Gestures settings control advanced features, such as whether swiping to the left or right moves forward or backward in Safari and how Mission Control is activated.

4. Some settings contain a drop-down menu to fine-tune the gesture.

5. As you mouse over a particular setting, a video demonstrating the action appears in the right side of the window.

6. Close the System Preferences.

If You Have to Choose...

Choose the trackpad. Even if you are a life-long mouser, you'll find that Apple's trackpad gesture support integrates perfectly into El Capitan and makes performing common tasks similar to using an iPad.

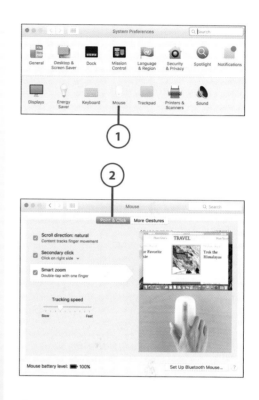

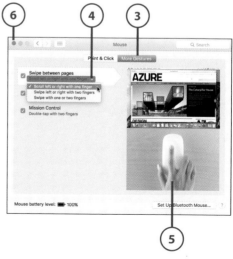

Adjusting Your Display

Your Mac's display is your window into your computer, so it's important that you configure your display to best suit your needs. For detailed CAD or drawing, you might want to use the full resolution. Gamers looking for the fastest framerates or late-night typing might call for a larger (lower resolution) option. Using the Display settings, you can control the image so that it is right for the task at hand.

Setting Display Resolution

The display resolution is the number of pixels that are viewable on the screen at any time. Lower the resolution for a larger image—or raise it, for smaller details. To control the screen resolution on your system, follow these steps:

1. Click the System Preferences icon on the Dock and then click the Displays icon.

2. Click the Display button at the top of the panel.

3. Click the Scaled radio button. Alternatively, the default radio button (Default for Display) chooses the best option for your system.

4. Choose one of the listed resolutions to immediately switch your display. Note that some resolutions might look fuzzy on your screen because your Mac has to scale the images.

5. Close the System Preferences.

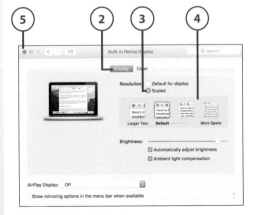

What Are Mirroring Options?

When setting your display resolution, you'll notice a checkbox for showing Mirroring Options in your menu bar. This is for working with external displays that can mirror your Mac's screen. You can read more about this feature in Chapter 13.

Controlling Display Brightness

Display brightness is a personal setting; some individuals like muted, dimmed displays and others like colors offered by full-brightness settings. To set the brightness of your display, follow these steps:

1. Click the System Preferences icon on the Dock and then click the Displays icon.

2. Click the Display button at the top of the panel.

3. Drag the Brightness slider left or right to dim or brighten the display.

4. Click the Automatically Adjust Brightness and Ambient Light Compensation checkboxes to have your screen dim or brighten depending on the time of day and your room's ambient lighting. Note that some of these settings are available only on modern MacBooks.

5. Close the System Preferences.

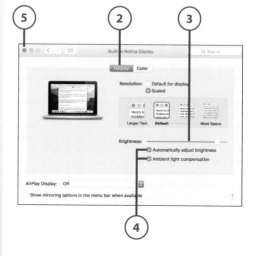

Adjusting Brightness from Your Keyboard

You can also adjust display brightness using the dim/bright keys (shared with F1 and F2) on your keyboard.

Choosing a Color Profile

Color profiles help keep colors consistent between computers with different monitors. By choosing a color profile that is calibrated for your display, you're ensured that colors you see on one machine match a similarly calibrated display on another machine. To choose a calibration profile, follow these steps:

1. Click the System Preferences icon on the Dock and then click the Displays icon.

2. Click the Color button at the top of the panel.

3. Click the preferred profile in the Display Profile list. The changes are immediately applied.

4. Close the System Preferences.

Where Do These Profiles Come From?

You can add profiles to your system by installing software or by running the calibration procedure, which creates your own personalized color profile.

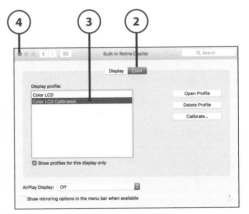

Calibrating the Display

If you'd like to calibrate your display manually, El Capitan provides a wizard-like interface for choosing the best display settings for your Mac.

1. Click the System Preferences icon on the Dock and then click the Displays icon.

2. Click the Color button at the top of the panel.

3. Hold down Option and then click Calibrate.

4. The Display Calibrator Assistant starts.

5. Click the Expert Mode checkbox to get the best results. (This isn't visible if you didn't hold down Option while starting calibration.)

6. Click Continue to proceed through the assistant.

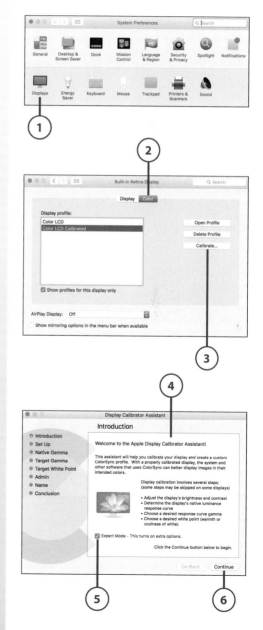

7. Follow the onscreen instructions to test the output of your display and click Continue to move on to the next screen.

8. When finished, enter a name for the new calibrated profile.

9. Click Continue to save the profile.

10. The new profile is added to the color profile list.

11. Close the System Preferences.

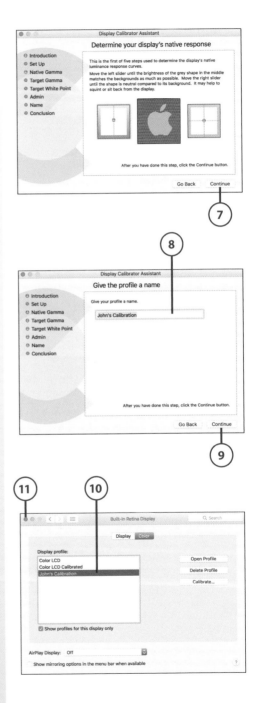

Setting Sound Input and Output

Sound has never been an afterthought on Macintosh systems, and yours is no different. Your system is equipped with a stereo sound system, head-phone jack, microphone jack (shared with the headphone jack in recent models), and even digital audio out. You can configure these input and out-put options to reflect your listening needs.

Setting the Output Volume

Volume, as you might expect, is one control that is needed system-wide. To control the output volume of your system, follow these steps:

1. Click the speaker icon in the menu bar.

2. Drag the slider up to increase the volume, or slide it down to decrease the volume.

3. Drag the slider all the way to the bottom to mute all output sounds.

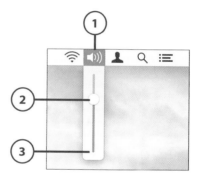

Keyboard Volume Controls

You can also use the special controls located on the F10, F11, and F12 keys to mute, decrease, and increase the system volume.

Adding the Volume Control to the Menu Bar

If sound control is not visible in your menu bar, it has been manually removed. You can re-add it to the menu using the Show Volume in the Menu Bar option in the Sound System Preferences panel.

Configuring Alert Sounds

Your Mac generates alert sounds when it needs to get your attention. To configure the sounds, and how loud they play, follow these steps:

1. Click the System Preferences icon on the Dock, and then click the Sound icon.

2. Click the Sound Effects button at the top of the panel.

3. Scroll through the alert sound list to see all of the available alert sounds.

4. Click a sound to select it as your alert sound and hear a preview.

5. Choose which sound output device (usually your internal speakers) should play the alert sound.

6. Use the alert volume slider to adjust the volume of alerts that your system plays. This is independent of the system output volume.

7. Check Play User Interface Sound Effects to play sounds when special events occur—such as emptying the trash.

8. Close the System Preferences when finished configuring the sound effects.

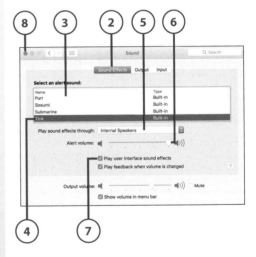

Choosing and Adjusting an Output Device

To configure your sound output options with a bit more flexibility than just changing the volume, you need to adjust the output settings for the device that is being used for playback—typically your speaker.

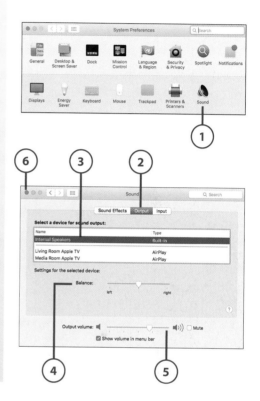

1. Click the System Preferences icon on the Dock and then click the Sound icon.

2. Click the Output button at the top of the panel.

3. Choose the output device to configure (probably your speakers).

4. Use the Balance setting to adjust audio to the left or right speaker.

5. Set or mute the Output Volume.

6. Close the System Preferences when finished.

Shhh…We're Watching TV!

Your Mac can connect to a TV and output sound via built-in HDMI or Thunderbolt to HDMI adapter (depending on your model). Once connected, your TV set will be shown as a new output device!

>>>*Go Further*

HOW DO I USE HEADPHONES OR DIGITAL AUDIO?

When headphones are plugged into your Mac, the sound output settings alter to reflect the change. All sound is directed to the headphones rather than the internal speakers.

Your Mac also sports a home-theater-worthy digital optical output, disguised as the headphone jack. To use the digital output, you need a mini TOSLINK adapter, which provides a standard TOSLINK plug for connecting to stereo equipment. These cables from Amazon.com easily get the job done: www.amazon.com/6ft-Toslink-Mini-Cable/dp/B000FMXKC8.

Picking and Calibrating an Input Device

In addition to sound output, you can also input sound on your Mac using either the built-in microphone or the line-in jack on the back. To configure your input device, follow these steps:

1. Click the System Preferences icon on the Dock and then click the Sound icon.

2. Click the Input button at the top of the panel.

3. Choose the device to use for input.

4. Use the Input Volume slider to adjust the gain on the microphone—this is how much amplification is applied to the signal.

5. Click the Use Ambient Noise Reduction checkbox if you're working in an environment with background noise.

6. Speak at the level you want your computer to record. The Input level graph should register near the middle when you use a nor-mal speaking level. If it doesn't, readjust the input volume slider.

7. Close the System Preferences.

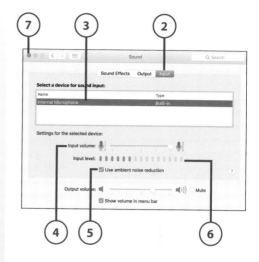

Quick Sound Input/Output Access

If you work frequently with audio and need quick access to your input and output device settings, you can skip the Sound Preferences panel entirely. Just hold down Option when clicking the speaker icon in your menu bar and, instead of showing you the volume, it lets you pick between all your input and output devices.

Keeping the Input Volume Under Control

It might be tempting to turn the input volume up as high as it goes so that the microphone detects even little noises. Keep in mind, however, that the higher the input volume for wanted sounds, the higher the volume for unwanted sounds as well!

Recording Audio and Video

It has always been possible to record audio and video "out of the box" with a new Macintosh, but not without jumping through a bunch of seemingly unnecessary hoops or trudging through unwieldy software. With El Capitan, Apple has made it easy to take advantage of your Mac's built-in capabilities to record audio, video, and even screen actions.

Recording Audio

To create and save a new audio recording, first make sure that you've configured your sound input settings correctly (including ambient noise reduction, if needed) then follow these steps:

1. Open the QuickTime Player application. (You can find it in the Launchpad or the Applications folder.)

2. Choose File, New Audio Recording.

3. Use the drop-down menu to the right of the record button in the Audio Recording window to choose an input source and recording quality.

4. If you want to hear audio through the speakers as it is recorded, drag the volume slider to the right.

5. Click the Record button to begin recording.

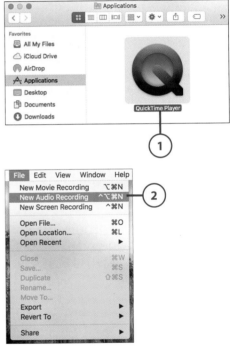

6. Click the Stop button to stop recording.

7. Use the playback controls to listen to your creation.

8. Choose File, Export to save the audio, if desired.

Recording with the FaceTime HD Video Camera

Although FaceTime enables you to see video of yourself on your computer, it doesn't give you the option to record. If you want to take a recording of what the built-in camera sees, follow these steps:

1. Open the QuickTime Player application. (You can find it in the Launchpad or the Applications folder.)

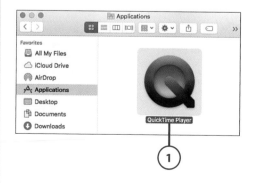

2. Choose File, New Movie Recording.

3. Use the drop-down menu on the right side of the recording controls to choose a camera (if you have more than one), input microphone, and recording quality.

4. If you want to hear audio through the speakers as it is recorded, drag the volume slider to the right.

5. Click the Record button to begin recording.

6. Click the Stop button to stop recording.

7. Use the playback controls to view the video you've recorded (not shown).

8. Choose File, Export to save the movie, if desired. (The available options vary depending on the quality of your camera.)

Lights, Camera, Screen Actions

In addition to audio and video, you can record whatever is happening on your screen. QuickTime Player offers a New Screen Recording option under the File menu that does exactly what you'd think.

>>>Go Further
VIDEO AND PHOTO FUN!

If you want to record and share videos and photos, or you want to just play around with your Mac's HD camera, try Photo Booth—located in the El Capitan Dock (or Launchpad or the Applications folder). Photo Booth provides a simple interface for taking pictures and video, applying effects, and sharing the results.

Use your Mac as a speakerphone.

Move between devices with Handoff.

In this chapter, you learn about El Capitan and how it can integrate with your iDevices, including:

→ Connecting your iOS Device with El Capitan
→ Transferring files with AirDrop
→ Using Handoff to move between devices
→ Making and receiving phone calls on your Mac
→ Sending SMS messages on your Mac
→ Using your iOS device as a hotspot

Using El Capitan with Your iDevices

Apple has designed OS X to work hand-in-hand with iOS devices, like the iPhone and iPad. El Capitan makes your iOS device an extension of your Mac—making it simple to move files back and forth, edit documents across devices, and even make use of the calling features of your iPhone.

Enabling El Capitan and iOS Communication

In order to communicate, your iOS device and Mac need a few simple settings tweaked—namely, they must both have active Bluetooth and Wi-Fi. Fortunately, these are the default settings for El Capitan, so chances are, you're already all set. If you (or someone else who uses your computer) have altered these settings, it's easy to change them back.

Verifying Your Wi-Fi and Bluetooth Settings

Follow these steps to check and enable your Wi-Fi and Bluetooth settings on both your Mac and your iOS device:

1. Open the Bluetooth System Preferences.

2. If Bluetooth is Off, click Turn Bluetooth On.

3. Close the Preferences.

4. Use the Wi-Fi menu to verify that your Wi-Fi is on and connected to your wireless access point.

5. Swipe up on your iOS device and use Control Center to verify that Bluetooth and Wi-Fi are enabled. Enable them, if need be.

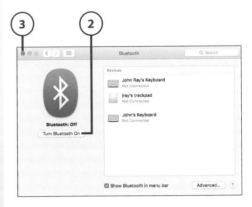

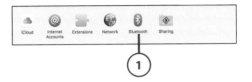

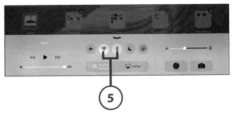

Using AirDrop

Earlier in the book you learned how to use AirDrop to share files between Macs. With El Capitan, it can also be used to share files between your Mac and iOS devices. Let's look at both scenarios now—sending files from the Mac to iOS and vice versa.

Sending Files to iOS via AirDrop

To send a file to your iOS device, make sure you've enabled Wi-Fi and Bluetooth and then complete these steps:

1. Click AirDrop in the Finder sidebar.

2. After a few seconds, your iOS device appears.

3. Drag the file you want to transfer to the device icon.

4. iOS prompts you for the transfer. Touch Decline to stop the copy process or Accept to begin.

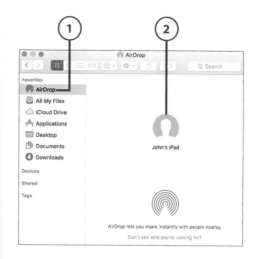

5. iOS opens the file automatically when the transfer completes.

When in Doubt, iOS Asks

If iOS doesn't know what to do with a file you've sent, it prompts you with a list of applications that can open it. Just choose your app and away you go.

Sending Files to El Capitan via AirDrop

To send a file from your iOS device to El Capitan, the process is similar. First, open the file on your iOS device and then complete the following steps:

1. Click AirDrop in the El Capitan Finder sidebar.

2. After a few seconds, your iOS device appears.

3. Touch the Share icon on your iOS device.

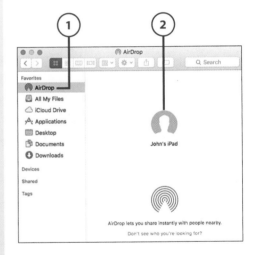

Where Is Share?

The Share button frequently appears in apps that create or manage content (Photos and Notes, for example). Unfortunately, there isn't a standard place it is located on the screen.

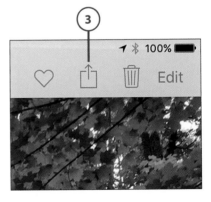

4. Select the items you want to transfer.

5. Touch the icon of the machine to which you want to transfer them.

6. El Capitan automatically downloads the files to the Downloads folder.

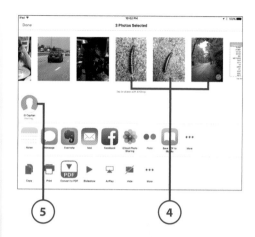

Enable AirDrop Access!

If you don't see your iOS device (or Mac) in AirDrop, chances are you've disabled it or set it to be restrictive about whom it can communicate with. You can configure AirDrop to allow access from Everyone to Just Contacts, using the Control Center on iOS and the AirDrop window (see Chapter 3, "Connecting Your Mac to a Network," for details) on OS X.

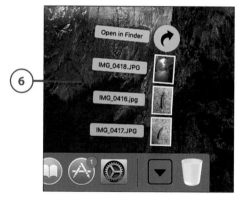

Using Handoff to Move Between Devices

The El Capitan Handoff feature is uniquely Apple. When you're in the middle of a task and want to move from your Mac to your iPad or iPhone, you can seamlessly switch to your device and pick up where you left off—no need to save files and sync with cloud services. Handoff gives you a slick and fast way to move around without having to even think about the process.

Enabling Handoff

By default, Handoff should be enabled on your Mac and iOS device, but you might still want to verify this setting yourself. To verify your Handoff settings, complete the following actions:

1. Open the General System Preferences panel.

2. Click the Allow Handoff Between This Mac and Your iCloud Devices checkbox.

3. Close the System Preferences.

4. On your iOS device, open the Settings app and navigate to the General category.

5. Use the Handoff & Suggested Apps area to enable Handoff.

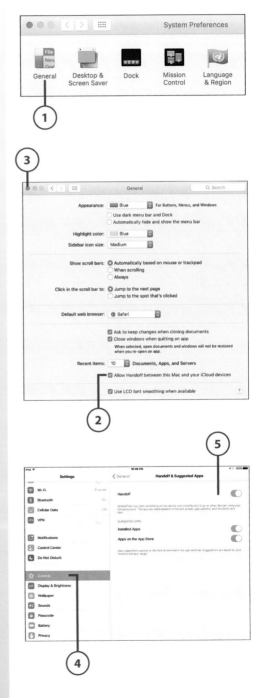

It's Not All Good

Different iCloud Accounts? No Handoff!

To use Handoff, your Mac and iOS device must both be logged into the same iCloud account. See Chapter 4, "Setting Up iCloud and Internet Accounts," for more information on activating iCloud on your Mac. On your iOS device, you configure your iCloud account on Device setup and can modify it with the Settings app under the iCloud category.

Handing Off from El Capitan to iOS

To handoff from an El Capitan application to iOS, follow these steps:

1. Open the application and use it as you normally would on OS X. (Here, Safari is in use.)

2. Activate your iOS device. An icon for the corresponding app appears in the lower left of the lock screen.

3. Swipe up from the lower left of the lock screen.

4. The application (and whatever content you were viewing/editing) is immediately visible on your iOS device.

Handoff Support

Handoff works with a variety of apps, including Safari, Mail, Pages, Keynote, and Numbers. Developers will obviously add Handoff to their apps where it makes sense, so these instructions are just general guidelines. Which apps it works with will change over time.

>>>Go Further

HANDING OFF TO AN UNLOCKED DEVICE

If your iOS device is already unlocked, you can access handoff through the iOS application switcher (double-click the Home button). A Handoff indicator will appear at the bottom of the switcher.

Handing Off from iOS to El Capitan

Handing off from iOS to El Capitan is just as easy. To handoff from your iOS application to your Mac, just complete these actions:

1. Open the application and use it as you normally would on your iOS device. (Here, Mail is being used on an iPad.)

2. Your Mac displays an icon for the corresponding app alongside the dock. Click the icon.

3. The application opens and displays the content you were editing/viewing, ready to be completed.

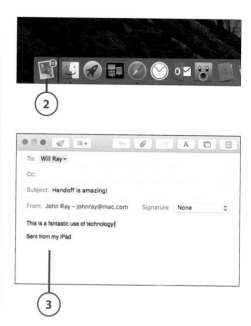

Using Your iPhone to Cell-Enable Your Mac

An exceptionally cool feature of El Capitan's iOS integration is the ability to enable your Mac to act as a speakerphone and make and receive phone calls through your iPhone, as well as send and receive SMS messages.

These features require your iPad and iPhone to be connected to the same network with Bluetooth enabled, and for them to both be logged into the same iCloud account. After that, enabling the cellular capabilities and using them is a piece of cake!

Keep an Eye on Your iPhone

When you start using El Capitan with your iPhone, you'll likely see a few prompts on your iPhone screen asking for permission to handle calls and send text messages. I'd love to tell you *when* these appear, but they seem a bit unpredictable. Just pay attention to your phone and make sure you accept any requests to enable the features we're about to explore.

Enabling El Capitan Cellular Calls

FaceTime controls the phone capabilities of El Capitan. To enable cellular calls, start FaceTime and then complete the following steps.

1. Choose FaceTime, Preferences to view the application preferences.

2. Make sure the Settings button is selected at the top of the window.

3. Check the Calls from iPhone checkbox to enable your Mac to place calls through your iPhone.

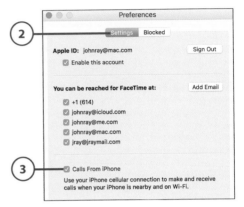

Placing a Phone Call

To place a phone call, you again use FaceTime. Your iPhone must be on, connected to Wi-Fi, and somewhere in the general proximity of your Mac. Open FaceTime and then follow along:

1. Type a name or phone number in the field at the top of the FaceTime window.

2. If the number matches a contact, the name is shown; if not, only a phone number is visible. Click the phone icon beside the name or number.

3. From the menu that appears, choose the number you want to call from under the Call Using iPhone section.

4. A window appears showing the call duration.

5. Click Mute to silence your microphone.

6. Click End to hang up.

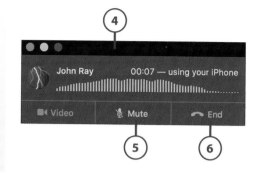

Receiving a Phone Call

To receive a phone call, again it's FaceTime—but, like other FaceTime video/audio chats, the application doesn't even need to be running! Follow these steps to receive a phone call on El Capitan:

1. Wait for a phone call. A window appears with the name of the caller.

2. Click Accept to begin the call or Decline to ignore the call.

3. The window updates to show the call duration.

4. Click Mute to silence your microphone.

5. Click End to hang up.

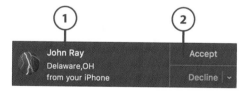

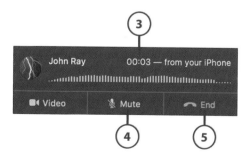

It's Not All Good

Minutes Are Minutes

When making or receiving iPhone calls on El Capitan, you *will* be using your standard cell phone minutes. Even with all the fancy networking involved in making the iOS/El Capitan integration work, you still can't get away from your cell phone network provider!

Text Messaging with El Capitan

With El Capitan's iPhone integration, you can send and receive messages from anyone. Doing so is identical to messaging with other Macs and iOS devices as described in Chapter 7, "Being Social with Messages, FaceTime, Twitter, and Facebook."

1. Within Messages, begin typing the name or number of a contact.

2. If the contact auto-completes, choose the number you want to text message. If not, just type the full number. You'll notice that Messages designates the contact as a Text Message contact, rather than an iMessage (Mac/iOS) contact.

3. Converse with your text-messaging buddy as you would any other contact.

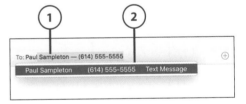

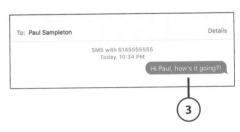

Receiving Is Believing

Receiving text messages (prior to sending one) is identical to receiving any other communication in Messages. If the app is running, it appears as a new conversation in the main window. If Messages is closed, you receive a notification of the new message with the option of responding. This service is so well-integrated, you won't even know you're chatting via SMS.

Using Your iOS Device as an Instant Hotspot

El Capitan offers the ability to quickly share your iPhone or iPad's cellular Internet connection—assuming your plan already includes support for personal hotspots. To use this feature, you don't need to do anything except make sure that your devices are signed into the same iCloud account.

Sharing Your iOS Internet Connection

To share your iOS connection via a Personal Hotspot, follow these steps.

1. Make sure your iOS device is on and has a cellular connection (not pictured).

2. Open the Wi-Fi menu and select the Personal Hotspot item that appears from the list of available hotspots.

3. That's it. No more configuration and no passwords. You're immediately online! Use the Wi-Fi menu to monitor the signal strength and battery life of your iOS device.

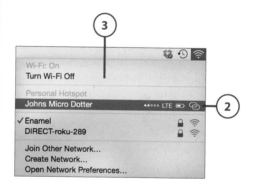

>>>Go Further
FOR OUR CLOSING ACT...

If you happen to be an iOS developer (or just want to do something cool), there's one other piece of iOS/OS X integration you might be interested in: screen recording. To record the screen of an iOS 8 (or later) device, just connect it to your Mac with a Lightning cable. The device's screen becomes a video input source, just like a camera. Once connected, you can open QuickTime and use the movie recording features to record action on the iOS device screen.

Connect your Mac to external displays and peripherals using System Preferences.

13

Connecting Peripherals to Your Mac

The Mac comes with everything you need to get started using the system, but that doesn't mean that you can't expand it. Your Mac can interface with many different devices—frequently without requiring any additional software to be installed.

In this chapter we look at the different types of peripherals that work with your Mac out-of-the-box.

Connecting USB Input Devices

The Mac can connect to a variety of devices using the standard USB (Universal Serial Bus) ports located on the back. This section walks you through connecting a generic keyboard and mouse. Keep in mind, though, that there are *hundreds* of different input devices.

You should always refer to the documentation that came with your device. If the manual doesn't mention the Macintosh (such as for a Windows-specific keyboard), try plugging in the device to see what happens!

USB Device Compatibility

The USB standard includes a variety of different profiles that define how a device can be used (input, audio output/input, and so on). These standards are supported on both Macintosh and Windows platforms. Just because a device does not specifically say it supports the Mac, doesn't mean that it won't work anyway.

The latest MacBooks support USB-C, an emerging standard for USB connections. If you're the lucky owner of a new Mac with USB-C, you might need Apple's USB-C adaptor to connect to the more common USB standard peripherals.

Configuring a USB Keyboard

Your Mac comes with a perfectly usable keyboard, but if you have a favorite *wired* keyboard, you can plug it in and start using it almost immediately. To use a standard USB keyboard with your Mac, follow these steps:

1. Plug the keyboard into a free port on your Mac (not pictured).

2. If the keyboard is an Apple or Mac-specific keyboard, it is recognized and immediately usable (not pictured).

3. If you are using a generic USB keyboard, the Keyboard Setup Assistant launches and you are asked to identify the keyboard. Click Continue.

4. Walk through the steps presented by the setup assistant, pressing the keyboard keys when requested. If the assistant can't identify the keyboard, you are asked to manually identify it.

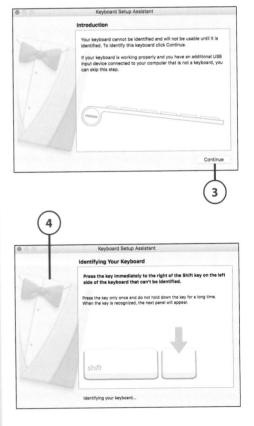

5. Click Done at the conclusion of the setup assistant. The keyboard setup is complete, and the keyboard is ready to be used.

Manually Configuring the Keyboard Type

If the setup assistant does not start automatically when you plug in a USB keyboard, you can start it by opening the System Preferences window and clicking the Keyboard icon. In the Keyboard panel, click Change Keyboard Type.

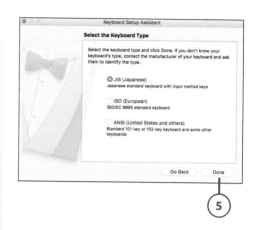

Configuring a USB Mouse

The Apple mouse is nice, but some of us like options! Want to use a shiny USB mouse with a zillion buttons? No problem. Like keyboards, USB mice plug right in and start working in a matter of seconds.

1. Open the System Preferences and click the Mouse icon.

2. Plug a USB mouse into your Mac (not pictured).

3. After a few seconds the Mouse panel updates to show the available options for your device.

4. Uncheck Scroll Direction: Natural if you prefer a scroll wheel that behaves in a traditional manner (down to go up, and vice versa).

5. Adjust the Tracking Speed, Scrolling Speed (if the mouse includes a scroll wheel), and Double-Click Speed by dragging the sliders left or right.

6. Choose which button acts as the primary button.

7. Close the System Preferences panel when you've finished your configuration.

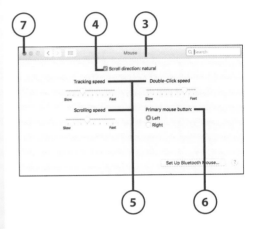

Using Bluetooth Devices

The Mac's built-in Bluetooth enables it to wirelessly connect to a variety of peripheral devices, including keyboards, mice, headsets, and so on. As with USB peripherals, your first step toward installing a device is to read the manufacturer's instructions and install any drivers that it came with.

After installing the software that came with the peripheral, you use the Apple Bluetooth System Preferences panel to choose and *pair* your device.

>>>Go Further
WHAT IS PAIRING?

When you're working with Bluetooth peripherals, you'll notice many references to pairing. Pairing is the process of making two devices (your Mac and the peripheral) aware of one another so they can communicate.

In order to pair with your computer, your device needs to be in pairing mode, which should be described in the device's manual.

Pairing a Bluetooth Mouse or Trackpad

To pair a Bluetooth device with your Mac, you follow the same basic steps, regardless of the type of peripheral. This task's screenshots show an Apple Magic Trackpad being paired with the Mac.

1. Open the Bluetooth System Preferences panel.

2. Make sure that your Mac's Bluetooth system is On.

3. Devices that are paired with your Mac are shown at the top of the list on the left, and new devices are shown at the bottom.

4. Click Pair to pair a new mouse or trackpad with your Mac.

5. After a few seconds, the device is paired and available.

6. Click the X beside a device in the list to remove the pairing at any time.

7. Close the System Preferences when finished.

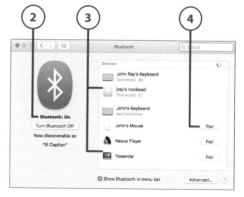

Setting Up Bluetooth Devices from Almost Anywhere

You might notice that there is a Set Up Bluetooth [Keyboard, Mouse, Trackpad] option within the keyboard, mouse, and trackpad system preferences panels. You can use these as shortcuts to immediately start searching for a Bluetooth device of that type. The Bluetooth System Preferences panel, however, is the central point for pairing all devices.

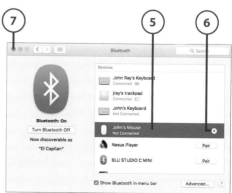

8. Your new device is listed in the Bluetooth System Preferences panel (not shown).

9. Use the corresponding (Mouse/Trackpad) Preferences panel to configure your device.

Monitoring Your Battery

When you're using an Apple Bluetooth device or keyboard, the corresponding preferences panels display battery status for the devices. You can also monitor battery status by adding the Bluetooth status to your menu bar by selecting Show Bluetooth Status in Menu Bar in the Bluetooth System Preferences panel.

Pairing a Bluetooth Keyboard

Some Bluetooth devices, such as keyboards, require an additional step while pairing: the entry of a passkey on the device you are pairing with. To pair a keyboard with your system, follow these steps:

1. Follow steps 1–5 of the "Pairing a Bluetooth Mouse or Trackpad" task, selecting the keyboard device from the list of detected devices, then clicking Pair.

2. The setup process prompts you to enter a passkey on your device. Type the characters exactly as displayed on screen, including pressing Return, if shown.

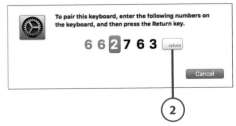

3. If the passkey was successfully entered, the device is configured and paired.

4. Open the Keyboard Preferences panel and configure the device as described in Chapter 11's section "Updating Keyboard and Dictation Settings."

It's Not All Good

Dealing with Troublesome Passkeys

If, for some reason, you enter the passkey and get an error, look for a Passcode Options button in the lower-left corner of the window during setup. Clicking this button *might* allow you to bypass the passkey or choose one that is easier to enter on your device.

Connecting a Bluetooth Headset

Wireless headphones and headsets can help untether us from our computers when conferencing or listening to music. Your Mac with El Capitan supports high-quality audio over Bluetooth connections, and setup is a cinch:

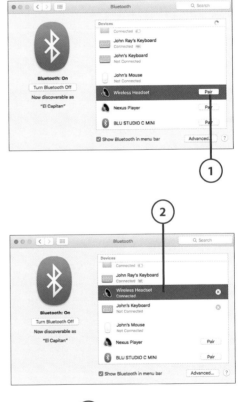

1. Follow steps 1–5 of the "Pairing a Bluetooth Mouse or Trackpad" task, selecting the headset device from the list of detected devices, then clicking Pair.

2. The headset is added to your system. You might need to cycle the power on and off the headset before it will work, however.

3. To set the headset for audio input or output, use the Sound System Preferences panel, as described in Chapter 11's section, "Setting Sound Input and Output."

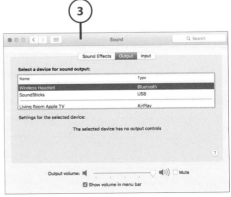

Adding and Using the Bluetooth Status Menu

Apple Bluetooth devices report their status directly to your computer, giving you a heads up on battery issues and other status problems. To use the Bluetooth status menu, follow these steps.

1. Open the System Preferences window and click the Bluetooth icon.

2. Click the Show Bluetooth in Menu Bar checkbox.

3. Close the System Preferences.

4. The Bluetooth menu is added to your display.

5. Each paired device has an entry in the menu for quick control of its features and display of battery levels (Apple devices only).

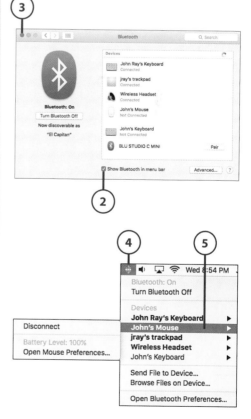

Using External Displays and Projectors

Even the smallest Macintosh screens are larger than the biggest monitors we
had a decade ago, yet somehow we manage to fill them. As I'm sure you've
encountered, there are times when using an external monitor or a projector
is helpful. As long as you have the right cables, running an external monitor is
plug-and-play—no rebooting required.

What Kind of External Displays Can I Run?

All modern Macs have USB-C, Thunderbolt, or a Mini DisplayPort video output,
which can be adapted to many different standards using a plug-in dongle from
Apple. Earlier models used a miniDVI port, which, similarly, could be output to
VGA or DVI monitors with the appropriate adapter.

Extending Your Desktop to Another Monitor

To use another monitor to extend
your desktop, follow these steps:

1. Plug the monitor into your Mac
   using the appropriate adapter
   cable (not shown).

2. The monitor is initialized and
   displays your desktop at the
   highest resolution (not shown).

3. Open the Displays System
   Preferences panel.

4. A unique window is shown
   on each connected monitor,
   enabling you to customize its
   characteristics.

5. Close the System Preferences (not
   shown).

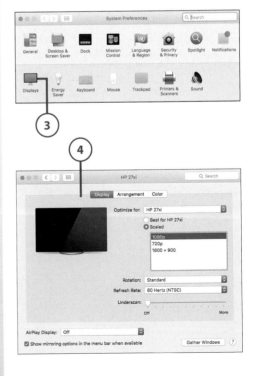

Setting Monitor Arrangements

After a monitor has been connected to your system, you can choose how it is arranged in relationship to your Mac display and whether or not it displays the menu bar.

1. Open the Displays System Preferences panel.

2. Click the Arrangement button at the top of the window.

3. Drag the visual representation of the monitors so that it best represents your physical setup (that is, external monitor on the left, right, above, and so on).

4. If you want, change your primary display by dragging the small white line representing the menu bar from one display to the other.

5. Close the System Preferences.

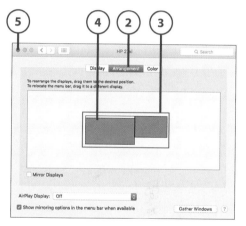

>>>Go Further
MANAGING MULTIPLE MONITORS

When the Displays System Preferences panel is opened with two or more monitors connected, a unique copy of the preferences panel is shown on each monitor, representing that monitor's settings.

Within each window, you can adjust the color and resolution of your external display using the same approach described in Chapter 11's section, "Adjusting Your Display." You can also use the Gather Windows button to pull all open application windows onto that display.

Adding the Display Mirroring Menu to Your Menu Bar

If you frequently want to mirror your display (rather than extend your desktop), or display content on an Apple TV, you can either use the Displays System Preferences panel or add a global "mirroring" menu to the menu bar.

1. Open the Displays System Preferences panel.

2. Click the Show Mirroring Options in the Menu Bar When Available checkbox.

3. Close the System Preferences.

4. The menu item appears when external displays (or Apple TVs) are available to use.

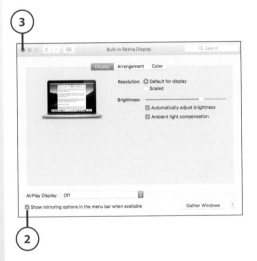

Using Mirrored Displays

When you plug another display into your Mac, it is initialized and activated as an extension to your desktop at the highest resolution it supports. If you'd prefer to mirror the content between your displays, do the following:

1. Click the display mirroring menu item in your menu bar.

2. Choose Mirror Built-in Retina Display. Your screen might go blank or flash for a moment.

3. Once Mirroring has started, you can choose which display size is mirrored (the built-in display, or the connected monitor).

4. Choose Use as Separate Display to switch back to using two separate displays.

Adapting Resolutions

If the external display is set as your primary monitor or cannot be adjusted to match your internal LCD, your Mac might instead change the resolution on its display to match the external monitor. This change reverts when you turn off mirrored video. To change the display resolution from the default, use the Displays System Preferences panel, as pictured in the previous section.

Connecting to an Apple TV (or Other Device) with AirPlay (New!)

Taking display connections to the next level, El Capitan makes it simple to wirelessly share your display with an Apple TV (2nd or 3rd generation). Couple an Apple TV with a monitor or a projector, and you have a wireless presentation system for classrooms, businesses, or just at-home fun.

AirPlay works in one of four modes: mirroring, desktop extension, video/image sharing, and audio playback. Before reading any further, make sure you've added the display mirroring menu to your display (if it isn't there already) using the steps in the preceding section, "Adding the Display Mirroring Menu to Your Menu Bar."

Although the Apple TV is the only AirPlay device that currently supports video, there are many speaker systems, amplifiers, and other devices (including Apple's own AirPort Express) that can receive audio over AirPlay.

It's Not All Good

Old Mac? You Might Be Out of Luck!

El Capitan is only capable of mirroring and extending your display if you have recent Mac hardware. If you don't see the mirroring menu (and you have an Apple TV), your Mac is likely too old to use El Capitan AirPlay features. That said, I strongly encourage you to check out AirParrot—a commercial piece of software that offers all the AirPlay features of El Capitan (and more) on *any* Mac (http://airparrot.com).

Mirroring Your Display to an Apple TV

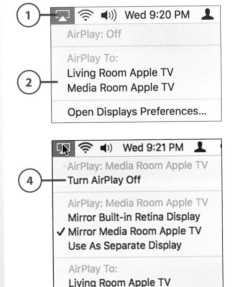

To display your Mac monitor on an Apple TV, both devices must be turned on and connected to the same network. When things are powered up, follow these steps to mirror your display:

1. Click the display mirroring menu in the menu bar.

2. All available Apple TV devices are shown. Choose the one you want to mirror to.

3. After a few seconds, your Mac desktop is visible on the display connected to the Apple TV via AirPlay (not shown).

4. To disconnect from AirPlay, choose Turn AirPlay Off from the mirroring menu.

Mirror, Mirror on the Preferences Panel

You can also choose an AppleTV to mirror to directly from the Displays System Preferences panel. If an AppleTV is detected, an AirPlay pop-up menu is added to the preferences.

Setting the AirPlay Apple TV Resolution

For the best mirroring performance, your Mac display should match the resolution of the display connected to the Apple TV—otherwise, your desktop will be enlarged and might look blurry. To adjust the resolution of the mirrored display, use these options.

1. Click the display mirroring menu in the menu bar.

2. Choose Mirror Built-in Display to scale the Apple TV image to match your Mac's display.

3. Choose Mirror <AirPlay Device> to change your Mac resolution to match the resolution of the display connected to your Apple TV (this is the preferred approach).

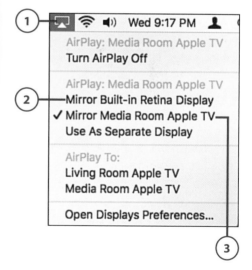

Extending Your Desktop to an Apple TV

In addition to mirroring, El Capitan actually enables your Mac to use an Apple TV as an entirely new monitor—extending your desktop as if you had plugged a new display directly into your computer!

1. Connect to the Apple TV as described in "Mirroring Your Display to an Apple TV."

2. Choose Use as Separate Display from the AirPlay Menu.

3. The Apple TV is added as an external display and can be configured using the Displays Preferences panel like any other display.

4. To disconnect from AirPlay, choose Turn AirPlay Off from the mirroring menu.

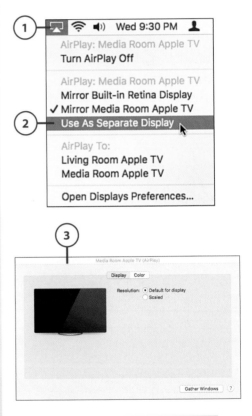

Sharing Multimedia to an Apple TV

In addition to acting as a monitor for your Mac, your Apple TV can also play video, audio, and other multimedia content (such as slideshows), if supported by your software. While viewing video, audio, or other multimedia content, look for an AirPlay icon, then, complete the following:

1. Click the icon to display and choose from any available Apple TV.

2. After choosing an Apple TV, the content that was playing on your Mac is automatically transferred to the Apple TV.

3. Choose Computer to return the display to your local Mac.

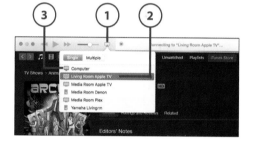

Sending System Audio to an Apple TV

Any application that outputs audio to your default system audio device can be sent transparently, via AirPlay, to an Apple TV. To send your system audio to an Apple TV connected to a sound system, follow these steps:

1. Open the Sound System Preferences panel.

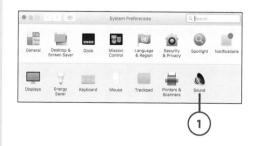

2. Click the Output button at the top of the panel.

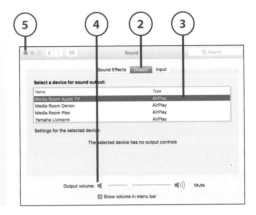

3. Choose the AirPlay device you want to use for audio.

4. Adjust audio and work with the device just like you would with your normal Mac speakers.

5. Close the System Preferences.

Connecting and Using a Printer

Out of the box, El Capitan supports a range of popular printers just by plugging them in. Occasionally, however, you might need to install a driver before you can successfully print.

Drivers

Drivers are just pieces of software that help your Mac communicate in the same language as physical hardware, like printers.

As with any peripheral that you want to use, be sure to read and follow the manufacturer's instructions before proceeding.

Your Mac can connect to printers either over a network or via a USB direct connection. Regardless of the approach, configuration is straightforward.

Setting Up a USB Printer

To connect to a printer via a USB connection, set up the printer as directed by the manufacturer, then follow these steps:

1. Connect the USB plug from the printer to your Mac and turn on the printer. If the printer is auto-detected, it might prompt you to download software (not shown).

2. Open the System Preferences window and click the Printers & Scanners icon.

3. In many cases, the printer is detected and configured automatically and is immediately available for use. If this is the case, it is displayed in the Printers list, and you may close the Printers & Scanners System Preferences panel.

4. If the printer is not detected, click the + button below the Printers list and choose Add Printer or Scanner from the pop-up menu.

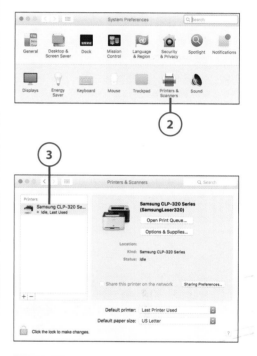

5. A window is shown displaying all of the available printers detected by your Mac. Choose the printer from the list.

6. Your Mac searches for the software necessary to use the printer and displays the chosen printer name in the Use drop-down menu.

7. If the correct printer name is shown in the menu, jump to step 11.

8. If the correct printer name is not displayed in the Use drop-down menu, choose Select Software from the menu.

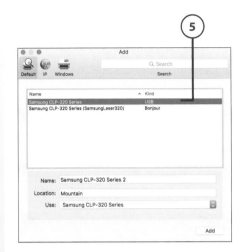

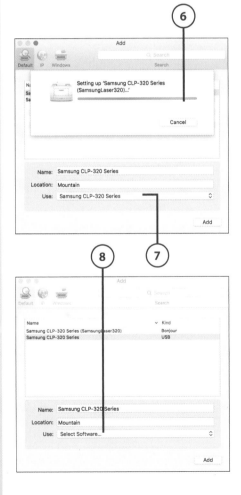

9. A window appears that shows all the printers supported in El Capitan. Click your printer within the list.

10. Click OK.

11. Click Add to finish adding the printer. If there are options (such as a duplexer) that your Mac can't detect, it might prompt you to configure printer-specific features.

12. Close System Preferences and begin using your printer.

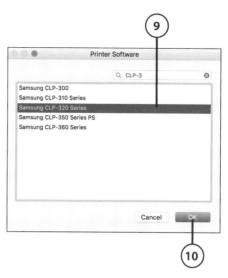

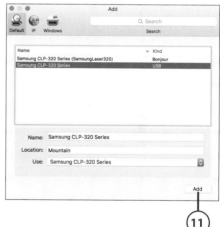

>>>*Go Further*

SETTING UP A NETWORK OR AIRPORT PRINTER

To add a network printer, follow the steps described in Chapter 6's section, "Accessing a Network Printer."

Airport-connected printers, even though they might not technically be network printers, are configured identically to network printers. Airport makes them available over Bonjour, a configuration-free networking technology developed by Apple.

Printing to a Printer

The options available when printing can vary depending on the application that you're printing from, but once you're used to the process, you'll be able to find your way around any software's printing options.

To output to one of your configured printers, complete the following steps in the application of your choice:

1. Choose File, Print from your application's menu bar.

2. Click the Show Details button to display all the available options, if needed.

Where Is the Page Setup Option?

Apple has been working to streamline the printing process. In many applications, the Page Setup functionality has been combined with the standard Print function.

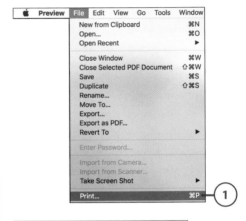

3. Select the printer you want to print to.

4. Set the number of copies and page range options.

5. Set the paper size and orientation, if desired.

6. Use the advanced printing options pop-up menu to choose specific printing options for your printer or options related to the application you're using.

7. Review the results of your settings in the preview area on the left side of the window.

8. Use the controls below the preview to step through the pages in the document.

9. Use the Presets menu to save your settings if you want to recall them in the future.

10. Click Print to output to the printer.

Printing to PDF

In addition to printing to a printer, you can print a document to a PDF, or open it directly as a PDF in Preview. To print to a PDF, click PDF and choose Save as PDF in the Print dialog box. To open the document as a PDF in Preview, choose Open PDF in Preview.

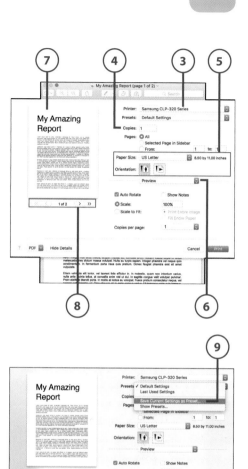

Connecting and Using a Scanner

Although it's not a heavily advertised feature of El Capitan, the operating system can detect and drive a range of scanners without any additional drivers or software. This means that you can connect a scanner to your Mac and almost immediately begin scanning images.

Adding a Scanner

To connect a USB scanner to your Mac, complete any initial setup instructions provided in the hardware manual and then follow these steps:

1. Plug the scanner into your Mac and turn it on (not shown).

2. Open the System Preferences and click the Printers & Scanners icon.

3. The scanner, if supported, appears in the Scanners listing on the left side of the panel.

4. Choose the application you want to start when the Scan button is pressed on the scanner. I recommend Preview because it is a convenient application for working with images.

5. Close the System Preferences.

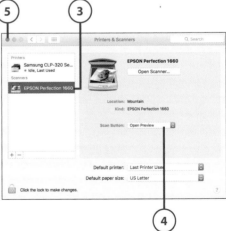

Network Scanners

El Capitan supports many network scanners, such as the popular Canon Pixma All-In-One line. For these devices, make sure you install any software the manufacturer provided and then follow the instructions for scanning with a wired scanner. OS X should automatically recognize the scanner, as long as you are connected to the same network.

Scanning in Preview

Preview (in the Applications folder, click Preview) serves as the image hub on your Mac. It views images and PDFs, and allows annotations, cropping, image rotation, and more. With El Capitan, it can also act as your scanning software. To scan an image directly into Preview, do the following:

1. Open Preview, or press the scan button on the scanner if Preview is set as the default scanning application.

2. Choose Import from Scanner from the File menu.

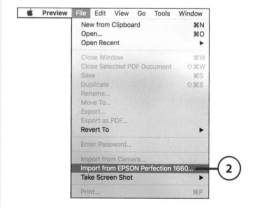

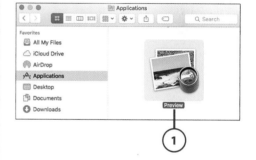

3. The basic scanning window appears. If you want to choose your scanning area or set the resolution, click Show Details and skip to step 8.

4. Use the pop-up menu in the lower-left corner to choose the size of the document you're scanning.

5. Choose Detect Separate Items from the pop-up menu to automatically scan individual photos, pictures, and so on into separate images within a single scan.

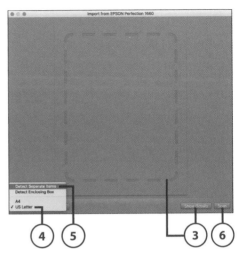

6. Click Scan. Preview performs a detailed scan, and then opens the result in a new window, where you can save it if desired.

Scanning Options

Originally, the Image Capture utility (found in the Applications folder) handled scanning in OS X. El Capitan has expanded that capability to Preview, but Image Capture is still available if you'd like to give it a try.

7. Repeat step 6 as needed for all of your images.

8. In detailed scanning mode, full controls for the scanner are shown on the right side of the window. Choose the scan's resolution, size, orientation, and color depth.

9. Configure the format for scanned images.

10. Adjust any image filters and clean-up features you want to apply to the scan.

11. Click Overview to perform a low-resolution scan of your document and display it in the preview area on the left.

12. Adjust the bounding rectangle to fit your document. If you've chosen to detect separate items, you will see multiple bounding rectangles.

13. Click Scan to begin scanning.

14. The result opens in a new window, where you can save it if desired.

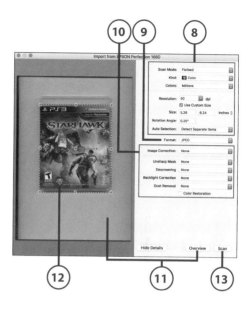

Add and manage user accounts.

Create full system backups using Time Machine.

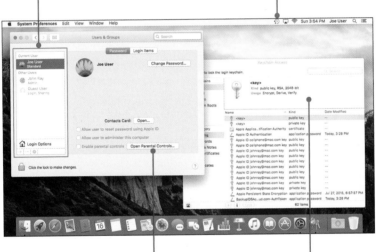

Apply parental controls to users.

Use Keychain Access to manage sensitive information.

In this chapter, you learn the steps that you can take to secure your Mac and its data, including:

→ Creating user accounts
→ Applying parental controls
→ Keeping passwords in Keychain
→ Encrypting your account data
→ Activating the El Capitan firewall
→ Backing up your files and information
→ Using Time Machine to restore backups
→ Accessing previous files with Versions

Securing and Protecting Your Mac

Security on a computer is important—increasingly we store our lives on our computers. We save our memories, our music and video, and our important documents. Having a computer stolen (or losing the contents of your hard drive) can be more traumatic than losing a credit card. Practicing appropriate account, application, and information security can ensure that even if the worst happens, your data remains private.

In addition to protecting your information from theft and unauthorized access, you should take steps to ensure the data's availability—in other words, you should ensure that your files are available when you need them. By backing up your computer, you can be sure that even in the event your computer is stolen or its hard drive crashes, your work is protected.

Working with Users and Groups

El Capitan can accommodate multiple users—family members, friends, co-workers, and even guests. By creating and using different accounts, you can limit access to files. In addition, you can combine individual users into groups that have access controls.

Creating User Accounts

When creating a user account, you can control what the users can do by assigning them an account type. There are five account types in El Capitan:

Administrator—An account with full control over the computer and its settings

Standard—An account that can install software and work with the files within the individual account but not across the entire computer

Managed with Parental Controls—A standard user account that includes parental controls to limit account and application access

Sharing Only—An account that can only be used to access shared files, but not to log into the system

Guest—A preconfigured account that allows the user to log in and use the computer but that automatically resets to a clean state upon logout

By default, the first account you create on your computer is an Administrator account, but you should create additional user accounts based on what the users need to do.

Unlock Your Preferences

Before making changes to many of the system preferences, you need to click the Lock icon in the lower-left corner of the preference panel and supply your username and password. This extra step is frequently required to help prevent unwanted changes to your Mac.

Adding Accounts

To add any type of account to the system, follow these steps:

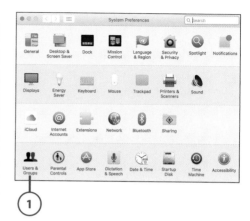

1. Open the System Preferences window and click the Users & Groups icon.

2. Click the + button below the user list to add a new user.

3. The account creation window appears. Use the New Account pop-up menu to choose the account type you want to create.

4. Enter the full name of the user you're adding.

5. Type the account name for the user. This is the username the person uses to access all El Capitan services.

6. Choose whether to use an iCloud password or a separate password for the account. (A separate password is demonstrated here.)

7. Type a new password for the account into the Password and Verify fields.

8. If desired, provide a hint for the password. The hint is displayed after three unsuccessful login attempts.

9. Click Create User.

10. Close the System Preferences.

Enabling the Guest Account

The Guest account provides a simple means of giving anyone access to the computer for a short period of time. To control the Guest account, follow these steps:

1. Open the System Preferences window and click the User & Groups icon.

2. Click the Guest User item within the account list.

3. Check/uncheck the Allow Guests to Log in to This Computer checkbox.

4. To allow guest access to shared folders, click Allow Guest Users to Connect to Shared Folders.

5. Close the System Preferences.

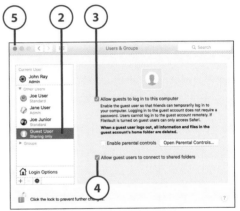

Applying Parental Controls

If you've created a managed account with Parental Controls, or have enabled the Guest account, you can configure which applications a user can run, when the user can run the programs, and what parts of the Internet the user can access.

1. Open the System Preferences window and click the Parental Controls icon.

2. Choose the account you want to configure.

3. Click Enable Parental Controls.

4. Click the Apps button to choose which applications the user can use, what people the user can email and use Game Center with, and whether or not the camera can be used.

5. Use the Web button to restrict access to websites.

Managed Versus Standard

If you've created a Standard account type, you can convert it to a Managed account with Parental Controls by selecting it in the Parental Controls list and then clicking the Enable Parental Controls button.

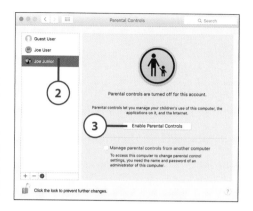

6. Click the Stores button to set permissions for the iTunes and iBooks stores and restrict purchases to specific media ratings.

7. Click the Time button to set limits on the days of the week and length of time each day that a user can control the computer.

8. Use the Privacy button to choose what data applications may access within the user's account—such as the user's location or Facebook settings.

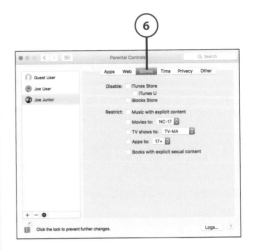

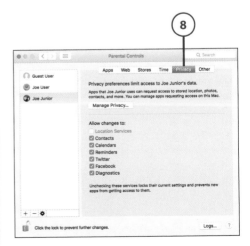

9. Use Other to configure whether dictation is allowed, limit printer and scanner administration and DVD burning, hide profanity in the dictionary, prevent changes to the Dock, and activate a "Simple Finder" mode.

10. Close the System Preferences.

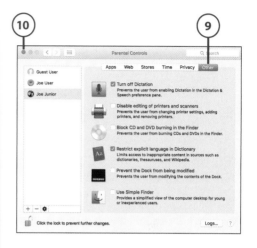

iCloud Password Without the Cloud

If you choose to create an account using an iCloud password only, you'll have to provide the account name to El Capitan. There's nothing wrong with this approach, but keep in mind that the computer needs to be connected to the Internet to sync with your iCloud password. If your system isn't Internet connected, or connects rarely, you might have trouble with this feature.

Creating Groups

For individuals who should have the same kind of access rights (such as your co-workers), you can group them together. You can then use that group in other parts of El Capitan (such as setting file permissions) to refer to all of the accounts at one time.

1. Open the System Preferences window and click the Users & Groups icon.

2. Click the + button below the account list to add a new account.

3. The account creation window appears. Use the New Account pop-up menu to choose Group.

4. Enter a name for the group.

5. Click Create Group.

6. The group appears in the account list. Make sure it is selected.

7. Click the checkboxes in front of each user who should be a member of the group.

8. Close the System Preferences.

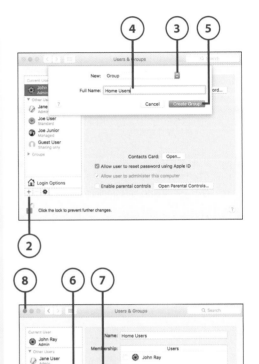

Configuring General Account Security

To better protect user accounts from potential security problems, El Capitan has a range of security settings in one place. To configure the best possible security for your account, follow these steps:

1. Open the System Preferences window and click the Security & Privacy icon.

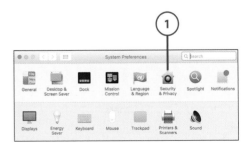

2. Click the General button at the top of the panel.

3. Check the Require Password checkbox and set the pop-up menu to Immediately so that a password is required to wake your computer after the screen saver kicks in.

4. If desired, set a message to display when the screen is locked.

5. Check Disable Automatic Login to disable access to your Mac without a valid username and password.

6. Click the Advanced button.

7. Check Log Out After 60 Minutes of Inactivity. You might want to adjust the time to a shorter period. After this option is set, you are automatically logged out of your Mac if you don't use it for the designated amount of time.

8. Choose to require an administrator password to access locked preferences.

9. Click OK.

10. Close the System Preferences.

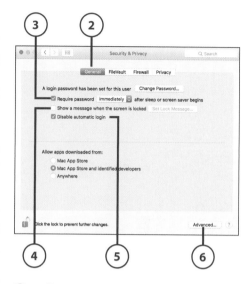

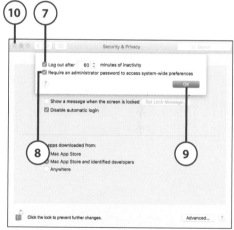

Assigning File Permissions for Users and Groups

After you've created users and groups, you can begin protecting files and folders so that certain users can access them but others can't:

1. Select a file or folder in the Finder.

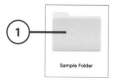

Sample Folder

2. Choose Get Info from the File menu.

3. Open the Sharing & Permissions section of the information window.

4. Click the + button to add a user or group to the permission list.

5. Choose a user or group from the window that opens.

6. Click Select.

Permissions, Permissions Everywhere

When setting permissions on a folder, you can apply those same permissions to everything *in* the folder by clicking the gear icon at the bottom of the permission settings and choosing Apply to Enclosed Items.

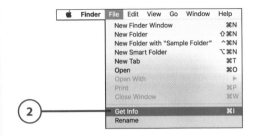

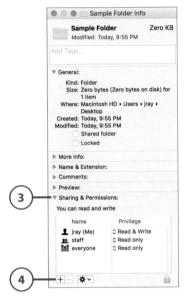

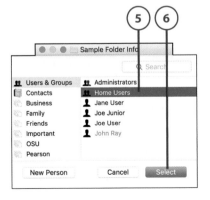

7. Use the pop-up menu in the Privilege column to the right of the user or group to set whether the user can read only, read and write, or write only.

8. To remove access for a user or group, select it and click –.

9. Close the Info window.

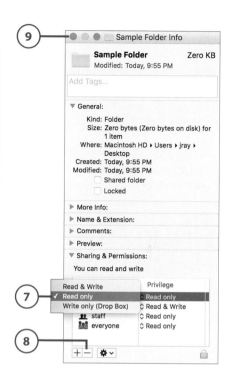

Choose Your Permissions

In addition to these permissions, you can set permissions for network shares. The sharing permissions (see Chapter 6, "Sharing Files, Devices, and Services") define who can access a folder over the network. The file permissions, however, can also limit access to the files and folders within a share, or who can see the files and folders when they're logged directly into your computer.

Tracking Passwords with Keychain Access

When you use Safari, connect to file shares, or use other secure services, you're frequently prompted to Save to Keychain. When you save your passwords, you're storing them in a special system-wide database that manages secure information—called the keychain.

Unknown to many, you can use the Keychain Access utility (found in the Applications/Utilities folder or in the Utilities Launchpad group) to view and modify records in your keychain. You can even use Keychain Access to store arbitrary data (such as notes, passwords, and so on) that you'd like to have encrypted. Keychain values can only be accessed when the keychain is unlocked.

There are multiple different keychain databases you can access or create. By default, passwords and account information are stored in a keychain named Login, which is automatically unlocked when you log into your account.

Viewing Keychain Items

You can access your Login keychain entries at any time. To view an item that has been stored in your keychain, follow along with these steps:

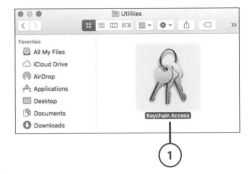

1. Open the Keychain Access application from the Applications/Utilities folder or Launchpad.

2. Choose the keychain you want to view (Login is where most items are located).

3. Select the category of data you want to view.

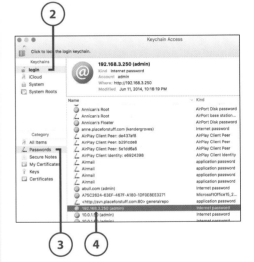

4. Double-click the keychain entry to open a window displaying the details.

5. Click Show Password to authenticate and display the keychain password in clear text.

6. Close the keychain entry window.

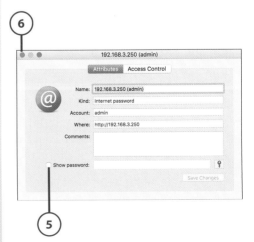

Adding Data to the Keychain

There are two types of information you can manually store in a keychain—secure notes and password items. Notes can be arbitrary text, and password items are generally a username, password, and a name for the item you're adding.

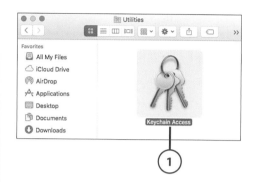

Collect the information you want to add and then follow these steps:

1. Open the Keychain Access application.

2. Choose the keychain you want to add data to.

3. Select the Passwords or Secure Notes categories to set which type of information you are storing.

4. Click the + button at the bottom of the Keychain Access window.

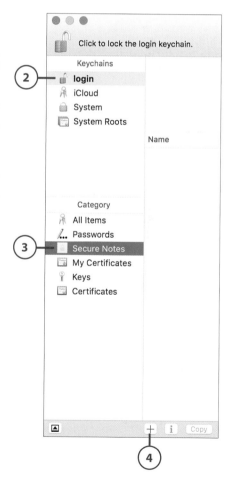

5. Enter your note or account information in the form that appears.

6. Click Add.

7. The new entry appears in the keychain.

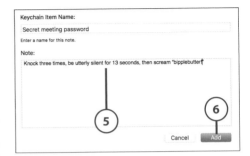

Using the Password Assistant

When adding a new password, you might notice a key icon by the password field. Clicking the key launches a password assistant that creates a secure password for you. The key icon and password assistant are found throughout the El Capitan interface where passwords are required.

Creating a New Keychain

The Login keychain stores almost everything related to accounts you've configured in El Capitan, but because it is designed to be automatically unlocked at login, you might want to create another keychain that is only unlocked when you want it to be. To do so, follow these steps:

1. Open the Keychain Access application and choose File, New Keychain from the menu.

2. Enter a name for the keychain and then click Create.

3. You are prompted for a password to secure the new keychain. Enter a secure password in the New Password and Verify fields.

4. Click OK.

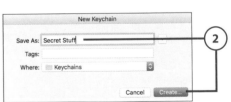

5. The new keychain is displayed in the keychain list and you can store any data you'd like in it.

6. Continue adding items or choose Keychain Access, Quit Keychain Access to exit (not shown).

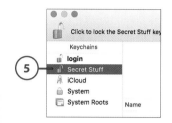

Adding a Keychain Menu Item

To quickly unlock and lock keychains, you can add a keychain item to your menu bar:

1. Open the Keychain Access application and choose Keychain Access, Preferences from the menu.

2. Click the General button at the top of the window.

3. Click Show Keychain Status in Menu Bar.

4. Close the Preferences.

5. The Keychain Lock menu item is added, giving easy access to unlocking and locking your keychains.

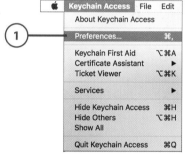

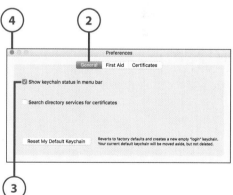

Encrypting Your El Capitan Disk

One of the best ways to secure sensitive information is through encryption. The Keychain Utility provides an encryption feature for small pieces of data, but not for your documents. To fully encrypt all data on your Mac, you can make use of FileVault disk-level encryption.

Activating FileVault

To turn on FileVault encryption for your Mac, complete the following steps:

1. Open the System Preferences window and click the Security & Privacy icon.

2. Click the FileVault button at the top of the panel.

3. Click Turn On FileVault.

4. Choose whether your iCloud account can unlock FileVault if you forget your password. Alternatively, you can have FileVault create a recovery key that you must manually store in a secure location.

5. Click Continue.

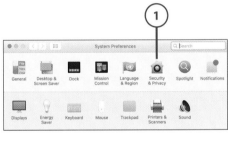

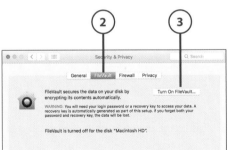

6. Click Enable User and supply each user's password for those who should be able to unlock the protected disk. By default, the person activating FileVault will have access, so if your Mac has only one account, you won't have to do this step.

7. Click Continue.

8. Click Restart to restart your Mac and begin encrypting your drive. This process takes place in the background so you can continue to use your computer as you normally would.

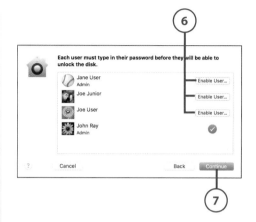

Effortless Encryption

FileVault encryption is completely transparent. Your entire disk is encrypted and made available to you when you log in. If another user tries to access files in your account, or even removes the drive from your computer to try to access its contents, they won't be able to.

Application Execution Security

With El Capitan, you can limit your computer's ability to run applications from sources other than the App Store or from developers who have registered an ID with Apple. Why would you want to do this? Because software from unknown sources can be hazardous to your system's health!

Setting Application Execution Limits

By default, El Capitan enables you to install and use applications from the App Store and apps published separately from properly registered developers. To change this to better suit your sense of well-being, follow these steps:

1. Open the System Preferences window and click the Security & Privacy icon.

2. Click the General button at the top of the panel.

3. Use the radio buttons at the bottom of the window to choose which applications you want to be allowed on your system.

4. Close the System Preferences.

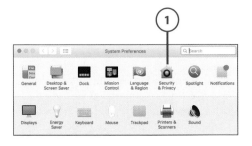

Everyone Is Affected!

The application limits you set here apply to the entire system, so software previously installed and functional might stop working if you make changes.

Many power users want to set the limit to allow applications downloaded from anywhere; this provides the most flexibility. Most of us, however, will be best protected using the Mac App Store and Identified Developers setting.

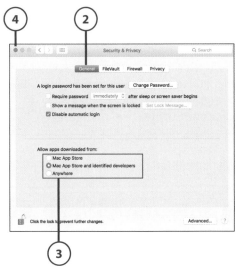

Adding Network Security with the Built-In Firewall

Many applications open themselves to connections from the outside—opening you, in turn, to Internet attacks. Firewalls block these connections before your computer accepts them. El Capitan offers an easy-to-configure firewall that lets you choose what network services your Mac exposes to the world.

Activating the El Capitan Firewall

To turn on the El Capitan firewall, follow these steps:

1. Open the System Preferences window and click the Security & Privacy icon.

2. Click the Firewall button at the top of the panel.

3. Click Turn On Firewall.

4. The circle beside the Firewall: Off label turns green and the label changes to Firewall: On to indicate that the firewall is active.

5. Close the System Preferences, or continue configuring Incoming Services.

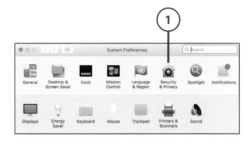

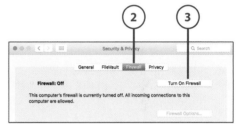

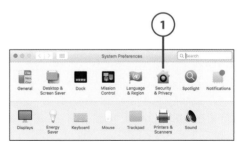

Configuring Incoming Services

After your firewall is active, you need to choose which connections to allow and which to block. To define how the firewall reacts to incoming requests, use this process:

1. Open the System Preferences window and click the Security & Privacy icon.

2. Click the Firewall button at the top of the Panel.

3. Click Firewall Options.

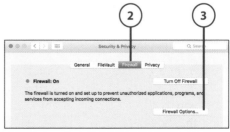

4. To block all incoming connections, click the Block All Incoming Connections checkbox.

5. Use the pop-up menu beside each of your running applications to choose whether it should allow or block incoming connections.

6. Add or remove applications from the list using the + and – buttons.

7. If you want applications that have been signed (where the publisher is a known and registered entity) to automatically accept connections, click the Automatically Allow Signed Software to Receive Incoming Connections checkbox.

8. Enable stealth mode if you'd like your computer to appear offline to most network device scans.

9. Click OK to save your configuration.

10. Close the Security & Privacy Preferences panel.

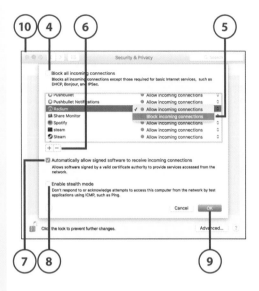

Advantages of a Signature

An application being signed does not make it more or less susceptible to network attack. It does, however, give you a degree of certainty that the application is not a Trojan horse or spyware specifically designed to infect your computer.

Hiding Location Information and Application Data

If you have an iOS device, you're probably accustomed to it asking you if it can share your location with an application. In El Capitan, the operating system can also determine your approximate location and share that information as well. It can also collect information on your application usage and send it to Apple for use in "improving its products." If you'd prefer not to make this information available, follow these steps:

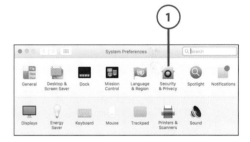

1. Open the System Preferences and click the Security & Privacy icon.

2. Click the Privacy button at the top of the panel.

3. Select a category of information to protect, such as your location, your contacts (address book), and information about your application usage.

4. Use the controls associated with each type of data to enable or disable access to it.

5. Close the System Preferences.

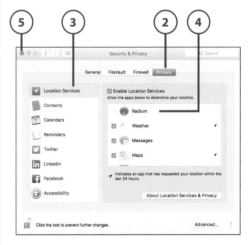

Sharing Isn't Always Bad

Before disabling all these services, be aware that sending information to Apple can be critical for them to correct bugs in El Capitan—applications that use your location or contacts will prompt you before they do so, so they can't use location information without permission.

Backing Up Important Information

An often-overlooked part of security is information availability—in other words, ensuring that information is available when it is needed. If your hard drive fails, your data is unavailable, and items of value can be lost!

Backups are the best way to keep your system ready if disaster strikes. Apple provides an extremely simple backup mechanism in the form of Time Machine, a transparent solution built into El Capitan.

Quick Backups

You can create ad-hoc backups in El Capitan by inserting a writeable DVD or CD into your drive and then copying the files you want to protect onto the optical media (which is just like when you add them to a disk).

Using Time Machine

The Time Machine feature in El Capitan is a backup solution that is painless to use, covers your entire system, and can restore files from multiple different points in time. Even better, configuration for Time Machine is actually easier than traditional backup solutions like Apple Backup!

>>>Go Further
TIME CAPSULE BACKUPS

To use Time Machine, you need a hard drive or network share to use as your backup volume. You can use any external drive, but it should have at least twice the capacity of your internal hard drive. An easy solution is to use an Apple Time Capsule wireless access point (www.apple.com/timecapsule/).

Before continuing, you should make sure that you can mount your Time Machine volume (either locally or over the network) on your Mac. (Chapter 8, "Managing Who, Where, When, and What," and the online Chapter 16, "Upgrading Your Mac," can help here.)

Activating Time Machine

After mounting your Time Machine backup volume on your Mac, follow these steps to configure Time Machine to begin backing up your system:

1. Open the System Preferences window and click the Time Machine icon.

2. Click the ON/OFF switch to turn Time Machine On.

3. Choose an available disk(s) from the list that appears.

4. Click Encrypt Backups if you'd like your backup data to be stored in a fully encrypted format.

5. Click Use Disk. (If using a network volume, enter your username and password, then click Connect.)

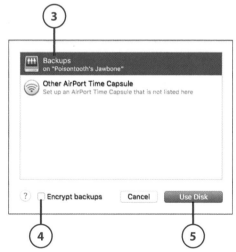

6. The Time Machine backups are scheduled and begin after a few seconds.

7. Close the System Preferences.

Customizing the Time Machine Backups

To further customize your Time Machine backup, including files that you want skipped, complete these steps:

1. Open the System Preferences window and click the Time Machine icon.

2. Click Options.

3. Use the + and − to add or remove individual files, folders, and volumes to the Time Machine exclusion list. These items are skipped during the backup.

4. Click Notify After Old Backups Are Deleted to receive warnings as old information is removed to make space for new data. Use the Backup While on Battery Power checkbox to have your MacBook use Time Machine while running off its battery.

5. Click Save.

6. Close the System Preferences.

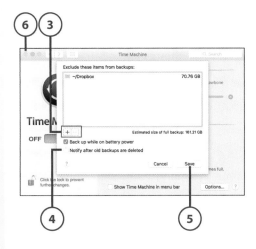

Adding a Time Machine Menu Item

To monitor your Time Machine backups and quickly launch a Time Machine restore, you can add a menu item to your menu bar:

1. Open the System Preferences window and click the Time Machine icon.

2. Check Show Time Machine in Menu Bar.

3. The menu item is added to your menu bar. A small triangle appears in the icon when a backup is running.

4. Click the Time Machine menu item to start and stop backups and enter the Time Machine restore process.

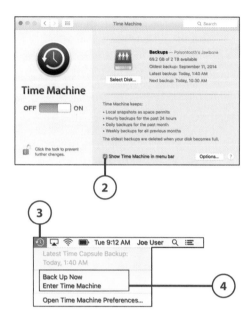

Recovering Data

Recovering data from a Time Machine backup is one of the more unique experiences you can have in El Capitan. Follow these steps to enter the Time Machine and recover files from the past:

1. Open the Time Machine using the application (Applications/Time Machine) or Time Machine menu item.

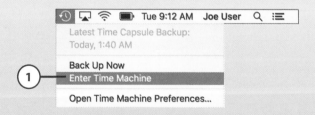

2. Navigate to a location on your disk that holds (or held) the file or folder you want to restore. For example, if you deleted an application and want to restore it, open the Applications folder.

3. Use the arrows on the right (or directly click the timeline) to choose a point in time. The window updates to show the state of the file system at the chosen time.

4. When viewing the files/folders you want to restore, click the Restore button under the file system window. The files are restored to match the snapshot.

5. Click Cancel to exit.

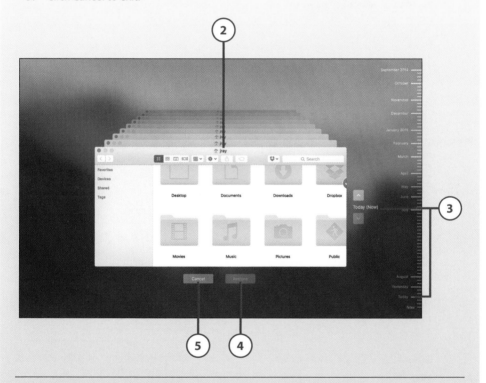

Find the Missing Files

Searches are active in Time Machine. Use the Search field on the Finder window to help identify files to restore.

Restoring a Machine from Scratch

If your Mac suffers a complete hard drive failure, you can use your Time Machine backup to recover everything on your system. Make sure you have a bootable disk or can boot from the recovery partition (Command+R); see the online Chapter 15, "Troubleshooting Your System," for details.

1. Boot from your media or the El Capitan recovery partition, and then click Restore from Time Machine Backup.

2. Click Continue.

3. When the Restore Your System window appears, click Continue.

4. Choose your Time Machine disk from the list that appears.

5. Select the backup and backup date that you want to restore, and follow the onscreen steps to complete the restoration (not shown).

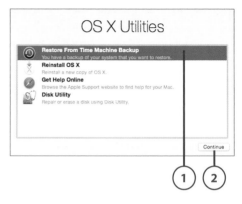

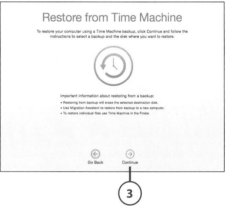

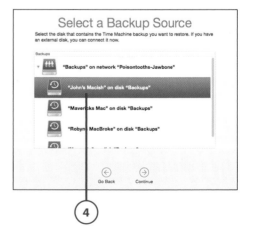

El Capitan's Recovery Feature

If your hard drive is still functional, you can boot off the El Capitan recovery partition that is automatically created when you install the operating system. To do
this, simply hold down Command+R while turning on or restarting your computer.

Even if your drive has failed, many Mac models made in 2010 and later can boot
using the Internet and Apple's remote servers. Command+R first tries to boot
from a local recovery partition; if that fails, it then tries using the Internet recovery
method. The recovery feature gives you access to disk repair and formatting tools,
Time Machine restores, and even a full reinstall of the operating system.

Using File Versions

El Capitan also includes a Time Machine-like feature called Versions. Unlike
Time Machine, however, Versions keeps revisions of your files' contents. As
you make changes, El Capitan automatically saves the changes so that you
can browse your editing history over time.

Manually Saving a Version

The El Capitan versioning system is built to automatically save versions of your files as
you edit—no manual saving is required. If you'd like to explicitly tell the system to save a
version, you can, by following these steps:

1. Make the desired changes to your document.

2. Choose File, Save.

3. A new version is added to the document's version history (not shown).

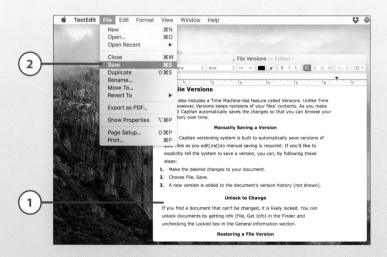

Unlock to Change

If you find a document that can't be changed, it is likely locked. You can unlock documents by getting info (File, Get Info) in the Finder and unchecking the Locked box in the General information section.

Restoring a File Version

Accessing the version history of a document is very similar to using Time Machine. To view and access the version history of a file, do the following:

1. Within the document that has history you want to access, choose File, Revert To, Browse All Versions from the menu bar.

2. The Version screen is displayed.

3. The current document is located on the left.

4. Use the timeline on the right to browse through different versions of your file.

5. The previous versions of the file are displayed on the right.

6. You can copy and paste text from the document on the right into the document on the left, but you cannot make changes to the previous versions.

7. To completely restore a previous version of the file, view the version you want to restore on the right, and then click the Restore button.

8. Click the Done button to exit the file version history.

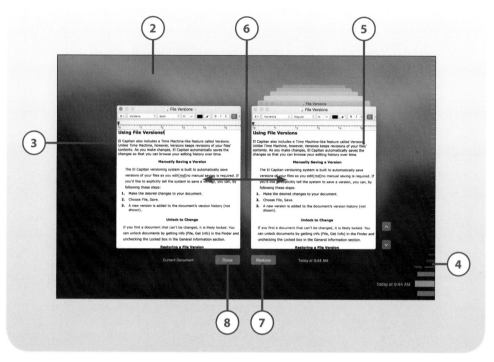

It's Not All Good

Don't Rely on Versions without Testing!

It is up to the individual developer to add Versions support to their apps, so verify that it works in your application before relying on it. If your app doesn't support Versions, you can still use Time Machine to recall earlier copies of its documents.

>>>Go Further

USE ICLOUD FOR OFF-SITE STORAGE

To move critical files to iCloud, you can click a document's name in the title bar when editing and then use the Where drop-down menu to choose one of the options under iCloud Library. Choose the name of your application (followed by iCloud) to move to an iCloud folder specifically for that application, or just pick iCloud Drive to place it at the top level of your iCloud drive storage. The file immediately moves to the cloud. Using iCloud ensures that all your iCloud-connected devices have access to the file as well. Learn more about iCloud in Chapter 4, "Setting Up iCloud and Internet Accounts."

Index